Turkish
phrase book

**Berlitz Publishing / APA Publications GmbH & Co.
Verlag KG, Singapore Branch, Singapore**

Contacting the Editors
Every effort has been made to provide accurate information in this publication, but changes are inevitable. The publisher cannot be responsible for any resulting loss, inconvenience or injury. We would appreciate it if readers would call our attention to any errors or outdated information by contacting Berlitz Publishing, 193 Morris Ave., Springfield, NJ 07081, USA. Fax: 1-908-206-1103, e-mail: comments@berlitzbooks.com

Satisfaction guaranteed—If you are dissatisfied with this product for any reason, send the complete package, your dated sales receipt showing price and store name, and a brief note describing your dissatisfaction to: Berlitz Publishing, Langenscheidt Publishing Group, Dept. L, 36-36 33rd Street, Long Island City, NY 11106. You'll receive a full refund.

Cover photo: © Imageshop.com

Contents

Vowels

Turkish vowels do not have exact equivalents in English. The Turkish **a**, for instance, is shorter and harder than any English *a*, and this generally applies to all the other vowels. The main exception is **i**, which is located somewhere between the *i* in fish and the *ee* in beer. These characteristics give Turkish a distinctly "alien" sound, but they also make it better articulated than English and easier for foreigners to understand.

Certain vowels are followed by an *h* in the pronunciation, to emphasize the shortness of the sound.

a	like *a* in p*a*rachute; always a hard sound	a	**kara** **araç**	<u>ka</u>ra <u>a</u>rach
e	like *e* in n*e*t	e	**sene** **evet**	<u>se</u>ne <u>eh</u>-vet
ı	like *ir* in sh*ir*t or *er* in hott*er*	er/ir	**tatlı** **ızgara**	<u>tat</u>ler ırz-<u>ga</u>ra
i	like *ee* in f*ee*l	ee	**siyah**	<u>see</u>-yah
o	like *o* in *o*range	o	**otel** **otlar**	<u>oh</u>-tel <u>ot</u>-lar
ö	similar to *ur* in f*ur*	ur	**börek** **dört**	<u>bur</u>-rek durrt
u	like *u* in p*u*ll or *oo* in p*oo*r	u/oo	**uzak** **doğru**	<u>oo</u>zak <u>door</u>-ru
ü	like *ew* in f*ew*	ew	**üç** **üzüm**	ewch <u>ew</u>zewm

Dipthongs

ay	like *igh* in s*igh*	i	**bay**	bi
ey	like *ay* in d*ay*	ay	**bey**	bay
oy	like *oy* in b*oy*	oy	**koy**	koy

Stress

Letters underlined in the transcriptions should be read with slightly more stress (i.e., louder) than the others, but don't overdo this as Turkish is not a heavily stressed language.

The Turkish alphabet

The Turkish alphabet has no *q, w,* or *x,* but there are five accented letters – **ç, ğ, ö, ş, ü** – which follow their unaccented equivalents, and a dotless **ı** that precedes **i**.

A	*ah*		**M**	*meh*
B	*be*		**N**	*ne*
C	*je*		**O**	*o*
Ç	*che*		**Ö**	*ur*
D	*de*		**P**	*peh*
E	*eh*		**R**	*reh*
F	*fe*		**S**	*se*
G	*geh*		**Ş**	*sheh*
Ğ	*yoo<u>mushak</u> geh*		**T**	*te*
H	*heh*		**U**	*oo*
I	*er*		**Ü**	*ew*
İ	*ee*		**V**	*veh*
J	*zheh*		**Y**	*yeh*
K	*keh*		**Z**	*zeh*
L	*leh*			

Basic Expressions

ESSENTIAL

Yes./No.	**Evet./Hayır.** *eh-vet/hi-yer*
Okay.	**Tamam.** *tamam*
Please.	**Lütfen.** *lewt-fen*
Thank you.	**Teşekkür ederim.** *teshek-kewr ederim*
Thank you very much.	**Çok teşekkür ederim.** *chok teshek-kewr ederim*

Greetings/Apologies
Selamlaşma/Özür dileme

Hello./Hi!	**Merhaba./Selam!** *mer-habah/seh-lam*
Good morning.	**Günaydın.** *gewn-eye-dern*
Good afternoon.	**İyi günler.** *eeyee gewnlair*
Good evening.	**İyi akşamlar.** *eeyee ak-sham-lar*
Good night.	**İyi geceler.** *eeyee geh-jeh-lair*
Good-bye.	**Hoşçakal. /Güle güle.** *hosh-cha kal/gew-leh gew-leh*
Excuse me!	**Afedersiniz!** *aff-edair-seeniz*
Sorry!	**Özür dilerim!** *urz-ewr dilereem*
Don't mention it.	**Bir şey değil.** *beer shey day-eel*
Never mind.	**Önemli değil.** *urnemlee day-eel*

Communication difficulties
İletişim güçlükleri

Do you speak English?

İngilizce biliyor musunuz?
eengee<u>leez</u>-je beelee-yor musoonuz

Does anyone here speak English?

Burada İngilizce bilen biri var mı? *burada eengee<u>leez</u>-je bee-len <u>beer</u>ee var mer*

I don't speak Turkish.

Türkçe bilmiyorum. *tewrk-che bee<u>l</u>meeyorum*

Could you repeat that?

Tekrar edebilir misiniz?
tek-<u>rar</u> edeh-bee<u>leer</u> miseeniz

Excuse me? [Pardon?]

Efendim? *eh-<u>fen</u>dim*

Could you spell it?

Harfler misiniz? *harf-<u>lair</u> miseeniz*

Please write it down.

Lütfen yazar mısınız.
<u>lewt</u>-fen ya<u>zar</u> mersernerz

What does this mean?

Bunun anlamı nedir?
boonun an<u>lam</u>-er neh-deer

Please point to the phrase in the book.

Lütfen bu deyimi kitapta gösterir misiniz.
<u>lewt</u>-fen boo day-ee<u>mee</u> kitapta go-staireer miseeniz

I understand.

Anladım. *an<u>lad</u>irm*

I don't understand.

Anlamadım. *an<u>lam</u>adirm*

Do you understand?

Anladınız mı? *an<u>lad</u>ernerz mer*

GRAMMAR

Turkish uses a system of root words with different endings (suffixes ➤ 6). This often results in one word being an entire sentence. For example; "I am coming" would simply be **geliyorum**. This can sometimes make it difficult to identify the same word in different contexts. So try to stick to the standard phrases in this book at first.

– *Bir milyon lira.* (That's one million lira.)
– Anladım. (I don't understand.)
– *Bir milyon lira.* (That's one million lira.)
– Lütfen yazar mısınız … Ha,
"one million lira." Buyrun.
(Please write it down. … Ah,
"one million lira." Here you are.)

Questions Sorular

In Turkish, questions are indicated by a special suffix (➤ 6)
– **mi**, **mu**, or **mı** – which comes before the personal ending,
if there is one (➤ 169).

Are you coming? **Geliyor <u>mu</u>sunuz?**

Did you see (that)? **(Onu) Gördün <u>mü</u>?**

Where? Nerede?

Where is it?	**Nerede?** _neredeh_
Where are you going?	**Nereye gidiyor sunuz?** _<u>nere</u>-yeh gid<u>ee</u>yor soonuz_
across the road	**yolun karşı tarafında** _<u>yolun</u> kar-<u>sher</u> tarafernda_
around the town	**kentin yakınlarında** _kent-in yakernlar<u>ern</u>da_
at the meeting place [point]	**buluşma yerinde** _bul<u>ush</u>ma yair-inde_
from the U.S.	**ABD'den** _ah beh deh'den_
here (to here)	**burada (buraya)** _boorada (booraya)_
in Turkey	**Türkiye'de** _<u>tewr</u>kee-yeh'deh_
in the car	**arabada** _ar<u>a</u>ba-da_
inside	**içerde** _itch-<u>air</u>-deh_
near the bank	**bankanın yakınında** _banka<u>nern</u> yakern-<u>ern</u>da_
next to the post office	**postanenin yanında** _posst-<u>arne</u>-neen <u>yan</u>-ern-da_
opposite the market	**pazarın karşısında** _paz-<u>za</u>rern kar-sher-<u>sirn</u>da_
on the left / right	**solda/sağda** _solda/<u>saa</u>-da_
on the sidewalk [pavement]	**kaldırımda** _kalder<u>erm</u>da_
outside the café	**kafenin dışında** _kah-<u>feh</u>-neen dir<u>sher</u>nda_
there (to there)	**orada (oraya)** _orada/oraya_
to the hotel	**otele** _oh-teleh_
up to the traffic lights	**trafik ışıklarına kadar** _trafeek irsh<u>erk</u>-lar<u>er</u>na kad-ar_

12

When? Ne zaman?

When does the museum open?	**Müze ne zaman açılıyor?** *mewze neh za<u>man</u> a<u>cherl</u>-iyor*
When does the train arrive?	**Tren ne zaman geliyor?** *tren neh za<u>man</u> <u>gel</u>-iyor*
at 7 o'clock	**saat 7'de** *sa-art <u>yedee</u>-de*
after lunch	**öğle yemeğinden sonra** *owe-leh ye<u>me</u>-yeenden sonra*
around midnight	**gece yarısı civarında** *ge-<u>jeh</u> ya-rer-<u>ser</u> jee-va-rern-<u>da</u>*
10 minutes ago	**10 dakika önce** *on da-<u>keeka</u> <u>own</u>-je*
before Friday	**Cuma'dan önce** *jew-<u>madan</u> <u>own</u>-je*
by tomorrow	**yarına kadar** *<u>yar</u>-erna kad-ar*
every week	**her hafta** *hair <u>hafta</u>*
for 2 hours	**2 saat için** *ikee sa-art itch<u>in</u>*
from 9 a.m. to 6 p.m.	**saat 9.00'dan 18.00'e kadar** *sa-art <u>dokooz</u>-dan on <u>sekeez</u>-eh kad-ar*
in 20 minutes	**20 dakika içinde** *yirmee da-<u>keeka</u> itch-<u>in</u>deh*
always	**her zaman** *hair za<u>man</u>*
never	**hiçbir zaman** *hitch-beer za<u>man</u>*
not yet	**henüz değil** *<u>hen</u>-ewz <u>day</u>-eel*
now	**şimdi** *<u>shim</u>dee*
often	**sık sık** *sirk sirk*
on March 8	**8 Mart'ta** *<u>sekeez</u> <u>mart</u>-ta*
on weekdays	**hafta içinde** *<u>hafta</u> itch-<u>in</u>de*
sometimes	**bazen** *bar-zen*
soon	**yakında** *ya<u>kern</u>da*
then	**sonra** *<u>sonra</u>*
within 2 days	**2 gün içinde** *ikee gewn itch-<u>in</u>de*

13

What sort of ...? Ne gibi ...?

I'd like something ...	**... bir şey istiyorum.** *... beer shey istee-yorum*
It's ...	**... -dir.** *... deer*
beautiful / ugly	**güzel/çirkin** *gewzel/cheerkin*
better / worse	**daha iyi/daha kötü** *dah-ha eeyee/dah-ha kurtew*
big / small	**büyük/küçük** *bew-yewk/kewchewk*
cheap / expensive	**ucuz/pahalı** *ujooz/pahal-er*
clean / dirty	**temiz/kirli** *temeez/keerlee*
dark / light	**karanlık/aydınlık** *karan-lirk/eye-dirn-lirk*
delicious / disgusting	**lezzetli/berbat** *lez-zetlee/bair-bat*
early / late	**erken/geç** *air-ken/getch*
easy / difficult	**kolay/zor** *kol-eye/zor*
empty / full	**boş/dolu** *bosh/dol-loo*
good / bad	**iyi/kötü** *eeyee/kurtew*
heavy / light	**ağır/hafif** *eye-er/haf-feef*
hot / warm / cold	**sıcak/ılık/soğuk** *sir-jak/irlirk/soh-ook*
narrow / wide	**dar/geniş** *dar/gen-eesh*
next / last	**sonraki/sonuncu** *sonrakee/sonoon-ju*
old / new	**eski/yeni** *eskee/yenee*
open / shut	**açık/kapalı** *achirk/kapal-er*
pleasant / nice / unpleasant	**hoş/iyi/hoş değil** *hosh/eeyee/hosh day-eel*
quick / slow	**çabuk/yavaş** *chabook/yavash*
quiet / noisy	**sessiz/gürültülü** *sess-siz/gew-rewl-tew-lew*
right / wrong	**doğru/yanlış** *door-ru/yanlersh*
tall / short	**uzun/kısa** *oozun/kirsah*
thick / thin	**kalın/ince** *kalern/eenjeh*
vacant / occupied	**serbest/meşgul** *sair-best/mesh-gewl*
young / old	**genç/yaşlı** *gench/yash-ler*

The equivalent of the English "a/an" is often **bir**.

   an apple   **bir elma**

There is no equivalent of the English "the" (definite article) in Turkish. Instead, it is implied through context.

   car/the car   **araba**

   The car has been stolen.   **Araba çalındı.**

Turkish nouns and pronouns change their endings depending on their grammatical function. For example, "car" can be **araba**, **arabayı** or **arabaya** (➤ 169 for more details).

How much/many? Ne kadar/Kaç tane?

How much is that?	**Bu ne kadar?** *boo neh kaddar*
How many are there?	**Kaç tane var?** *katch tarneh var*
1/2/3	**bir/iki/üç** *beer/ikee/ewch*
4/5	**dört/beş** *durrt/besh*
none	**hiç** *hitch*
about one million lira	**yaklaşık bir milyon lira** *yakla-shirk beer meel-yon leerah*
a little	**biraz** *beeraz*
a lot of (traffic)	**(trafik) çok** *(trafeek) chok*
enough	**yeter** *yetair*
few/a few of them	**birkaç tane/birkaç tanesi** *beerkatch tarneh/beerkatch tarneh-see*
more than that	**daha fazla** *dah-ha fazlah*
less than that	**daha az** *dah-ha az*
much more	**çok daha** *chok dah-ha*
nothing else	**bu kadar** *boo kaddar*
too much	**çok fazla** *chok fazlah*

Why? Neden?

Why is that?	**Neden böyle?** *neh-den bow-leh*
Why not?	**Neden olmasın?** *neh-den olmasırn*
It's because of the weather.	**Hava durumu yüzünden.** *havah du-roomu neh-den-eeleh*
It's because I'm in a hurry.	**Çünkü acelem var.** *chewn-kew ah-jelem var*
I don't know why.	**Nedenini bilmiyorum.** *neh-den-eenee beelmeeyorum*

Who?/Which? Kim?/Hangi?

Who's it for?	**Bu kimin için?** *boo kimeen itchin*
(for) her/him	**onun (için)** *onoon (itchin)*
(for) me	**benim (için)** *benim (itchin)*
(for) you	**sizin (için)** *sizeen (itchin)*
someone	**birisi** *beereesi*
no one	**hiç kimse** *hitch kimseh*
Which one do you want?	**Hangisini istersiniz?** *han-gee-see-nee istair-seeniz*
this one/that one	**bunu/şunu** *boonu/shoo-nu*
one like that	**bunun gibi** *boonun gibee*
something	**bir şey** *beer shey*
nothing	**hiçbir şey** *hitch beer shey*

Whose? Kimin?

Whose is that?	**Bu kimin?** *boo kimeen*
It's ...	**... -dir.** *... deer*
mine/ours/yours	**benim/bizim/sizin** *benim/bizim/sizin*
his/hers/theirs	**onun/onun/onların** *onoon/onoon/onlarern*
It's ... turn.	**Sıra ...** *sir-ra*
my/our/your	**benim/bizim/sizin** *benim/bizim/sizin*
his/her/their	**onun/onun/onların** *onoon/onoon/onlarern*

GRAMMAR

The possessive endings are put on the <u>end</u> of the word:

my **-(i)m**	your **-(i)n**	her/his/its **-(s)i**
our **-(i)miz**	your (polite) **-(i)niz**	their **-leri**

For example: my bicycle = **bisikletim**   our car = **arabamız**

With the exception of "her/his/its" all the letters in parentheses are omitted if the noun ends in a vowel.

To express the English "have/has," you use the word with its possessive ending, followed by the word **var** meaning "there is":

I have a car. (literally, "my car there is")	**arabam var**
He has a bicycle.	**bisikleti var**

To say "don't/doesn't have" the word **yok** is used instead of **var**:

I don't have a ticket.	**biletim yok**
He/She doesn't have any money.	**parası yok**

How? Nasıl?

How would you like to pay?	**Nasıl ödemek istersiniz?**	
	nassirl urdemek istairseeniz	
by cash	**nakit** _nakeet_	
by credit card	**kredi kartı ile**	
	kredee karter ee-leh	
How are you getting here?	**Buraya nasıl geleceksiniz?**	
	booraya nassirl gel-eh-jek-seeniz	
by car/bus/train	**araba/otobüs/tren ile**	
	arabah/oto-bews/tren ee-leh	
on foot	**yürüyerek** _yew-rew-yair-ek_	
quickly	**çabucak** _chaboojak_	
slowly	**yavaş yavaş** _yavash yavash_	
too fast	**çok hızlı** _chok herz-ler_	
very	**çok** _chok_	
with a friend	**bir arkadaş ile** _beer arka-dash-la_	
without a passport	**pasaportsuz** _passaport-suz_	

Is it ...?/Are there ...? ... mi?/... var mı?

Is it free of charge?	**Bedava mı?** _bedava mer_	
It isn't ready.	**Hazır değil.** _haz-zer day-eel_	
Is there a shower in the room?	**Odada duş var mı?**	
	odda-da dush var mer	
Is there a bus into town?	**Kente otobüs var mı?**	
	kent-eh otobews var mer	
There it is/they are.	**İşte orada/oradalar.**	
	eesh-teh orada/orada-lar	
Are there buses into town?	**Kente giden otobüsler var mı?**	
	kent-eh gee-den otobews var mer	
There aren't any towels in my room.	**Odamda havlu yok.**	
	oddam-da have-loo yok	
Here it is/they are.	**İşte burada/buradalar.**	
	eesh-teh boorada/boorada-lar	
There it is/they are.	**İşte orada/oradalar.**	
	eesh-teh orada/orada-lar	

Can/May? ... bilir mi?

Can I ...?	**... bilir miyim?**
	... beeleer meeyeem
May we ...?	**... bilir miyiz?**
	... beeleer meeyeez
Can you show me ...?	**... gösterebilir misiniz?**
	... bana go-stair-eh-beeleer miseeniz
Can you tell me ...?	**... söyleyebilir misiniz?**
	... sow-leh-yeh-beeleer miseeniz
Can I help you?	**Yardımcı olabilir miyim?**
	yar-derm-jer ola-beeleer meeyeem
Can you direct me to ...?	**... yolunu gösterebilir misiniz?**
	... yoloonu go-stair-eh-beeleer miseeniz
I can't.	**Yardım edemeyeceğim.**
	yardirm edeh-mey-eh-jay-eem

What do you want? Ne istiyorsunuz?

I'd like ...	**... istiyorum.** *... istee-yorum*
Could I have ...?	**... rica edebilir miyim?**
	... ree-cah edair-beeleer meeyeem
We'd like ...	**... istiyoruz.** *... istee-yorooz*
Give me ...	**... verir misiniz.** *... vereer miseeniz*
I'm looking for ...	**... arıyorum.** *... ariyorum*
I need to ...	**... gerek.** *... gerek*
go ...	**... -e git.** *... eh geet*
find ...	**... -i bul.** *... ee bull*
see ...	**... -i gör.** *... ee gurr*
speak to ...	**... ile konuş.** *... ile konoosh*

– Afedersiniz. (Excuse me.)

– Evet? Yardımcı olabilir miyim?
(Yes? Can I help you?)

– Ayşe Hanım ile konuşabilir miyim?
(Can I speak to Miss/Mrs. Ayşe?)

– Bir dakika lütfen. (Just a moment, please.)

Other useful words
Başka yararlı sözcükler

fortunately	**iyi ki** *eeyee kee*
hopefully	**umarım** *oomarem*
of course	**tabii** *tabee-ee*
perhaps	**belki** *belkee*
unfortunately	**ne yazık ki** *neh yazirk kee*
and	**ve** *veh*
or	**ya da** *yah dah*
also	**ayrıca** *eye-rer-jah*
but	**ama** *ama*

Exclamations Ünlemler

At last!	**Sonunda!** *sonoondah*
Go on.	**Haydi.** *hi-dee*
Nonsense!	**Saçma!** *satch-ma*
That's true.	**Doğru.** *door-ru*
No way!	**Asla!** *ass-lah*
How are things?	**Ne haber?** *neh har-bair*
great	**şahane** *sha-har-neh*
terrific	**fevkalade** *fev-kaladeh*
very good	**çok iyi** *chok eeyee*
fine	**iyi** *eeyee*
not bad	**fena değil** *feh-nah day-eel*
okay	**iyi** *eeyee*
not good	**iyi değil** *eeyee day-eel*
fairly bad	**epeyce kötü** *eh-pay-je kurtew*
terrible	**berbat** *bair-bat*

Accommodations

There is a wide range of places to stay in Turkey, from luxury five-star hotels to small, family-run guest houses. Standards vary, although they are improving overall.

Here are some of the main categories of places to stay:

Otel *otel*

Most big towns and cities have either first- or second-class hotels. Luxury establishments are almost all confined to Ankara, Istanbul, Bursa, İzmir, Antalya, and Adana.

Motel *motel*

Motels are widespread. Rooms are nearly always equipped with a shower, a toilet, and a radio. Some include air conditioning and a refrigerator, too. Normally they sleep two people, but extra beds can usually be put in for children.

Pansiyon *panseeyon*

These guest houses offer a more intimate glimpse of Turkish life. Breakfast is included in the price, and there may be a kitchen where you can cook. Toilet rooms and bathrooms are usually communal.

Gençlik yurdu *genchlik yurdu*

Youth hostels are open to holders of International Student Travel Conference (ISTC) or International Youth Hostel Federation (IYHF) cards and visitors with "student" or "teacher" on their passports.

Tatil köyü *tateel kuryew*

These are resorts in seaside areas, classified A and B, which provide furnished apartments, sometimes with cooking facilities. They are close to shopping, and most have a swimming pool.

Reservations Yer ayırtma

In advance Önceden

Can you recommend a hotel in ...?
... -de bir otel önerebilir misiniz?
... deh beer oh-tel owe-nair-eh-beeleer miseeniz

Is it near the center of town?
Kent merkezine yakın mı?
kent-in merkez-eeneh yakern mer

How much is it per night?
Geceliği ne kadar?
geh-jeh-leeyee neh kaddar

Do you have a cheaper room?
Daha ucuz bir oda var mı?
dah-ha oojuz beer odda var mer

Could you reserve me a room there, please?
Lütfen, bana bir oda ayırır mısınız?
lewt-fen, bana beer odda eye-erer mersernerz

At the hotel Otelde

Do you have a room?
Boş odanız var mı?
bosh oddanerz var mer

I'm sorry. We're full.
Özür dilerim. Doluyuz.
urzewr deelerim. dolooyooz

Is there another hotel nearby?
Yakında başka bir otel var mı?
yakernda bashka beer oh-tel var mer

I'd like a single/double room.
Tek/iki kişilik bir oda istiyorum.
tek/ikee kisheelik beer odda istee-yorum

Can I see the room, please?
Lütfen, odayı görebilir miyim?
lewt-fen, oddayer gurr-eh-beeleer-meeyim

I'd like a room with ...
... bir oda istiyorum.
... beer odda istee-yorum

twin beds
iki yataklı *ikee yatakler*

a double bed
iki kişilik yataklı *ikee kisheelik yatakler*

a bath/shower
banyolu/duşlu *ban-yo-loo/doosh-loo*

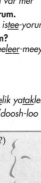

– Boş odanız var mı? (Do you have any vacancies?)
– Özür dilerim, doluyuz. (I'm sorry. We're full.)
– Yakında başka bir otel var mı?
(Is there another hotel nearby?)
– Evet efendim. Ambassador oteli çok yakında.
(Yes, ma'am/sir. The Ambassador is very near.)

21

Reception Resepsiyon

I have a reservation.	**Yer ayırtmıştım.** *yair eye-ert-mershterm*
My name is …	**Adım …** *adirm*
We've reserved a double and a single room.	**İki kişilik ve tek kişilik oda ayırtmıştık.** *ikee kisheelik veh tek kisheelik odda eye-ert-mershterk*
I've reserved a room for two nights.	**İki gece için bir oda ayırtmıştım.** *ikee geh-jeh itchin beer odda eye-ert-mershterm*
I confirmed my reservation by mail.	**Ayırttığım yeri mektup ile teyit etmiştim.** *eye-ert-ter-erm yairee mek-toop ee-leh teyeet et-mishtim*
Could we have adjoining rooms?	**Yan yana odalarda kalabilir miyiz?** *yan yanah oddalarda kala-beeleer meeyiz*

Amenities and facilities Olanaklar ve hizmetler

Is there (a) … in the room?	**Odada … var mı?** *oddada … var mer*
air conditioning	**havalandırma** *havalanderma*
TV/telephone	**televizyon/telefon** *televeez-iyon/telefon*
Does the hotel have (a) …?	**Otelde … var mı?** *oh-teldeh … var mer*
fax	**faks** *faks*
laundry service	**çamaşır yıkama hizmeti** *chamasherr yer-kama hiz-metee*
satellite TV	**uydu televizyon** *ooydu televeez-iyon*
sauna	**sauna** *sa-oona*
swimming pool	**yüzme havuzu** *yewzme havoozoo*
Could you put … in the room?	**Odaya … koyabilir misiniz?** *oddaya … koy-ah-beeleer miseeniz*
an extra bed	**ek yatak** *ek yatak*
a crib [child's cot]?	**çocuk yatağı** *chojook yata-yer*
Do you have facilities for children/the disabled?	**Çocuklar/özürlüler için ne gibi hizmetleriniz var?** *chojooklar/ur-zewr-lew-lair itchin neh gibee hizmet-lair-eeniz var*

How long ...? Ne kadar zaman?

We'll be staying ...	**... kalacağız.**
	... kalaja-yerz
overnight only	**yalnızca bir gece**
	yalnerz-jah beer geh-jeh
a few days	**birkaç gün** *beerkatch gewn*
a week (at least)	**(en az) bir hafta** *(en az) beer haf-tah*
I'd like to stay an extra night.	**Bir gece daha kalmak istiyorum.**
	beer geh-jeh dah-ha kalmak istee-yorum

– Merhaba. Yer ayırtmıştım. Adım John Newton.
(Hello. I have a reservation. My name's John Newton.)

– *Merhaba, Bay Newton.* (Hello, Mr. Newton.)

– İki gece için bir yer ayırtmıştım.
(I've reserved a room for two nights.)

– *Tamam. (Kayıt) formu(nu) doldurur musunuz?*
(Very good. Could you fill out this (registration) form?)

Lütfen pasaportunuzu görebilir miyim?	May I see your passport, please?
Lütfen bu formu doldurunuz/ burasını imzalayınız.	Please fill out this form/sign here.
Arabanızın plaka numarası nedir?	What is your license plate number?

YALNIZCA ODA	room only
KAHVALTI DAHİL	breakfast included
YEMEK VERİLİR	meals available
SOYAD/AD	last name/first name
EV ADRESİ/SOKAK/NUMARA	home address/street/number
UYRUK/MESLEK	nationality/profession
DOĞUM TARİHİ/YERİ	date/place of birth
PASAPORT NUMARASI	passport number
ARABA PLAKA NUMARASI	license plate number
(İMZA) YER/TARİH	place/date (of signature)
İMZA	signature

23

Price Fiyat

How much is it …?	**… ne kadar?**	… neh kaddar
per night/week	**geceliği/haftalığı**	geh-jeh-lee-yee/ haf-<u>tah</u>-ler-er
for bed and breakfast	**oda ve kahvaltı**	odda veh kah-<u>val</u>ter
excluding meals	**yemek hariç**	<u>ye</u>mek har-<u>eetch</u>
American Plan (A.P.) [full board])	**tam pansiyon**	tam pan-<u>see</u>-yon
Modified American Plan (M.A.P.) [half board])	**yarım pansiyon**	yar-<u>erm</u> pan-<u>see</u>-yon
Does the price include …?	**Fiyata … dahil mi?**	fee-<u>yat</u>-ah … da-<u>heel</u> mee
breakfast	**kahvaltı**	kah-<u>val</u>ter
sales tax [VAT]	**KDV**	kdv (kah-deh-veh)
Do I have to pay a deposit?	**Ön ödeme yapmam gerekiyor mu?**	own <u>urd</u>eme yap-mam gerek-eeyor mu
Is there a discount for children?	**Çocuklar için indirim var mı?**	cho<u>jook</u>lar itch<u>in</u> in<u>deer</u>im var mer

Decisions Karar verme

May I see the room?	**Odayı görebilir miyim?**	oddayer gurr-eh-bee<u>leer</u> meeyim
That's fine. I'll take it.	**Tamam. Odayı tutuyorum.**	ta<u>mam</u>. Oddayer too<u>tu</u>-yorum
It's too …	**Çok …**	chok
dark/small	**karanlık/küçük**	ka<u>ran</u>lerk/kew<u>chewk</u>
noisy	**gürültülü**	gew<u>rewl</u>-tew-lew
Do you have anything …?	**… var mı?**	… var mer
bigger/cheaper	**daha büyüğü/ucuzu**	dah-ha bew<u>yew</u>-ew/dah-ha oo<u>juz</u>-oo
quieter/warmer	**daha sessizi/sıcağı**	dah-ha sess-<u>seez</u>-ee/ser<u>ja</u>-er
No, I won't take it.	**Hayır, tutmuyorum.**	hi-<u>yer</u>, <u>toot</u>mu-yorum

Problems Sorunlar

The … doesn't work.	**… çalışmıyor.** *… chalershmer-yor*
air conditioning	**havalandırma** *havalanderma*
fan	**vantilatör** *van-tee-laturr*
heating	**ısıtıcı** *erser-terjer*
light	**ışık** *ersherk*
I can't turn the heat [heating] on/off.	**Isıtıcıyı açamıyorum/kapatamıyorum.** *erser-terjer-yer acha-meryorum/ kapata-meryorum*
There is no hot water/ toilet paper.	**Sıcak su/tuvalet kağıdı yok.** *serjak soo/too-valet ki-yarder yok*
The faucet [tap] is dripping.	**Musluk damlıyor.** *moosluk damler-yor*
The sink/toilet is blocked.	**Lavabo/tuvalet tıkalı.** *lavabow/too-valet terkaler*
The window/door is jammed.	**Pencere/kapı tutukluk yapıyor.** *pen-jereh/kap-er tootuk-looluk yaper-yor*
My room has not been made up.	**Odam hazırlanmamış.** *oddam haz-er-lan-mamersh*
The … is/are broken.	**… kırık.** *… kererk*
blinds/shutters	**panjurlar** *pan-joorlar*
lamp	**lamba** *lam-bah*
lock	**kilit** *keelit*
There are insects in our room.	**Odamızda böcek var.** *oddamerz-da burjek var*

Action Önlem

Could you have that seen to?	**Buna baktırabilir misiniz?** *bunah bakter-ah-beeleer miseeniz*
I'd like to move to another room.	**Başka bir odaya taşınmak istiyorum.** *bashka beer odda-yah tashernmak istee-yorum*
I'd like to speak to the manager.	**Müdürle görüşmek istiyorum.** *mewdewr-leh gurrewsh-mek istee-yorum*

25

Requirements Gereksinimler

The voltage in Turkey is generally 220 V, 50 cycle AC, though 110 V is also found, especially on the European side of Istanbul. Plugs mainly have two round pins (the Continental style). Check the voltage before using any plugs, electrical appliances, etc.

About the hotel Otel hakkında

Where's the …?	**… nerede?** … *neredeh*
bar	**bar** *bar*
bathroom [toilet]	**tuvalet** *too-valet*
dining room	**yemek salonu** *yemek salon-oo*
elevator [lift]	**asansör** *assan-surr*
parking lot [car park]	**otopark** *oto-park*
shower room	**duş** *doosh*
swimming pool	**yüzme havuzu** *yewzmeh havoozu*
tour operator's bulletin board	**gezi şirketinin ilan tahtası** *gezee sheer-ket-eenin eelan tah-ta-ser*
Does the hotel have a garage?	**Otelin garajı var mı?** *oh-telin garaj-er var mer*
Can I use this adapter here?	**Burada bu adaptörü kullanabilir miyim?** *boorada boo adap-turrew koollanah-beeleer meeyim*

YALNIZCA TIRAŞ MAKİNESİ İÇİN	razors [shavers] only
ACİL ÇIKIŞ	emergency exit
YANGIN KAPISI	fire door
RAHATSIZ ETMEYİNİZ	Do not disturb.
DIŞ HAT İÇİN …	Dial … for an outside line.
RESEPSİYON İÇİN …	Dial … for reception.
HAVLULARI ODADAN ÇIKARMAYINIZ	Do not remove towels from the room.

26

Personal needs Kişisel gereksinimler

The key to room ..., please.
Lütfen ... numaralı odanın anahtarını verir misiniz.
lewt-fen ... noo-mar-aller oddanern anah-tar-er vereer miseeniz

I've lost my key.
Anahtarımı kaybettim.
anah-tar-ermer kybettim

I've locked myself out of my room.
Kapıda kaldım.
kap-erda kalderm

Could you wake me at ...?
Beni saat ... -de uyandırabilir misiniz? *benee sa-art ... deh oyander-ah-beeleer miseeniz*

I'd like breakfast in my room.
Kahvaltımı odamda istiyorum.
kah-valt-er-mer oddam-dah istee-yorum

Can I leave this in the safe?
Bunu kasaya koyabilir misiniz?
boonu kassa-yah koy-ah-beeleer miseeniz

Could I have my things from the safe?
Kasadan eşyalarımı alabilir miyim?
kassa-dan esh-yah-larermer ala-beeleer-meeyim

Where can I find (a) ...?
... nerede bulabilirim?
....nereh-deh bull-ah-beeleerim

maid
oda hizmetçisini
odda heezmet-chee-see-nee

our tour guide
gezi rehberimizi *gez-ee reh-bair-eemiz*

May I have (an) extra ...?
Fazladan (bir) ... alabilir miyim?
fazlah-dan (beer) ... ala-beeleer meeyim

bath towel
banyo havlusu *ban-yo havloosu*

blanket
battaniye *bat-tanee-yeh*

hangers
askı *asker*

pillow
yastık *yasterk*

soap
sabun *sab-un*

Is there any mail for me?
Bana mektup var mı?
bana mektoop var mer

Are there any messages for me?
Bana mesaj var mı? *bana messaj var mer*

Could you mail this for me, please?
Lütfen bunu benim için postalar mısınız?
lewt-fen boonu benim itchin posstalar mersernerz

Renting Kiralama

We've reserved an apartment / cottage.

Bir apartman dairesi/kır evi ayırmıştık.
beer apart-man di-resee/keer ev-ee eye-yert-mershterk

in the name of …

… adına *… adderna*

Where do we pick up the keys?

Anahtarları nereden alacağız?
anah-tar-larer nereh-den ala-ji-yerz

Where is the …?

… nerede? *… neredeh*

electric meter

elektrik sayacı *elek-treek sy-ajer*

fuse box

sigorta kutusu *seegortah kutoosu*

valve [stopcock]

vana *vanah*

water heater

su ısıtıcı *soo erser-terjer*

Are there any spare …?

Yedek … var mı? *yedek … var mer*

fuses

sigorta *seegortah*

gas bottles

gaz tüpü *gazz tewpew*

sheets

çarşaf *charshaff*

Which day does the maid come?

Hizmetçi hangi gün geliyor?
heezmet-chee hangee gewn geleeyor

When do I put out the trash [rubbish]?

Çöpü ne zaman dökebilirim?
churp-ew neh zaman durkeh-beeleerim

Problems Sorunlar

Where can I contact you?

Sizinle nerede bağlantı kurabilirim?
seez-inleh neredeh bar-lanter koor-ah-beeleerim

How does the stove [cooker]/ water heater work?

Fırın/su ısıtıcı nasıl çalışıyor? *fer-ern/ soo erserter-jer nasserl chalersh-iyor*

The … is/are dirty.

… kirli. *… keer-lee*

The … has broken down.

… bozuldu. *… bozooldu*

We accidentally broke/lost …

Kazayla … kırdık/kaybettik.
kaz-eye-lah … kerderk/kybettik

That was already damaged when we arrived.

Geldiğimizde zaten hasarlıydı.
geldee-yeemiz-deh zar-ten hassar-luy-der

Useful terms Yararlı sözcükler

boiler	**kazan** *kazzan*
dishes [crockery]	**tabak çanak** *tabak chanak*
freezer	**dondurucu** *don-dur-ooju*
frying pan	**tava** *tavah*
kettle	**çaydanlık** *chaydan-lerk*
lamp	**lamba** *lambah*
refrigerator	**buzdolabı** *booz-dolaber*
saucepan	**tencere** *ten-jereh*
stove [cooker]	**fırın** *fer-ern*
utensils [cutlery]	**çatal bıçak** *cha-tal berchak*
washing machine	**çamaşır makinesi** *chama-sher makeene-see*

Rooms Odalar

balcony	**balkon** *bal-kon*
bathroom	**banyo** *ban-yo*
bedroom	**yatak odası** *yatak odda-ser*
dining room	**yemek odası** *yemek odda-ser*
kitchen	**mutfak** *moot-fak*
living room	**oturma odası** *ot-oorma odda-ser*
toilet	**tuvalet** *too-va-let*

Youth hostel Gençlik yurdu

Do you have any places left for tonight?	**Bu gece için yer var mı?** *boo geh-jeh itch-in yair var mer*
Do you rent out bedding?	**Yatak takımı kiralıyor musunuz?** *yatak takerm-er keeraler-yor musoonuz*
What time are the doors locked?	**Kapılar saat kaçta kapanıyor?** *kap-er-lar sa-art katch-tah ka-paner-yor*
I have an International Student Card.	**Uluslararası Öğrenci Kartım var.** *ooloos-lar-araser ur-ren-jee karterm var*

REQUIREMENTS ➤ 26; CAMPING ➤ 30

Camping Kamp yapma

Turkey's Ministry of Tourism has rated many campsites ranking them according to size rather than facilities offered. Besides these sites, there are many other campsites scattered across the country, particularly along the coasts and near tourist centers. They are open from April/May through October. The ministry also produces a countrywide map showing some 130 registered campsites and listing their facilities, such as showers, toilets, kitchen, and laundry facilities.

If you want to camp on private land, get permission from the owner first.

Reservations Yer ayırtma

Is there a campsite near here?	**Yakınlarda bir kamp alanı var mı?**
	yakern-larda beer kamp alarn-er var mer
Do you have space for a tent/ trailer [caravan]?	**Çadır/karavan için yeriniz var mı?**
	chader/karavan itchin yair-eeniz var mer
What is the charge …?	**… ücret nedir?** *… ewj-ret neh-deer*
per day/week	**günlük/haftalık** *gewn-lewk/hafta-lerk*
for a tent/car	**çadır/araba için** *chader/arabah itchin*
for a trailer [caravan]	**karavan için** *karavan itchin*

Facilities Hizmetler

Are there cooking facilities on site?	**Yemek pişirmek için mutfak var mı?**
	yemek pisheermek itchin moot-fak var mer
Are there any electrical outlets [power points]?	**Elektrik prizi var mı?**
	elek-treek preezee var mer
Where is/are the …?	**… nerede?** *… neredeh*
drinking water	**içme suyu** *itchmeh soo-yoo*
trashcans [dustbins]	**çöp bidonları** *churp beedon-larer*
laundry facilities	**çamaşırhane** *chamasher-harneh*
showers	**duş** *doosh*
Where can I get some butane gas?	**Nerede bütan gazı bulabilirim?**
	neredeh bewtan gazzer bull-ah-beeleerim

KAMP YAPMAK YASAKTIR	no camping
İÇME SUYU	drinking water
ATEŞ/MANGAL YAKMAK YASAKTIR	no fires/barbecues

Complaints Şikayetler

It's too sunny here.	**Burası çok güneşli.** *booraser chok gewneshlee*
It's too shady / crowded here.	**Burası çok gölgede/kalabalık.** *booraser chok gurlge-deh/ kalabalerk*
The ground's too hard / uneven.	**Zemin çok sert/bozuk.** *zemeen chok sairt/bozook*
Do you have a more level spot?	**Daha düz bir yer var mı?** *dah-ha dewz beer yair var mer*
You can't camp here.	**Burada kamp yapamazsınız.** *boorada kamp yapa-maz-sernerz*

Camping equipment Kamp donanımı

butane gas	**bütan gazı** *bewtan gazzer*
campbed	**kamp yatağı** *kamp yat-eye-yer*
charcoal	**odun kömürü** *odoon kurmewrew*
flashlight [torch]	**el feneri** *el fenair-ee*
groundcloth [groundsheet]	**su geçirmez yaygı** *soo gecheer-mez yi-ger*
guy rope	**germe halatı** *germeh halarter*
hammer	**çekiç** *chekitch*
kerosene [primus] stove	**gaz ocağı** *gaz ojaher*
knapsack	**sırt çantası** *sert chantaser*
mallet	**tokmak** *tokmak*
matches	**kibrit** *kibreet*
(air) mattress	**hava yatağı** *havah yat-eye-er*
paraffin	**parafin** *parafin*
sleeping bag	**uyku tulumu** *oykoo tooloomu*
tent	**çadır** *chader*
tent pegs	**çadır kazıkları** *chader kazerk-lar-er*
tent pole	**çadır direği** *chader dee-ray-ee*

Checking out Otelden ayrılma

What time do we have to check out by?	**Saat kaçta otelden ayrılmamız gerekiyor?** sa-art katch-ta oh-tel-den eye-_rerl_-mamerz gerek-eeyor
Could we leave our baggage here until … p.m.?	**Bavullarımızı akşam saat … -e kadar burada bırakabilir miyiz?** bavool-larermerz-er aksham sa-art … eh kaddar boorada ber-akah-bee_leer_ meeyiz
I'm leaving now.	**Şimdi ayrılıyorum.** shim_dee_ eye-_rerl_-er-yorum
Could you order me a taxi, please?	**Lütfen bana bir taksi çağırabilir misiniz?** _lewt_-fen bana beer taksee char-ah-bee_leer_ miseeniz
It's been a very enjoyable stay.	**Buradan çok memnun kaldım.** booradan chok memnoon _kalderm_

Paying Ödeme

In a restaurant, leave a tip of around five percent even if the bill says service is included (**servis dahil**), and around 10 percent if it does not. Hotel porters should get a small tip. Taxi drivers and **dolmuş** drivers do not expect a tip, but you might have to round up the fare by a small amount as they may not always have the right change. Barbers and Turkish bath (**hamam**) attendants look for gratuities of around 20 percent. Attendants in public toilets deserve a few coins. Tips in U.S. dollars or pounds sterling are usually most appreciated.

May I have my bill, please?	**Lütfen hesabı alabilir miyim?** _lewt_-fen hes-_sab_-er ala-bee_leer_ meeyim
How much is my telephone bill?	**Telefon faturam ne kadar?** telefon fat_oo_ram neh kaddar
I think there's a mistake in this bill.	**Bu hesapta bir yanlışlık var.** boo hesapta beer yan_lersh_-lerk var
I've made … telephone calls.	**… telefon görüşmesi yaptım.** … telefon gur-_rewsh_-me-see _yap_term
I've taken … from the mini-bar.	**Minibar'dan … aldım.** minibar'dan … _alderm_
Can I have an itemized bill?	**Dökümlü hesap alabilir miyim?** dur_kewm_lew hehsap ala-bee_leer_ meeyim
Could I have a receipt, please?	**Lütfen fiş alabilir miyim?** _lewt_-fen fish ala-bee_leer_ meeyim

Eating Out

Restaurants

In Turkey, you will find any number of eating establishments to suit your mood. Whether you want a noisy, a romantic or an elegant evening, you should be able to find something to suit you. Some restaurants display a "tourist menu" in English and other languages and, in addition, offer one or more set menus. These restaurants have been rated first or second class by the Ministry of Tourism, but there is no appreciable difference.

Don't be fooled by the look of a restaurant. Appearances are not always to be trusted and you may find excellent food hiding behind a drab exterior.

Lokanta/Restaurant *lokanta/"restaurant"*

If a place calls itself a restaurant it is often geared to the business trade, with a certain number of international dishes. A **lokanta** tends to serve mainly Turkish food, sometimes with a tourist menu.

Balık lokantası *balerk lokanta-ser*

Fish restaurants, found along the coast and in ports. They offer fresh fish and seafood, as well as a splendid variety of appetizers (**meze**).

Kebapçı *kebapcher*

These restaurants serve various kinds of grilled meats or kebabs.

Köfteci *kurftejee*

These establishments specialize in **köfte**, a type of grilled croquette made from minced lamb.

Hazır yemek *hazer yemek*

A type of fast-food restaurant specializing in dishes that have been prepared beforehand and only need reheating. The menu will include soup, rice, and meat and vegetable dishes.

İşkembeci *ishkem-bejee*

Specialists in **İşkembe çorbasi** – mutton tripe soup.

Pideci *peedejee*

The closest thing to a pizzeria. Flat bread (**pide**) served hot out of the oven and garnished with minced meat, tomatoes and/or cheese.

Tatlıcı *tatlerjer*

If you have a sweet tooth these are a must – restaurants serving a variety of desserts and sweet pastries. They also offer light chicken lunches.

Bufe *bewfeh*

Kiosks selling sandwiches, chicken dishes, soft drinks, and other snacks.

Gazino *gazeeno*

Family restaurant where you can choose between a light supper or full meal, often with some form of entertainment, such as music and dancing.

Meal times Yemek saatleri

Lunch is normally served between midday and around 2 p.m. Dinner is served from 7 to 12 p.m.

Turkish cuisine Türk mutfağı

Turkish cooking is characterized by its grilled meats, stuffed vegetables, and pastry desserts steeped in syrup. Shish kebab, stuffed grape leaves, and baklava are among the dishes enjoyed the world over.

To dine out successfully in Turkey you need to dispense with some common habits. It is usually not worth bothering with the menu other than for an idea of prices. For starters (**meze**), go and see what is cooking in the kitchen and order a selection. Do not order your main course until you have had your fill of appetizers, served with fresh bread to soak up the tasty oil and juices. If you choose fish, you pick out your choice from a display cabinet and establish its price in advance. Do not overlook Turkish desserts; ask the waiter to tell you what is available.

Although Islam forbids alcohol, drinking is allowed under Turkish law, and alcoholic drinks are widely available. Likewise, pork is forbidden, but you may find it offered in some tourist-oriented restaurants. If you are visiting during Ramadan, the month of fasting, out of courtesy you should try to avoid eating or smoking in public places during daylight hours.

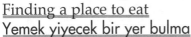

A table for …, please.	**Lütfen … kişilik bir masa.**
	lewt-fen … keesheelik beer massa
1/2/3/4	**bir/iki/üç/dört**
	beer/ikee/ewch/durrt
Thank you.	**Teşekkür ederim.** *teshek-kewr ederim*
The bill, please.	**Hesap lütfen.** *hesap lewt-fen*

Finding a place to eat
Yemek yiyecek bir yer bulma

Can you recommend a good restaurant?	**İyi bir lokanta önerebilir misiniz?** *eeyee beer lokanta owe-nair-eh-beeleer miseeniz*
Is there a(n) … restaurant near here?	**Yakınlarda bir … lokantası var mı?** *yakernlarda beer … lokanta-ser var mer*
Chinese	**Çin** *chin*
fish	**balık** *balerk*
inexpensive	**ucuz** *oocuz*
Italian	**İtalyan** *eetalyan*
vegetarian	**vejetaryen** *veje-tar-yen*
traditional local restaurant	**geleneksel yerel yemekler sunan lokanta** *gelenek-sel yair-el yemek-lair soonan lokanta*
Where can I find a(n) …?	**Nerede bir … bulabilirim?** *neredeh beer … bull-ah-beeleerim*
burger stand	**büfe** *bew-feh*
café	**kafe** *kafeh*
café / restaurant	**kafe/lokanta** *kafeh/lokanta*
with a terrace / garden	**teraslı/bahçeli** *tair-ass-ler/bah-che-lee*
fast-food restaurant	**hazır yemek lokantası** *hazzer yemek lokanta-ser*
ice-cream parlor	**dondurmacı** *dondur-majer*
pizzeria	**pizzacı** *pizza-jer*
steak house	**et lokantası** *ett lokanta-ser*

DIRECTIONS ➤ 94

Reservations Yer ayırtma

I'd like to reserve a table …	**… bir masa ayırtmak istiyorum.**
	… beer massah eye-ert-mak istee-yorum
for two	**iki kişi için** *ikee keeshee itchin*
for this evening/ tomorrow at …	**bu gece/yarın saat … için**
	boo geh-jeh/yarern sa-art … itchin
We'll come at 8:00.	**Saat 8.00'de geleceğiz.**
	sa-art sekeez-deh gel-eh-jayeez
A table for two, please.	**İki kişilik bir masa lütfen.**
	ikee keesheelik beer massah lewt-fen
We have a reservation.	**Yer ayırtmıştık.** *yair eye-ert-mershterk*

Saat kaç için?	For what time?
Adınız nedir?	What's the name, please?
Özür dilerim. Doluyuz.	I'm sorry. We're very busy/full.
… dakika içinde bir masa boşalacak.	We'll have a free table in … minutes.
Lütfen … dakika sonra geri geliniz.	Please come back in … minutes.
Sigara içilen bölümde mi içilmeyen bölümde mi?	Smoking or non-smoking?

Where to sit Oturacak yer

Could we sit …?	**… oturabilir miyiz?**
	… otoorah-beeleer meeyiz
over there/outside	**orada/dışarda** *orada/der-sharda*
in a non-smoking area	**sigara içilmeyen bir yerde**
	seegara itcheel-may-en beer yair-deh
by the window	**pencere kenarında** *penjair-eh kenarernda*

– Bu gece için bir masa ayıtmak istiyorum.
(I'd like to reserve a table for this evening.)
– Kaç kişi için? (For how many people?)
– Dört kişi. (Four.)
– Saat kaç için? (For what time?)
– Saat 8.00'de geleceğiz. (We'll come at 8:00.)
– Adınız nedir? (And what's the name, please?)
– Smith (Smith.)
– Tamam. Görüşmek üzere. (Very good. We'll see you then.)

TIME ➤ 220; NUMBERS ➤ 216

Ordering Yemek siparişi vermek

Waiter!	**Garson!** *gar-son*
May I see the wine list, please?	**Şarap listesini görebilir miyim lütfen?** *sharap leeste-see-nee gur-rebeeleer meeyim lewt-fen*
Do you have a set menu?	**Fiks mönü var mı?** *fix murnew var mer*
Can you recommend some typical local dishes?	**Tipik yerel yemekler önerebilir misiniz?** *tipeek yair-el yemek-lair owe-nair-eh-beeleer miseeniz*
Could you tell me what … is?	**… -in ne olduğunu söyleyebilir misiniz?** *… een neh oldoo-yu-noo sow-leh-ye-beeleer miseeniz*
What kind of … do you have?	**Ne tür … var?** *neh tewr … var*
I'd like …/I'll have …	**… istiyorum.** *… istee-yorum*
a bottle/glass/carafe of …	**bir şişe/bardak/sürahi …** *beer shee-sheh /bar-dak/sew-rah-ee*

Siparişinizi vermeye hazır mısınız?	Are you ready to order?
Ne istersiniz?	What would you like?
Ne içmek istersiniz?	What would you like to drink?
… -i öneririm.	I recommend …
… yok.	We don't have …
Afiyet olsun.	Enjoy your meal.

– *Siparişinizi vermeye hazır mısınız?*
(Are you ready to order?)
– Özgün bir yerel yemek önerebilir misiniz?
(Can you recommend a typical local dish?)
– *Evet. Ahtapot salatasını öneririm.*
(Yes. I recommend the octopus salad.)
– Tamam. Ben onu istiyorum.
(Okay. I'll have that, please.)
– *Elbette. Ne içmek istersiniz?*
(Certainly. And what would you like to drink?)
– Lütfen bir sürahi kırmızı şarap.
(A carafe of red wine, please.)
– *Elbette. (Certainly.)*

DRINKS ➤ 49; MENU READER ➤ 52

37

Accompaniments Yan siparişler

Could I have … without the …?	**… -i … -siz isteyebilir miyim?** … ee … seez istay-eh-bee<u>leer</u> meeyim
With a side order of …	**Yanında … istiyorum.** yan<u>er</u>nda … is<u>tee</u>-yorum
Could I have a salad instead of vegetables, please?	**Sebze yerine salata isteyebilir miyim lütfen?** seb-zeh yair-<u>een</u>-deh sal<u>a</u>tah istay-eh-bee<u>leer</u> meeyim <u>lewt</u>-fen
Does the meal come with …?	**Yemeğin yanında … geliyor mu?** ye<u>may</u>-een yan<u>er</u>nda … ge<u>lee</u>-yor moo
vegetables/potatoes	**sebze/patates** seb-zeh/pa<u>tat</u>-tes
rice/pasta	**pilav/makarna** pee-lav/ma<u>kar</u>nah
Do you have any …?	**… var mı?** … var mer
ketchup/mayonnaise	**ketçap/mayonez** ket-chap/<u>mi</u>-yonez
I'd like … with that.	**Yanında … istiyorum.** yan<u>er</u>nda … is<u>tee</u>-yorum
vegetables/salad	**sebze/salata** seb-zeh/sal<u>a</u>tah
potatoes/French fries	**patates/patates kızartması** pa<u>tat</u>-tes/pa<u>tat</u>-tes ker-<u>zart</u>ma-ser
sauce	**sos** soss
ice	**buz** booz
May I have some …?	**Biraz … isteyebilir miyim?** bee<u>raz</u> … istay-eh-bee<u>leer</u> meeyim
bread	**ekmek** ek-mek
butter	**tereyağı** tereh-<u>yaa</u>-er
lemon	**limon** leemon
mustard	**hardal** har-<u>dal</u>
pepper	**biber** bee-bair
salt	**tuz** tooz
oil and vinegar	**sıvı yağ ve sirke** server yaa veh seer-<u>keh</u>
sugar	**şeker** shek-air
artificial sweetener	**yapay tatlandırıcı** yap-<u>eye</u> tat-<u>lander</u>-erjer
vinaigrette [French dressing]	**sirkeli salata sosu** seer-<u>keh</u>-lee sal<u>a</u>tah sossoo

General requests Genel istekler

Could I/we have a(n) (clean) ..., please?	**Lütfen (temiz) bir ... isteye bilir miyiz?** _lewt_-fen (temeez) beer ... istay-eh bee_leer_ meeyiz
ashtray	**kül tablası** kewl _tabla_-ser
cup/glass	**fincan/bardak** fern-jan/bar-dak
fork/knife	**çatal/bıçak** cha-tal/ber-chak
plate/spoon	**tabak/kaşık** tabak/ka-sherk
napkin [serviette]	**peçete** _peche_-teh
I'd like some more ..., please.	**Biraz daha ... istiyorum lütfen.** beeraz dah-ha ... _istee_-yorum _lewt_-fen
That's all, thanks.	**Bu kadar, teşekkürler.** boo kaddar teshek-_kewr_-lair
Where are the bathrooms [toilets]?	**Tuvalet nerede?** too-_va_-let neredeh

Special requirements Özel istekler

I can't eat food containing ...	**... içeren yiyecek yiyemem.** ... itch-_air_-en yee-_ye_jek yee-_ye_-mem
salt/sugar	**tuz/şeker** tooz/shek-air
Do you have any dishes/drinks for diabetics?	**Şeker hastaları için özel yemek/içki var mı?** shek-air has_tal_ar-er itch_in_ urzel yemek/itch_kee_ var mer
Do you have vegetarian dishes?	**Etsiz yemeğiniz var mı?** etseez ye_may_-eeniz var mer

For the children Çocuklar için

Do you have a children's menu?	**Çocuklar için yemek listesi var mı?** cho_jook_-lar itch_in_ yemek _leeste_-see var mer
Could you bring a child's seat, please?	**Çocuk sandalyesi getirebilir misiniz lütfen?** cho_jook_ san-_darl_-yesee geteer-eh-bee_leer_ miseeniz _lewt_-fen
Where can I change the baby?	**Bebeğin altını nerede değiştirebilirim?** bebay-een al_tern_-er neredeh day-eeshteer-eh-_bee_leerim
Where can I feed the baby?	**Bebeğe nerede yemek verebilirim?** bebay-ye neredeh yemek vereh-_bee_leerim

CHILDREN ➤ 113

Fast food/Café Hazır yemek/Kafe

Something to drink İçecek bir şeyler

I'd like (a) …	**Bir … istiyorum.** *beer … istee-yorum*
beer	**bira** *beerah*
tea/coffee	**çay/kahve** *chay/kah-ve*
black/with milk	**sütsüz/sütlü** *sewtsewz/sewtlew*
I'd like a … of red/white wine.	**Bir … kırmızı/beyaz şarap istiyorum.** *beer … ker-merzer/bay-yaz sharap istee-yorum*
glass/carafe/bottle	**bardak/sürahi/şişe** *bar-dak/sew-rah-ee/shee-sheh*
bottled/draft [draught]	**şişe/fıçı** *shee-sheh/fer-cher*

And to eat Ve yiyecek bir şeyler

A piece/slice of …, please.	**Bir parça/dilim … lütfen.** *beer par-chah/deelim … lewt-fen*
I'd like two of those.	**Şundan iki tane istiyorum.** *shoon-dan ikee tarneh istee-yorum*
burger/fries	**burger/patates kızartması** *boorger/patat-tes ker-zartma-ser*
omelet/pizza	**omlet/pizza** *om-let/pizza*
sandwich/cake	**sandöviç/kek** *sand-urvitch/kek*
ice cream	**dondurma** *dondurmah*
chocolate/strawberry/vanilla	**çikolatalı/çilekli/vanilyalı** *cheeko-latahler/chee-leklee/vaneel-yahler*
A … portion, please.	**Bir porsiyon … lütfen.** *beer porsee-yon … lewt-fen*
small	**küçük** *kew-chewk*
regular [medium]	**orta boy** *ortah boy*
large	**büyük** *bew-yewk*
It's to go [take away].	**Paket olacak.** *pa-ket olajak*
That's all, thanks.	**Bu kadar, teşekkürler.** *boo kaddar, teshek-kewr-lair*

DRINKS ➤ 49

> – Ne istersiniz? *(What would you like?)*
> – Iki kahve lütfen. *(Two coffees, please.)*
> – Sütsüz, sütlü? *(Black or with milk?)*
> – Sütlü, lütfen. *(With milk, please.)*
> – Yiyecek bir şeyler? *(Anything to eat?)*
> – Bu kadar, teşekkürler. *(That's all, thanks.)*

Complaints Şikayetler

I have no knife/fork/spoon.	**Bıçağım/çatalım/kaşığım yok.** *bercha-yerm/cha-tal-erm /kash-er-erm yok*
There must be some mistake.	**Bir yanlışlık olmalı.** *beer yanlersh-lerk ol-marler*
That's not what I ordered.	**Benim siparişim bu değil.** *benim see-par-eeshim day-eel*
I asked for …	**… istemiştim.** *… istemeeshtim*
I can't eat this.	**Bunu yiyemem.** *boonu yee-yemem*
The meat is …	**Et …** *et…*
overdone	**çok pişmiş** *chok peesh-meesh*
underdone	**az pişmiş** *az peesh-meesh*
too tough	**çok sert** *chok sait*
This is too …	**Bu çok …** *boo chok*
bitter/sour	**acı/ekşi** *ah-jer /ek-shee*
The food is cold.	**Yemek soğuk.** *yemek soh-ook*
This isn't fresh.	**Bu taze değil.** *boo tarzeh day-eel*
How much longer will our food be?	**Yemek için daha ne kadar bekleyeceğiz?** *yemek itchin dah-ha neh kaddar bek-lay-eh-jayeez*
We can't wait any longer. We're leaving.	**Daha fazla bekleyemeyeceğiz. Gidiyoruz.** *dah-ha fazlah bek-lay-eh-may-eh-jayeez. gidee-yoruz*
This isn't clean.	**Bu temiz değil.** *boo temeez day-eel*
I'd like to speak to the head waiter/manager.	**Şef garson/müdür ile konuşmak istiyorum.** *shef gar-son/mewdewr eeleh konooshmak istee-yorum*

41

Paying Hesabı ödeme

Service charges are normally included in the bill. Credit cards are accepted at an increasing number of restaurants, but these tend to be limited to large cities and tourist resorts.

I'd like to pay.	**Hesabı ödemek istiyorum.** *he<u>sab</u>-er <u>ur</u>demek i<u>stee</u>-yorum*
The bill, please.	**Hesap lütfen.** *hesap <u>lewt</u>-fen*
We'd like to pay separately.	**Ayrı ayrı ödemek istiyoruz.** *eye-<u>rer</u> eye-<u>rer</u> <u>ur</u>demek i<u>stee</u>-yoruz*
It's all together, please.	**Hepsi birlikte, lütfen.** *hepsee beer<u>lik</u>te, <u>lewt</u>-fen*
I think there's a mistake in this bill.	**Sanırım bu hesapta bir yanlışlık var.** *san-er-<u>rerm</u> boo he<u>sap</u>ta beer yan<u>lersh</u>lerk var*
What's this amount for?	**Bu tutar ne için?** *boo too<u>tar</u> neh it<u>chin</u>*
I didn't have that. I had …	**Bunu almadım. … aldım.** *boonu al<u>ma</u>derm. … <u>al</u>derm*
Is service included?	**Servis dahil mi?** *sairvees dah-<u>heel</u> mee*
Can I pay with this credit card?	**Bu kredi kartı ile ödeme yapabilir miyim?** *boo kredee kart-er eeleh <u>ur</u>demeh yapa-bee<u>leer</u> meeyim*
I forgot my wallet.	**Cüzdanımı unutmuşum.** *jewz-<u>dan</u>ermer oonutmooshum*
I don't have enough cash.	**Yanımda yeterli para yok.** *yan<u>erm</u>da yet-airlee parah yok*
Could I have a receipt, please?	**Lütfen fiş verir misiniz?** *<u>lewt</u>-fen fish ve<u>reer</u> miseeniz*
That was a very good meal.	**Yemek çok güzeldi.** *yemek chok gew<u>zel</u>-dee*

– Garson! Hesap lütfen. *(Waiter! The bill, please.)*
– Elbette. Buyrun. *(Certainly. Here you are.)*
– Servis dahil mi? *(Is service included?)*
– Evet, dahil. *(Yes, it is.)*
– Bu kredi kartı ile ödeme yapabilir miyim?
(Can I pay with this credit card?)
– Evet, elbette. *(Yes, of course.)*
– Teşekkür ederim. Yemek çok güzeldi.
(Thank you. That was a very good meal.)

Course by course Yemekler

Breakfast Kahvaltı

Turkish breakfast is usually a continental breakfast, sometimes
with the addition of sheep's milk cheese and black olives.

I'd like …	**… istiyorum.**
	… is*tee*-yorum
bread	**ekmek** *ek-mek*
butter	**tereyağı** *tereh-yaa-er*
eggs	**yumurta** *yoo*murta
boiled / fried / scrambled	**katı/sahanda/çırpma**
	*kat-ter/sa*han*da/*çher*pma*
fruit juice	**meyve suyu** *may-veh soo-yoo*
grapefruit / orange	**greyfurt/portakal** *grey-foort/porta*kal*
honey	**bal** *bal*
jam / marmalade	**reçel/marmelat** *ret*chel*/mar-me*lat*
milk	**süt** *soot*
rolls	**küçük yuvarlak ekmek**
	*kew-chewk yoo*var*-lak ek-mek*
toast	**kızarmış ekmek** *ker-*zar*mersh ek-mek*

Appetizers [Starters] Mezeler

Turkish **meze** are often the highlight of a meal, or even the complete meal
itself. Vegetarians will not go hungry as there is a good variety of dishes
made from vegetables and beans.

arnavut ciğeri	*arna-voot jee-air-ee*	fried liver morsels
beyaz peynir	*bay-yaz pay-neer*	white cheese
börek	*bur-rek*	hot filo pastries
dolma	*dol-mah*	stuffed grape leaves
imam bayıldı	*eemam by-yerl-der*	stuffed eggplant [aubergine]
patlıcan salatası	*patler-jan sa*la*ta-ser*	eggplant [aubergine] salad
pilaki	*pee*lak*-ee*	beans in olive oil
tarama	*taramah*	taramasalata *(fish roe pâté)*

Soups Çorbalar

balık çorbası	*balerk chorba-ser*	fish soup
et suyu	*et soo-yoo*	broth (thin soup of meat or fish stock)
et suyuna çorba	*et soo-yoo-na chorbah*	consommé
kremalı çorba	*krema-ler chorba*	cream soup
patates çorbası	*patat-tes chorba-ser*	potato soup
sebze çorbası	*seb-zeh chorba-ser*	vegetable soup
soğan çorbası	*so-arn chorba-ser*	onion soup
tavuk çorbası	*tavook chorba-ser*	chicken soup

Fish and seafood Balık ve deniz ürünleri

ahtapot	*ah-tapot*	octopus
alabalık	*ala-balerk*	trout
deniz tarağı	*deneez tara-er*	clams
ıstakoz	*ersta-koz*	lobster
istiridye	*eesteer-eedyeh*	oysters
kalamar	*kala-mar*	squid
karides	*kar-eedes*	shrimp [prawns]
lüfer	*lew-fair*	bluefish
midye	*meed-yeh*	mussels
morina balığı	*moreena bal-er-er*	cod
pisi balığı	*pee-see bal-er-er*	plaice
ringa balığı	*reenga bal-er-er*	herring [whitebait]
ton balığı	*ton bal-er-er*	tuna

Kılıç şiş *kerlerch shish*
Swordfish kebabs grilled with bay leaves, tomatoes, and green peppers.

Çınarcık usulü balık *cher-narjerk oosulew balerk*
Fried swordfish, sea bass and shrimp, served garnished with mushrooms and flavored with brandy.

Uskumru pilakisi *ooskumroo peela-keesee*
Mackerel fried in olive oil, with potatoes, celery, carrots, and garlic.
Served cold.

Meat and poultry Et ve kümes hayvanları

bonfile	bon-fee-leh	steak
böbrek	bur-brek	kidneys
but	boot	leg
but eti	boot et-ee	saddle
ciğer	jee-air	liver
dana	dan-ah	veal
domuz	domooz	pork
fileto/sığır filetosu/ but/dana pirzolası	feeleto/ser-er feeleto- soo/boot/dan-ah peerzo-la-ser	fillet/sirloin/rump/ T-bone steak
hindi	hindi	turkey
jambon	jambon	ham
kemikli et	kemeek-lee et	cutlet
kuzu	koozu	lamb
ördek	urdek	duck
pirzola	peerzola	chops
sığır eti	ser-er et-ee	beef
sosis	sosees	sausages
sülün	sewlewn	pheasant
tavuk	tavook	chicken
tavşan	tav-shan	rabbit

Şiş köfte *shish kurfteh*
Minced lamb croquettes on a skewer, grilled over charcoal.

Yoğurtlu kebab *yo-oort-loo kebab*
Kebab on toasted bread with pureed tomatoes and seasoned yogurt.

Çerkez tavuğu *cher-kez tavoo-oo*
Circassian chicken: boiled chicken with rice and nut sauce.

Çiğ köfte *chee kurfteh*
Raw meatballs made from minced meat, cracked wheat, and chili powder.

Kuzu dolması *koozu dolmaser*
Lamb stuffed with savory rice, liver and pistachios.

Kuzu güveç *koozoo gew-vetch*
Lamb stew with onions, garlic, potatoes, tomatoes, and herbs.

Vegetables Sebzeler

bezelye	*bezel-ye*	peas
biber	*bee-bair*	peppers
(kırmızı, yeşil)	*(ker-merzer/yesheel)*	(red, green)
domates	*domar-tes*	tomatoes
havuç	*havooch*	carrots
hıyar	*huy-yar*	cucumber
kabak	*kabak*	zucchini [courgettes]
kereviz	*kair-eveez*	celery
lahana	*laha-na*	cabbage
mantar	*man-tar*	mushrooms
marul	*marool*	lettuce
patates	*patat-tes*	potatoes
patlıcan	*pat-lerjan*	eggplant [aubergine]
pirinç	*peerinch*	rice
sarı şalgam	*sar-er shalgam*	rutabaga [swede]
sarmısak	*sar-mersak*	garlic
soğan	*so-arn*	onions
şalgam	*shalgam*	turnips
taze fasulye	*tarzeh fasool-ye*	green beans
taze soğan	*tarzeh so-arn*	shallots [spring onions]

Dolma *dolmah*
Turkish cuisine is famous for its stuffed vegetables (**dolma**), which come in two main varieties: a vegetarian stuffing with tomatoes, onions, olive oil, and garlic; and a minced meat stuffing with cheese, onions, and tomatoes. They are eaten hot or cold, often with yogurt.

Kabak musakkası *kabak moosak-kaser*
Vegetarian moussaka with eggplant [aubergine] and zucchini [courgette].

Türlü *tewr-lew*
Cooked mixed vegetables and beans, served hot.

İmam bayıldı *ee-mam bayerl-der*
Eggplant [aubergine] stuffed with tomatoes and cooked in olive oil; eaten cold.

Salad Salatalar

çoban salatası	*cho-ban salata-ser*	shepherd's salad
domates ve soğan salatası	*domar-tes veh so-arn salata-ser*	tomato and onion salad
karışık salata	*kar-er-sherk salata*	mixed salad
patates salatası	*patat-tes salata-ser*	potato salad
yeşil salata	*yesheel salata*	green salad

Cheese Peynirler

beyaz peynir	*bay-yaz pay-neer*	white cheese
kaşar	*kashar*	hard cheese
otlu peynir	*ot-loo pay-neer*	herb cheese
tulum peyniri	*tooloom pay-neer*	goat cheese

Herbs and spices Otlar ve baharatlar

dere otu	*dereh o-too*	dill
karanfil	*karanfeel*	cloves
kırmızı biber	*kermerzer beebehr*	chili
kekik	*kekik*	thyme
kimyon	*keemyon*	cumin
kişniş	*kishnish*	coriander
maydanoz	*my-danoz*	parsley
nane	*naneh*	mint
safran	*safran*	saffron

Fruit Meyveler

ahududu	_ahoo-doodu_	raspberries
çilek	_chee-lek_	strawberries
elma	_el-mah_	apples
erik	_ereek_	plums
greyfurt	_grey-foort_	grapefruit
karpuz	_kar-pooz_	watermelon
kavun	_kavoon_	melon
kiraz	_kee**raz**_	cherries
muz	_mooz_	bananas
nar	_nar_	pomegranates
portakal	_porta**kal**_	oranges
şeftali	_shef-**talee**_	peaches
üzüm	_ew**zewm**_	grapes

Dessert Tatlılar

aşure	_a**shooreh**_	mixed grain, bean, and fruit dessert
ayva tatlısı	_eye-vah **tatler**-ser_	quince dessert
baklava	_**bak**-lavah_	filo pastry filled with honey and pistachio nuts
kabak tatlısı	_kabak **tatler**-ser_	pumpkin dessert
kadayıf	_ka-**dye**-yerf_	shredded wheat dessert
kazandibi	_ka**zand**ibee_	oven-browned milk dessert
muhallebi	_moo**halleh**-bee_	(milk) pudding
sütlaç	_**sewt**-latch_	rice pudding
tavuk göğsü	_ta**vook** go-**oos**-oo_	(milk) pudding with thin ribbons of chicken breast

Drinks İçecekler

Alcoholic drinks Alkollü içecekler

Although Turkey is a Muslim country and alcohol is strictly forbidden under Islamic law, it is reasonably relaxed about drinking, particularly in tourist areas.

The national drink is **rakı**. This is a spirit made from distilled grapes and aniseed, similar to French pastis or Lebanese arak. It is nearly 90 percent proof and is usually drunk with water, which turns it milky white.

Turkey also has a long history of wine production, although almost all of it is exported today. The best Turkish wines, particularly white, come from the İzmir region.

There are locally produced beers and some spirits, such as gin and brandy. Imported brands are also available, but they are much more expensive.

Do you have … beer?	**… birası var mı?**	… beera-ser var mer
bottled/draft [draught]	**şişe/fıçı**	_shee_-sheh/fer-cher
Can you recommend a … wine?	**Bir … şarap önerebilir misiniz?**	beer … sharap owe-nair-eh-bee_leer_ miseeniz
red/white/blush [rosé]	**kırmızı/beyaz/pembe**	ker-mer_zer_/bay-_yaz_/pembeh
dry/sweet/sparkling	**sek/tatlı/köpüklü**	sek/tat-ler/kur-_pewk_-lew
I'd like the house wine, please.	**Yerli şaraptan istiyorum lütfen.**	yair-lee sharap-tan i_stee_-yorum _lewt_-fen
I'd like a glass of rakı.	**Bir kadeh rakı istiyorum lütfen.**	beer ka_deh_ raker i_stee_-yorum _lewt_-fen
I'd like a single/double …	**Tek/duble … istiyorum.**	tek/doobleh … i_stee_-yorum
brandy/gin/whisky/vodka	**konyak/cin/viski/votka**	kon-yak/jeen/veeskee/vot-ka
neat [straight]	**sek**	sek
on the rocks [with ice]	**buzlu**	booz-loo
with water/tonic water	**su/tonik ile**	soo/toneek eeleh

Non-alcoholic drinks Alkolsüz içkiler

If you don't want anything alcoholic, you'll find a satisfying variety of soft drinks to try. These range from carbonated bottled drinks like cola to fruit juices and mineral water. Although tap water is safe to drink, it is heavily chlorinated. Mineral water is a cheaper, pleasant-tasting alternative.

There are also a number of traditional drinks like **ayran**, a refreshing drink made of yogurt mixed with mineral water and a pinch of salt; **şıra**, unfermented grape juice; and **boza**, a calorie-packed sourish drink made from fermented millet. **Boza** can only be bought in winter, and is best bought from cake shops, where it is served sprinkled with cinnamon.

Although coffee is the drink that one associates with Turkey, tea is the early morning drink, and the one most often drunk during the day. You should also try some of the available herbal infusions; mint is particularly refreshing.

I'd like …	**… istiyorum.** … _istee_-yorum
(hot) chocolate	**(sıcak) kakao** (_serjak_) _kaka_-o
cola/lemonade	**kola/limonata** _kolah/leemonatah_
fruit juice	**meyve suyu** _may_-veh soo-yoo
orange/pineapple/tomato	**portakal/ananas/domates** _portakal/ananas/domar_-tes
turnip juice	**şalgam suyu** _shalgam_ soo-yoo
milkshake	**sütlü meyve suyu** sewt_lew may_-ve soo-yoo
mineral water	**maden suyu** mar-den soo-yoo
carbonated	**gazlı** _gazler_
non-carbonated [still]	**gazsız** _gazserz_
natural yogurt drink	**ayran** eye-_ran_
hot herbal drink	**salep** _sa_-lep

Coffeehouse Kahvehane

The coffeehouse is an institution in Turkey. Usually rather modest establishments, they are ubiquitous in towns, and there is at least one coffeehouse even in the smallest village.

The coffeehouse is the exclusive gathering place of the men. Women are generally unwelcome but well-educated Turkish ladies and female business travelers from the West will generally not be turned away.

You will see men sitting in groups vigorously discussing politics, the weather, soccer, etc. Other customers will be concentrating on a game of backgammon or playing dominoes.

For a small fee, the waiter will bring you a water pipe (**nargile**). Always smoke the water pipe in a group, passing the mouthpiece around. Draw the smoke up very slowly. Even if you are a heavy smoker, the water pipe may give you a mild feeling of euphoria.

More often than not, there will be no food sold at a coffeehouse. Sometimes a vendor might pass through selling sesame rolls (**simit**) or meat pies.

I'd like a cup of Turkish coffee.	**Bir Türk kahvesi lütfen.** *beer tewrk kave_see_ _lewt_-fen*
regular sweetness	**orta şekerli** *ortah sheker_lee_*
extra sweet	**şekerli** *sheker_lee_*
without sugar	**sade** *sa_deh_*
Can you prepare a water pipe for me?	**Bana nargile hazırlayabilir misiniz?** *bana nargeeleh hazerr-lah-ya-bee_leer_ miseeniz*
We'd like a backgammon board / some dominoes, please.	**Bize tavla/domino getirebilir misiniz?** *beezeh tavlah/domino geteereh-bee_leer_ miseeniz*

Menu Reader

This Menu Reader is an alphabetical glossary of terms that you may find in a menu. Certain traditional dishes are cross-referenced to the relevant page in the *Course by course* section, where they are described in more detail.

baharatlı	*bahar-rat-ler*	spicy
bol yağda kızartma	*bol yaa-da ker-zartma*	deep-fried
buğulama	*boo-yoo-lama*	steamed
çok az pişmiş	*chok az peeshmeesh*	very rare
dolma	*dolma*	stuffed ➤ 46
ekmek kırıntıları ile kızartılmış	*ek-mek ker-rernter-lar-er eeleh ker-zarterlmersh*	breaded
fırında nar gibi yapmak	*ferernda nar gibee yapmak*	oven-browned
fırında pişmiş	*ferernda peeshmeesh*	baked
hafif ateşte pişmiş	*hafeef ateshteh peeshmeesh*	braised
hafif kanlı	*hafeef kan-ler*	rare
haşlama	*hashlama*	poached
haşlanmış	*hashlanmersh*	boiled
ızgara	*erzgarah*	grilled
iyi pişmiş	*eeyee peeshmeesh*	well-done
kızarmış	*ker-zarmersh*	roasted
kızartma	*ker-zartma*	fried
kremalı	*krema-ler*	creamed
kuşbaşı kesim	*kooshbash-er keseem*	diced
orta ateşte	*orta ateshteh*	medium
salamurada yatırmak	*salamoorada yatermak*	marinated
sote	*so-tay*	sautéed
tütsülenmiş	*tewt-sew-len-mish*	smoked
yahni	*yah-nee*	stewed

A
acı hot *(spicy)*

acı biber chili pepper

acı biber sosu hot pepper sauce

acı sos spicy sauce

ada çayı sage

ağır strong *(flavor)*

ahtapot octopus

ahududu raspberries

akşam yemeği dinner

alabalık trout

alkollü içki alcoholic drink

alkolsüz içkiler non-alcoholic drink/soft drink

ananas pineapple

anasonlu likör aniseed liqueur

aperatif aperitif

ardıç böğürtleni juniper berries

armut pear

arnavut ciğeri fried liver morsels

aşure mixed grain dessert ➤ 48

av eti game

avakado avocado

ayran natural yogurt drink ➤ 50

ayva tatlısı quince dessert

B
badem almonds

badem ezmesi marzipan

bademli pasta almond tart

badem şekeri sugared almonds

baharat spices, herbs

baharatlı spicy

bakla broad beans

baklava filo pastry filled with honey ➤ 48

bal honey

balık fish

balık çorbası fish soup

barbunya kidney beans

bardak glass

barlam hake *(similar to cod)*

bazlama flapjack

beç tavuğu guinea fowl

bektaşi üzümü gooseberry

beyaz white *(wine)*

beyaz peynir white cheese

beyaz sos white sauce

beyaz üzüm white grapes

beyin brains

beze meringue

bezelye peas

bıldırcın quail

biber pepper *(condiment)*

biberiye rosemary

biftek steak

bira beer

bisküvit cookies [biscuits]

bol yağda kızartma deep-fried

bonfile steak

boza millet drink ➤ 50

böbrek kidney

böğürtlen blackberries

börek hot filo pastries ➤ 43

Brüksel lahanası Brussel sprouts

bufa balığı lamprey *(fish)*

buğulama steamed

buğulama balık steamed fish

but rump steak

but eti saddle

buz ice

buzlu iced/on the rocks *(drink)*

buzlu su iced water

C **ceviz** walnuts

ciğer liver

cin gin

cin soda gin fizz

cin tonik gin and tonic

Ç **çaça balığı** sprats *(young herring)*

çapak balığı bream; sea bream

çavdar ekmeği rye bread

çay tea *(beverage)*

çeşitli kuruyemiş assorted nuts

çiğ raw

çiğ börek fritters

çikolata chocolate

çikolatalı tatlı truffles

çilek strawberries

çırpma scrambled *(egg)*

çoban salatası shepherd's salad

çok soslu highly seasoned

çorba soup

çörek bun

çulluk woodcock

D **dana** beef

dana eti veal

dana kıyma minced beef

dana pirzolası T-bone steak

defne yaprağı bay leaf

deniz tarağı clams/cockles

deniz ürünleri seafood

dereotu dill

dil tongue

dil balığı sole

dilim slice

dilimli sliced

dişi koyun sutünden peynir ewe's milk cheese

doldurulmuş stuffed

dolma stuffed grape leaves

dolma zeytin stuffed olives

domates tomatoes

domates ketçabı ketchup

domates sosu tomato sauce

domates ve soğan tomato and onion salad

domuz pork

domuz paçası meat loaf in aspic made from pork [brawn]

domuz pastırması bacon

domuz sosisi pork sausages

dondurma ice cream

duble double *(alcohol)*

dut mulberry

düğme mantar button mushrooms

E ekmek bread

ekmek kırıntıları bread crumbs

ekmek kırıntıları ile kızartılmış breaded *(cutlet, etc.)*

ekşi sour *(taste)*

elma apples

elma şarabı cider

elmalı pasta apple pie/tart

enginar artichokes

erik plums

et meat *(general)*

et sosu gravy

et suyu broth *(thin soup of meat or fish stock)*

et suyuna çorba consommé

et ve sebze suyu meat and vegetable broth

evde yapılmış homemade

ezme pâté

F fasulye beans

fasulye sürgünü bean sprouts

fesleğen basil

fıçı birası draft [draught] beer

fındık hazelnuts

fırında patates roast potatoes

fırında pişmiş baked

fileto fillet

frenk maydanozu chervil

frenk soğanı chives

G garnitür
garnish, trimming

gazlı carbonated

gazoz lemonade

gazsız non-carbonated [still] (*drink*)

geyik eti venison

göğüs breast

gözleme waffles

greyfurt grapefruit

guava meyvesi guava

günün yemeği dish of the day

güveç casserole

güvercin pigeon

H hadım horoz capon

hafif light (*sauce, etc.*) / mild (*flavor*)

hamsi anchovies

hamur işi pastry

hardal mustard

havuç carrots

haşlama patates boiled potatoes

haşlanmış mısır sweet corn

hıyar cucumber

hıyar turşusu gherkins

hindi turkey

hindiba chicory / endive

hindistan cevizi coconut

horoz mantarı chanterelle mushrooms

hurma dates / fresh dates

I ıspanak spinach

ıstakoz lobster

ızgara grilled

ızgara tavuk grilled chicken

İ ilik marrow

imam bayıldı stuffed eggplant [aubergine] ➤ 46

incik shank (*top of leg*)

incir figs

istiridye oysters

istiridye mantarı oyster mushrooms

işkembe tripe

J jambon ham

jöle jelly

K **kabak** zucchini [courgette] / pumpkin

kabak tatlısı pumpkin dessert

kadayıf shredded wheat dessert

kafeini alınmış decaffeinated

kahvaltı breakfast

kahve coffee

kalamar squid

kalkan turbot / halibut

kalp heart

Karaman kimyonu caraway

karanfil cloves

karbonatlı carbonated

karışık baharat mixed spices

karışık ızgara mixed grill

karışık salata mixed salad

karışık sebze mixed vegetables

karides shrimp [prawns]

karnıbahar cauliflower

karpuz watermelon

kaşar hard *(cheddar-like)* cheese

katı hard-boiled *(egg)*

kavun melon

kaymak cream

kaymaklı creamy

kaynamış hamur dumpling

kayısı apricots

kaz goose

kazandibi oven-browned (milk) pudding

kebap kebab

kebere tomurcuğu caper

keçi goat

keçi sütünden peynir goat cheese

kek cake

kekik thyme

keklik partridge

kemikli on the bone

kemikli et cutlet

kepekli un whole wheat flour

kerevit crayfish

kereviz celery

keskin sharp *(flavor)*

kestane chestnuts

ketçap ketchup

kılıç balığı swordfish

kırmızı red *(wine)*

kırmızı biber red peppers / chili powder

kırmızı frenk üzümü red currants

kırmızı lahana red cabbage

kırmızı pancar beets [beetroot]

kırmızı tekir balığı red mullet

kıyılmış minced

kızarmış ekmek toast

kızarmış küçük ekmek parçaları gratin

kızarmış tavuk roast chicken

kızartılmış roast

kızartılmış sığır eti roast beef

kızartılmış tavuk roast chicken

kızgın yağda ve suda pişirilen biftek pot roast

kızartma fried

kiraz cherries

kivi kiwi fruit

kola cola

konserve meyve canned fruit

konserve sığır eti corned beef

konsantre meyve suyu fruit cordial [squash]

konyak brandy

koyun mutton

koz helvası nougat

köfte croquettes/meatballs ➤ 45

kömürde ızgara charcoal-grilled

köpüklü sparkling

köpüklü şarap sparkling wine

kraker crackers

krem karamel crème caramel

krema cream

kremalı çorba cream soup

küçük Hindistan cevizi nutmeg

küçük meyveli pasta tartlet (sweet)

küçük yuvarlak ekmek rolls

kümes hayvanları poultry

kurabiye cookies

kuru dry

kuru erik dried prunes

kuru fasulye string [haricot] beans

kuru hurma dried dates

kuru incir dried figs

kuru üzüm raisins

kuşkonmaz asparagus

kurutulmuş balık dried fish

kuzu lamb

kuzu dolması stuffed lamb ➤ 45

kuzu güveç lamb and potato stew ➤ 45

kuzu yahni lamb stew

kuzukulağı sorrel

L lahana cabbage

lahana salatası coleslaw

levrek sea bass

likör liqueur

lima fasulyesi butter beans

limon lemon/lemon grass

limon suyu lemon juice

limonata fresh lemonade

limonlu with lemon
lüfer bluefish

M **maden suyu** mineral water
makarna pasta
mandalina tangerine
mangalda pişmiş barbecued
mantar mushrooms
marmelat marmalade
marul lettuce
mayasız ekmek unleavened bread
maydanoz parsley
mayonez mayonnaise
menü menu
mercanköşk otu oregano
mercimek lentils
meyve fruit
meyve suyu fruit juice
meyve yahni stewed fruit
meyveli kek fruitcake
meyveli pasta tart/pie
meyveli süt milk shake
meze snack
mezeler appetizers ➤ 43
mezit whiting/haddock
mığrı conger eel

mısır corn [corn on the cob]
midye mussels
morina balığı cod
muhallebi (milk) pudding
muz banana
mürekkep balığı cuttlefish

N **nane** mint
nar pomegranates
nektarin nectarine
nohut chickpeas

O **oğlak** kid *(goat)*
olgun ripe
omlet omelet
omuz shoulder *(cut of lamb / other meat)*
orta şekerli regular sweetness *(coffee)*
otlu peynir herb cheese

Ö **öğle yemeği** lunch
öküz ox
öküz kuyruğu oxtail
ördek duck

P **paça** trotters *(pigs' feet)*

pandispanya sponge cake

patates potatoes

patates çorbası potato soup

patates kızartması French fries

patates salatası potato salad

patlıcan eggplant [aubergine]

patlıcan salatası eggplant [aubergine] salad

payelya paella

pekmez molasses [treacle]

pembe blush [rosé] *(wine)*

peynir cheese

pırasa leeks

pide pita bread

pilaki beans in olive oil

pilav rice

piliç spring chicken

pirinç rice

pirzola chops

pisi balığı plaice

pişmiş balık baked fish

porsiyon portion

portakal orange

portakal suyu orange juice

porto şarabı port

puf böreği shortcrust pastry

punç punch

püre mashed potatoes

R **rafadan** soft-boiled *(eggs)*

rakı aniseed-flavored spirit ➤ 49

ravent rhubarb

reçel jam

rendelenmiş grated

rezene fennel

ringa balığı herring

risotto risotto

rokfor blue cheese

rom rum

S **sade** non-carbonated [still] / plain / without sugar *(coffee)*

sade çorba consommé

sade kahve black *(coffee)*

sade un plain flour

safran saffron

sahanda fried *(egg)*

salam salami

salamura cured *(ham, etc.)* / marinated

salata salad

salata sosu vinaigrette [French dressing]

salep hot herbal drink

salyangoz snails

sandöviç sandwich

sardalye sardines

sarı kaymak custard

sarı şalgam rutabaga [swede]

sarmısak garlic

sarmısaklı in garlic

sarmısaklı mayonez garlic mayonnaise

sarmısaklı sos garlic sauce

sazan balığı roach *(fish)*

sebze vegetables *(general)*

sebze çorbası vegetable soup

sek very dry *(wine)*/neat [straight] *(spirits)*

sert kaymak whipped cream

sert peynir hard cheese

sert şarap full-bodied wine

sıcak hot *(temperature)*

sıcak çikolata hot chocolate

sıcak su hot water

sığır eti beef

sığır filetosu sirloin

sıra grape drink ➤ 50

sıvı yağda in oil

sirke salamurası marinated in vinegar

siyah ekmek black bread

siyah frenk üzümü black currants

siyah sucuk black pudding

siyah üzüm black grapes

sodalı ekmek soda bread

sofra şarabı table wine

soğan onions

soğan çorbası onion soup

soğancık shallots

soğuk çorba cold soup

soğuk içkiler cold drinks

soğuk tabak cold dish

soğutulmuş chilled *(wine, etc.)*

somon salmon

sos sauce

sosis sausages

soslu (cooked) in sauce

sote sautéed

spagetti spaghetti

spesiyalite specialties of the house

su water/juice

su kestanesi water chestnuts

su teresi watercress

sufle soufflé

sülün pheasant

sürahi carafe

süt milk

sütlaç rice pudding

sütlü with milk

sütlü meyve suyu milk shake

sütlü pelte blancmange

sütsüz black *(coffee)*

Ş **şalgam** turnip

şalgam suyu turnip juice

şarap wine

şarap listesi wine list

şeftali peach

şehriye noodles

şeker sugar/candy [sweets]

şekerleme candied fruit

şekerli with sugar/extra sweet *(coffee)*

şekerli çörek doughnut

şekerli krema icing

şeri sherry

şişe birası bottled beer

şişlenmiş skewered

şurup syrup

T **tahıl** cereal

talaş böreği vol-au-vent *(pastry filled with meat or fish)*

tarak scallops

tarama taramasalata ➤ 43

tarçın cinnamon

tarhun tarragon

tatlandırıcı sweetener

tatlı dessert

tatlı kırmızı biber sweet red peppers

tatlı patates sweet potato

tatlı su levreği perch

tatlı ve ekşi sos sweet-and-sour sauce

tavşan rabbit

tavuk chicken

tavuk ciğeri chicken liver

tavuk çorbası chicken soup

tavuk göğsü breast of chicken ➤ 48

tavuk sakatatı giblets

tavuk suyu çorba chicken broth soup

taze fresh

taze çökelek fresh curd cheese

taze fasulye green beans

taze incir fresh figs

taze lahana spring cabbage

taze meyve fresh fruit

taze soğan spring onions

tekir balığı mullet

tere cress

tereyağı butter

tırpana ray/skate

ton balığı tuna

tonik tonic water

tulum peyniri goat cheese

turp radish/horseradish

turunç bitter (Seville) orange

turunç suyu bitter orange juice

turşu pickle

tuz salt

tuzlu salted

tuzlu yer fıstığı salted peanuts

türlü ratatouille

tütsülenmiş smoked

tütsülenmiş ringa smoked herring

tütsülenmiş somon smoked salmon

tütsülenmiş yılan balığı smoked eel

U un flour

un ve yumurta içinde kızartma fried in batter

un ve yumurta sosunda in batter

uskumru mackerel ➤ 44

uyluk sweetbreads

Ü üzüm grapes

üzüm suyu grape juice

V vanilya vanilla

vermut vermouth

viski whisky

votka vodka

Y yaban domuzu wild boar

yaban havucu parsnips

yaban mersini blueberries

yaban ördeği wild duck

yabani mantar field mushrooms

yabani tavşan hare

yağda kızarmış tavuk fried chicken

yağlı fatty

yahni stew/stewed

yam yam

yarım şişe half bottle

yavru ahtapot baby octopus

yavru domuz suckling pig

yavru horoz cockerel

yavru kalamar baby squid

yavru ördek duckling

yayık ayranı buttermilk

yemek dish

yemek listesi menu

yemek üstü şarabı dessert wine

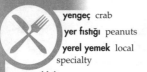

yengeç crab

yer fıstığı peanuts

yerel yemek local specialty

yeşil biber green peppers

yeşil fasulye green beans [French beans]

yeşil karnıbahar broccoli

yeşil salata green salad

yoğurt yogurt

yulaf lapası porridge

yumurta eggs

yumurta beyazı egg white

yumurta sarısı egg yolk

yumuşak peynir soft cheese

yılan balığı eel

Z

zencefil ginger

zengin rich *(sauce)*

zeytin olives

Travel

ESSENTIAL

1/2/3 ticket(s) to …	**… -e bir/iki/üç bilet.** *… eh beer/ikee/ewch beelet*
To …, please.	**… -e lütfen.** *… eh lewt-fen*
one-way [single]	**sırf gidiş** *serf gideesh*
round-trip [return]	**gidiş dönüş** *gideesh durnewsh*
How much …?	**… ne kadar?** *… neh kaddar*

Safety Güvenlik

Would you accompany me to the bus stop?	**Otobüs durağına kadar bana eşlik eder misiniz?** *oto-bews doo-ry-erna kaddar bana eshlik edair miseeniz*
I don't want to … on my own.	**Tek başıma … istemiyorum.** *tek basherma … istemee-yorum*
stay here	**burada kalmak** *booradah kalmak*
walk home	**eve yürümek** *ev-eh yewrew-mek*
I don't feel safe here.	**Burada kendimi güvende hissetmiyorum.** *booradah kendeemee gewvendeh hiss-setmee-yorum*

POLICE ➤ 159; EMERGENCY ➤ 224

65

Arrival Varış

British and U.S. citizens need to have a valid passport and purchase a visa either before leaving or from the visa desk before going through passport control on entry into Turkey. The cost is payable in pounds, dollars, or Turkish lira. Your passport stamp allows you to remain in Turkey for three months.

Duty free allowances are as follows:

You may bring in 200 cigarettes, 50 cigars, 200 g. tobacco, five 100 cc bottles of wine or spirits or seven 70 cc bottles.
(In addition, you can purchase 400 cigarettes, 100 cigars, and 500 g. tobacco from Turkish tax-free shops on entering the country.)

When you leave you can take out 200 cigarettes, 50 cigars, 250 g. tobacco, 1 liter of spirits, and 2 liters of wine.

Keep receipts for any expensive items that you have bought as proof of purchase.

If you buy an item of some value from a store that offers tax-free sales, you can be refunded the sales tax [VAT]. On leaving you need to show customs the item and its invoice in triplicate.

The purchase and export of antiquities is prohibited.

Passport control Pasaport kontrolu

We have a joint passport.	**Ortak pasaportumuz var.** *ortak passaport-oomuz var*
The children are on this passport.	**Çocuklar bu pasaportta kayıtlı.** *chojook-lar boo passaport-ta ky-yert-ler*
I'm here on vacation [holiday]/business.	**Tatil/iş için buradayım.** *tateel/ish itchin boora-dye-yerm*
I'm just passing through.	**Geçiyorum.** *getchee-yorum*
I'm going to …	**… -e gidiyorum.** *… eh gidee-yorum*
I'm on my own.	**Tek başımayım.** *tek basherm-eye-erm*
I'm with my family.	**Ailemle birlikteyim.** *eye-lem-leh beerlikte-yim*
I'm with a group.	**Grupla birlikteyim.** *groop-la beerlikte-yim*

Customs Gümrük

I have only the normal allowances.

Yalnızca gümrüksüz geçebilecek kadar var.
yalnerz-jah gewrewk-sewz geche-bilejek kaddar var

It's a gift.

Bir armağan. *beer arma-yarn*

It's for my personal use.

Kendi kişisel kullanımım için.
kendee keeshee-sel kool-lan-ermerm itchin

Gümrüğe tabi bir eşyanız var mı?	Do you have anything to declare?
Bunun için gümrük vergisi ödemeniz gerekir.	You must pay duty on this.
Bunu nereden aldınız?	Where did you buy this?
Lütfen şu çantayı açınız.	Please open this bag.
Başka bavulunuz var mı?	Do you have any more luggage?

I would like to declare …

… beyan etmek bulunmak istiyorum.
… bay-an etmek bulloon-mak istee-yorum

I don't understand.

Anlamadım. *anlamaderm*

Does anyone here speak English?

Burada İngilizce bilen biri var mı?
booradah eengeeleez-jeh bee-len beeree var mer

PASAPORT KONTROLU	passport control
SINIR	border crossing
GÜMRÜK	customs
BEYAN EDECEK EŞYASI OLMAYANLAR	nothing to declare
BEYAN EDECEK EŞYASI OLANLAR	goods to declare
VERGİSİZ EŞYALAR	duty-free goods

Duty-free shopping Vergisiz alışveriş

What currency is this in?

Bu hangi para birimi?
boo hangee parah bee-ree-mee

Can I pay in …

… cinsinden ödeyebilir miyim?
… jeen-seen-den ur-day-eh-beeleer meeyim

dollars

dolar *dol-ar*

Turkish lira

Türk lirası *tewrk leera-ser*

pounds

İngiliz sterlini *eengeeleez ster-leenee*

COMMUNICATION DIFFICULTIES ➤ 11

Plane Uçak

Turkish Airlines (**THY**) has regular flights connecting Istanbul, Ankara, Izmir, Antalya, Dalaman, and other useful destinations such as Samsun and Trabzon on the Black Sea and Kayseri near Cappadocia. It publishes a comprehensive timetable. Check-in formalities must be completed at least 20 minutes before departure. Discounts are available for families, parties of five or more, children aged two to 14, and those over 60. In summer, book in advance. Tickets cost about 25 percent more if purchased outside Turkey.

Tickets and reservations Bilet ve yer ayırtma

When is the ... flight to New York?	**New York'a ... uçak ne zaman?** *New York'ah ... oochak neh zaman*
first/next/last	**ilk/bir sonraki/en son** *eelk/ beer son-rakee/en son*
I'd like two ... tickets to New York.	**New York'a iki ... bilet istiyorum.** *New York'ah ikee ... beelet istee-yorum*
one-way [single]	**sırf gidiş** *serf gideesh*
round-trip [return]	**gidiş dönüş** *gideesh durnewsh*
first class	**birinci sınıf** *beerin-jee ser-nerf*
business class	**"business class"** *"business class"*
economy class	**ekonomi sınıfı** *ekon-omee ser-nerf-er*
How much is a flight to ...?	**... -e bilet ne kadar?** *... eh beelet neh kaddar*
Are there any supplements/discounts?	**Ek ücret/indirim var mı?** *ek ewj-ret/eendeerim var mer*
I'd like to ... my reservation for flight number 123.	**123 numaralı uçuş için ayırttığım yeri ... istiyorum.** *123 noomara-ler ooch-oosh itchin eye-yert-ter-erm yair-ee ... istee-yorum*
cancel	**iptal etmek** *eep-tal etmek*
change	**değiştirmek** *day-eesh-teer-mek*
confirm	**teyit etmek** *teyeet etmek*

Inquiries about the flight Uçuş hakkında sorular

How long is the flight?	**Uçuş ne kadar sürüyor?** *ooch-oosh neh kaddar sew-rew-yor*
What time does the plane leave?	**Uçak ne zaman kalkıyor?** *oochak neh zaman kalker-yor*
What time will we arrive?	**Ne zaman varacağız?** *neh zaman var-ah-jy-yerz*

Checking in Check-in yaptırmak

Where is the check-in desk for flight …?	**… numaralı uçuş için "check-in" masası nerede?** *… noomaraler ooch-oosh itchin "check-in" massah-ser neredeh*
I have …	**… var.** *… var*
three cases to check in	**bagaja verecek üç bavulum** *bagazha verejek ewch bavoolum*
two pieces of hand luggage	**iki parça el çantam** *ikee par-chah el chan-tam*
How much hand luggage is allowed free?	**Ne kadar el çantasını ücretsiz yanıma alabilirim?** *neh kaddar el chanta-serner ewj-ret-seez yanerm-ah ala-beeleerim*

Lütfen, biletiniz/pasaportunuz.	Your ticket/passport, please.
Koltuğunuz pencere kenarı mı koridor kenarı mı olsun?	Would you like a window or an aisle seat?
Sigara içilen bölüm mü içilmeyen bölüm mü?	Smoking or non-smoking?
Lütfen gidiş salonuna geçiniz.	Please go through to the departure lounge.
Kaç parça bavulunuz var?	How many pieces of baggage do you have?
Bavul ağırlığınız fazla.	You have excess baggage.
… Türk Lirası ek ücret ödemeniz gerekecek.	You'll have to pay a supplement of … Turkish lira.
El çantası için o çok ağır/büyük.	That's too heavy/large for hand baggage.
Bu çantaları kendiniz mi hazırladınız?	Did you pack these bags yourself?
Çantalarınızda keskin ya da elektronik eşya var mı?	Do they contain any sharp or electronic items?

VARIŞ	arrivals
GİDİŞ	departures
GÜVENLİK KONTROLU	security check
ÇANTALARINIZIN BAŞINDAN AYRILMAYINIZ	do not leave bags unattended

BAGGAGE ➤ 71

Information Danışma

Is there any delay on flight …? | **… numaralı uçuşta herhangi bir gecikme var mı?** … noo<u>ma</u>ra-ler ooch-<u>oosh</u>-tah hair-<u>han</u>gee beer ge<u>jeek</u>meh var mer

How late will it be? | **Ne kadar gecikecek?** neh kaddar ge<u>jeek</u>-ejek

Has the flight from … landed? | **… -den gelen uçak indi mi?** … den gel-en oochak een<u>dee</u> mee

Which gate does flight … leave from? | **… numaralı uçak hangi biniş kapısından hareket edecek?** … noo<u>ma</u>ra-ler oochak hangee beeneesh kap-er<u>sern</u>dan hareh-<u>ket</u> edejek

Boarding/In-flight Biniş/Uçakta

Your boarding pass, please. | **Biniş kartınız lütfen.** beeneesh karter-nerz <u>lewt</u>-fen

Could I have a drink/ something to eat, please? | **İçecek/yiyecek bir şey isteyebilir miyim lütfen?** <u>itch</u>-ejek/yee-<u>ye</u>jek beer shay istay-eh-bee<u>leer</u> meeyim <u>lewt</u>-fen

Please wake me for the meal. | **Lütfen beni yemek için uyandırın.** <u>lewt</u>-fen ben<u>ee</u> yemek itch<u>in</u> oy-<u>yan</u>der-ern

What time will we arrive? | **Ne zaman varacağız?** neh za<u>man</u> vara-<u>jy</u>-yerz

An airsickness bag, please. | **Lütfen bir tane sıhhi torba verirmisiniz.** <u>lewt</u>-fen beer tarneh serh-hee torbah ver<u>eer</u>miseeniz

Arrival Varış

Where is/are (the) …? | **… nerede?** … neredeh

buses | **otobüsler** oto-<u>bews</u>-lair

car rental | **araba kiralama şirketleri** arabah keer<u>ah</u>-lama sheer<u>ket</u>-lair-ee

currency exchange | **döviz bürosu** dur-<u>veez</u> bewrosu

exit | **çıkış** cher-kersh

taxis | **taksiler** taksee-lair

Is there a bus into town? | **Kente otobüs var mı?** kent-eh oto-<u>bews</u> var mer

How do I get to the … hotel? | **… otele nasıl gidebilirim?** … oh-teleh <u>nas</u>sirl gid-eh-<u>bee</u>leerim

Baggage Bavullar

Porter! Excuse me!	**Taşıyıcı! Afedersiniz!** *tasher-yer-jer! aff-edair-seeniz*
Could you take my luggage to …?	**Bavullarımı … götürebilir misiniz?** *bavool-larerm-er … gur-tewr-eh-beeleer miseeniz*
a taxi/bus	**taksiye/otobüse** *taksee-yeh/oto-bews-eh*
Where is/are (the) …?	**… nerede?** *… neredeh*
luggage carts [trolleys]	**el arabaları** *el araba-lar-er*
baggage check [left-luggage office]	**emanet** *emanet*
baggage claim	**bavul teslim bandı** *bavool tesleem bander*
Where is the luggage from flight …?	**… numaralı uçuşun bavulları nerede?** *… noomara-ler oochoosh-oon bavool-lar-er neredeh*

Loss, damage, and theft Kayıp, hasar ve çalinma

I've lost my baggage.	**Bavulumu kaybettim.** *bavool-oomu ky-bettim*
My baggage has been stolen.	**Bavulum çalındı.** *bavoolum chalern-der*
My suitcase was damaged.	**Bavulum hasar görmüş.** *bavoolum hassar gurmewsh*
Our baggage has not arrived.	**Bavullarımız gelmedi.** *bavool-larerm-erz gelmeh-dee*

Bavullarınız neye benziyordu?	What does your baggage look like?
Teslim etiketiniz var mı?	Do you have the claim check [reclaim tag]?
Bavullarınız …	Your luggage …
… gönderilmiş olabilir	may have been sent to …
bugün daha sonra gelebilir	may arrive later today
Lütfen yarın tekrar geliniz.	Please come back tomorrow.
Bavullarınızın gelip gelmediğini öğrenmek için bu numarayı arayınız.	Call this number to check if your baggage has arrived.

POLICE ➤ 159; COLOR ➤ 143

Train Tren

The Turkish State Railway (**TCDD**) runs comfortable trains on some major routes, but overall the Turkish rail system is not very comprehensive, and often a bus is the only option.

Among the best services are those between Istanbul and Ankara (10 hours) and Istanbul and İzmir (11 hours).

Istanbul has two main train stations: Sirkeci Garı for westbound trains and Haydarpaşa Garı for eastbound trains. Always opt for express or blue trains (**Mavi Express**) and reserve seats in advance.

To the station Tren garına

How do I get to the train station?	**Tren garına nasıl gidebilirim?** tren _gar_-ernah _nassirl_ gid-eh-_bee_leerim
Do trains to Ankara leave from Haydarpaşa station?	**Ankara'ya giden trenler Haydarpaşa garından mı hareket ediyor?** ankara'yah geeden tren-lair _hi_-dar-pasha _gar_-erndan mer hareh-_ket_ edee-yor
How far is it?	**Ne kadar uzakta?** neh kaddar oo_zak_-ta
Can I leave my car there?	**Arabamı orada bırakabilir miyim?** ara_bam_-er orada ber-akah-bee_leer_ meeyim

At the station Tren garında

Where is / are the ...?	**... nerede?** ... neredeh
baggage check [left-luggage office]	**emanet** _emanet_
currency exchange	**döviz bürosu** dur-_veez_ _bew_rosu
information desk	**danışma masası** dan-_ershma_ massah-ser
lost and found [lost property office]	**kayıp eşya bürosu** ky-_yerp_ esh-yah _bew_rosu
platforms	**peronlar** pair-onlar
snack bar	**büfe** bewfeh
ticket office	**bilet gişesi** bee_let_ geeshe-see
waiting room	**bekleme salonu** beklemeh salon-oo

DIRECTIONS ➤ 94

GİRİŞ	entrance
ÇIKIŞ	exit
PERONLAR	to the platforms
DANIŞMA	information
YER AYIRTMA	reservations
VARIŞ	arrivals
GİDİŞ	departures

Tickets Bilet

I'd like a … ticket to Ankara.	**Ankara'ya … bir bilet istiyorum.** *Ankara'yah … beer bee<u>let</u> i<u>stee</u>-yorum*
one-way [single]	**sırf gidiş** *serf gi<u>deesh</u>*
round-trip [return]	**gidiş dönüş** *gi<u>deesh</u> dur<u>newsh</u>*
first class	**birinci sınıf** *beerin-jee ser-<u>nerf</u>*
second class	**ikinci sınıf** *ikeen-jee ser-<u>nerf</u>*
concessions	**indirimli** *een<u>deer</u>im-lee*
I'd like to reserve a(n) … seat.	**… bir yer ayırtmak istiyorum.** *… beer yair eye-<u>yert</u>-mak i<u>stee</u>-yorum*
aisle seat	**koridor kenarında** *koree-dor ke<u>nar</u>ern-da*
window seat	**pencere kenarında** *<u>pen</u>-jereh ke<u>nar</u>ern-da*
Is there a sleeping car [sleeper]?	**Yataklı vagon var mı?** *ya<u>tak</u>-ler va-gon var mer*
I'd like a(n) … berth.	**… kuşet istiyorum.** *… koo<u>shet</u> i<u>stee</u>-yorum*
upper/lower	**üst/alt** *ewst/alt*

73

Price Fiyat

Train Tour (**Tren Tur**) cards offer unlimited travel for those under the age of 26, who can also travel around Turkey using a pan-European *Inter-rail* pass.

How much is that?	**Bu ne kadar?** *boo neh kaddar*
Is there a discount for ...?	**... için indirim var mı?** *... itchin eendeerim var mer*
children/families	**çocuklar/aileler** *chojook/eye-leh-lair*
senior citizens	**yaşlılar** *yash-ler-lar*
students	**öğrenciler** *ur-ren-jee-lair*

Queries Sorular

Do I have to change trains?	**Aktarma yapmak gerekiyor mu?** *aktarma yapmak gerek-eeyor moo*
Is it a direct train?	**Bu aktarmasız tren mi?** *boo aktarma-serz tren mee*
You have to change at ...	**... 'de aktarma yapmanız gerek.** *... deh aktarma yapma-nerz gerek*
How long is this ticket valid for?	**Bu bilet ne kadar süre ile geçerli?** *boo beelet neh kaddar sewreh eeleh getch-air-lee*
Can I take my bicycle on the train?	**Bisikletimi trene alabilir miyim?** *beeseeklet-eemee treneh ala-beeleer meeyim*
Can I return on the same ticket?	**Aynı biletle dönebilir miyim?** *eye-ner beelet-leh durneh-beeleer meeyim*
In which car [coach] is my seat?	**Koltuğum hangi vagonda?** *koltoo-oom hangee va-gonda*
Is there a dining car on the train?	**Trende yemekli vagon var mı?** *trendeh yemek-lee va-gon var mer*

– Ankara'ya bir bilet istiyorum lütfen.
(I'd like a ticket to Ankara, please.)
– Sırf gidiş mi, gidiş dönüş mü?
(One-way or round-trip?)
– Gidiş dönüş lütfen. (Round-trip, please.)
– Beş milyon lira. (That's five million lira.)
– Aktarma yapmam gerekiyor mu?
(Do I have to change trains?)
– Evet. Eskişehir'de aktarma yapmanız gerekiyor.
(Yes. You have to change at Eskişehir.)
– Teşekkür ederim. Hoşçakalın. (Thank you. Good-bye.)

Train times Tren saatleri

Could I have a timetable, please?	**Lütfen, bir tren tarifesi alabilir miyim?** _lewt-fen beer tren tareefeh-see ala-beeleer meeyim_
When is the … train to Ankara?	**Ankara'ya … tren ne zaman?** _Ankara'yah … tren neh zaman_
first/next/last	**ilk/bir sonraki/en son** _eelk/beer sonrakee/en son_
How frequent are the trains to …?	**… -e ne sıklıkta tren var?** _… eh neh serk-lerkta tren var_
once/twice a day	**günde bir/iki tane** _gewnveh beer/ikee tarneh_
five times a day	**günde beş tane** _gewnde besh tarneh_
every hour	**her saat** _hair sa-art_
What time do they leave?	**Kalkış saatleri ne?** _kalkersh sa-art-lair-ee neh_
on the hour	**saat başı** _sa-art bash-er_
20 minutes past the hour	**saat başını 20 geçe** _sa-art bash-er-ner yeermee getcheh_
What time does the train stop at …?	**Tren … -de saat kaçta duruyor?** _tren … deh sa-art katch-tah duroo-yor_
What time does the train arrive in …?	**Tren … -e saat kaçta varıyor?** _tren … eh sa-art katch-tah var-er-yor_
How long is the trip [journey]?	**Yolculuk ne kadar sürüyor?** _yoljoolook neh kaddar sew-rew-yor_
Is the train on time?	**Tren zamanında mı?** _tren zamanernda mer_

TIME ➤ 220; DIRECTIONS ➤ 94

Departures Gidiş

Which platform does the train to … leave from?	**… -e giden tren hangi perondan kalkıyor?** *… eh geeden tren hangee pair-ondan <u>kal</u>ker-yor*
Where is platform 4?	**4. peron nerede?** *durdun-joo pair-on neredeh*
over there	**orada** *orada*
on the left/right	**solda/sağda** *<u>sol</u>da/<u>saa</u>-da*
Where do I change for …?	**… için nerede aktarma yapacağım?** *… itch<u>in</u> neredeh ak<u>tar</u>ma yapah-<u>jy</u>-yerm*
How long will I have to wait for a connection?	**Bağlantı için ne kadar beklemem gerekiyor?** *baa-<u>lan</u>-ter itch<u>in</u> neh kaddar bekle<u>mem</u> gerek<u>ee</u>-yor*

Boarding Biniş

Is this the right platform for …?	**… treni bu perondan mı kalkıyor?** *… tren-ee boo pair-ondan mer <u>kal</u>ker-yor*
Is this the train to …?	**Bu … treni mi?** *boo … tren-ee mee*
Is this seat taken?	**Bu koltuk dolu mu?** *boo kol<u>took</u> doloo moo*
That's my seat.	**Bu koltuk benim.** *boo kol<u>took</u> benim*
Here's my reservation.	**Ayırttığım yer burası.** *eye-yert-<u>ter</u>-erm yair booraser*
Are there any seats/ berths available?	**Boş koltuk/kuşet var mı?** *bosh kol<u>took</u>/koo<u>shet</u> var mer*
Do you mind if …?	**… rahatsız olur musunuz?** *… ra<u>hat</u>-serz oloor musoonuz*
I sit here	**burada otursam** *boorada otoor-<u>sam</u>*
I open the window	**pencereyi açsam** *<u>pen</u>-jeh-reh-ye atch-<u>sam</u>*

76

On the trip Yolculuk sırasında

How long are we stopping here for?	**Burada ne kadar duracağız?** *boorada neh kaddar durah-jy-yerz*
When do we get to ...?	**...-e ne zaman geleceğiz?** *... eh neh zaman geleh-jay-yiz*
Have we passed ...?	**... -i geçtik mi?** *... ee getchtik mee*
Where is the dining/ sleeping car?	**Yemekli/yataklı vagon nerede?** *yemek-lee/yatak-ler va-gon neredeh*
Where is my berth?	**Kuşetim nerede?** *kooshet-eem neredeh*
I've lost my ticket.	**Biletimi kaybettim.** *beelet-eemee ky-bettim*

Long-distance bus [Coach] Şehirlerarası otobüsler

A comprehensive network of long-distance buses [coaches] serves all parts of Turkey. They are cheap, faster than trains, and comfortable if you take a modern air-conditioned vehicle. Tickets can be bought from agents, but the cheapest prices will be offered at the bus station itself, though you will have to stand in line.

Where is the bus [coach] station?	**Otobüs garajı nerede?** *oto-bews garaj-er neredeh*
When's the next bus [coach] to ...?	**... -e bir sonraki otobüs ne zaman?** *... eh beer sonrakee oto-bews neh zaman*
Where does it leave from?	**Nereden kalkıyor?** *nereh-den kalker-yor*
Where are the bus [coach] bays?	**Otobüs durakları nerede?** *oto-bews doorak-lar-er neredeh*
Does the bus [coach] stop at ...?	**Otobüs ... -de duruyor mu?** *oto-bews ... deh duroo-yor moo*
How long does the trip [journey] take?	**Yolculuk ne kadar sürüyor?** *yol-jewluk neh kaddar sew-rew-yor*
Are there ... on board?	**Otobüste ... var mı?** *oto-bews-teh ... var mer*
refreshments	**hafif yiyecek ve içecekler** *hafeef yee-yejek veh itch-ejek-lair*
toilets	**tuvalet** *too-va-let*

TIME ➤ 220

Shared taxis Dolmuş

There is also a type of shared taxi called a **dolmuş** which is found in Ankara, Istanbul, and İzmir. Like the local bus, the **dolmuş** runs over a specific route, picking up and discharging passengers who all pay the same fare.

Where does the shared taxi to … leave from?	**… dolmuşu nereden kalkıyor?** … dolmoo<u>shoo</u> <u>ne</u>reden kal<u>ker</u>yor
How much is the fare to …?	**… ne kadar?** … neh kaddar

Bus/Streetcar [Tram] Belediye otobüsü/Tramvay

City buses are incredibly cheap, although during the summer they can be hot and humid. Only cash is accepted on buses run by private companies. For the state-run city buses (**İETT** in Istanbul) you need to buy a ticket from the ticket office (**bilet gişesi**), which you can find near main bus terminals.

The only streetcar [tram] service in Turkey is a short one between Taksim and Tünel in Istanbul. And you will need to buy a city bus ticket before boarding.

Where is the bus station?	**Otobüs garajı nerede?** oto-<u>bews</u> ga<u>raj</u>-er neredeh
Where can I get a bus/ streetcar [tram] to …?	**… -e giden otobüse/tramvaya nerede binebilirim?** … eh <u>gee</u>den oto-<u>bews</u>-eh/ tram<u>vay</u>ah neredeh been-eh-<u>bee</u>leerim
What time is the … bus to Beyoğlu?	**Beyoğlu'na … otobüsü saat kaçta?** Bay-oloo'na … oto-<u>bews</u> sa-art katch-ta

Oradaki duraktan binmeniz gerekir.	You need that stop over there.
… numaralı otobüse binmelisiniz.	You need bus number …
… -de otobüs değiştirmelisiniz.	You must change buses at …

OTOBÜS DURAĞI	bus stop
SİGARA İÇİLMEZ	no smoking
ÇIKIŞ/ACİL ÇIKIŞ	exit/emergency exit

DIRECTIONS ➤ 94; TIME ➤ 220

Buying tickets Bilet satın almak

Where can I buy tickets?

Nereden bilet alabilirim?
nereh-den beelet ala-beeleerim

A … ticket to Ankara, please.

Ankara'ya … bir bilet lütfen.
Ankara'ya … beer beelet lewt-fen

one-way [single]

sırf gidiş *serf gideesh*

round-trip [return]

gidiş dönüş *gideesh durnewsh*

A book of tickets, please.

Bir bilet karnesi verir misiniz lütfen?
beer beelet karne-see vereer miseeniz lewt-fen

How much is the fare to …?

… -e bilet ücreti ne kadar?
… eh beelet ewjret-ee neh kaddar

Traveling Yolculuk etmek

Is this the right bus/streetcar [tram] to …?

Bu otobüs/tramvay … -e gidiyor mu?
boo oto-bews/tramvay … eh gidee-yor moo

Could you tell me when to get off?

İneceğim yeri söyler misiniz?
eeneh-jay-yim yair-ee sow-lair miseeniz

Do I have to change buses?

Aktarma yapmam gerekiyor mu?
aktarma yapmam gerekee-yor moo

How many stops are there to …?

… -e daha kaç durak var?
… eh dah-ha katch doorak var

Next stop, please!

Bir sonraki durak lütfen!
beer sonrakee doorak lewt-fen

BİLET GİŞESİ	ticket office
OTOMATİK BİLET MAKİNESİ	ticket vending machine

– Afedersiniz. Bu otobüs belediyeye gidiyor mu?
(Excuse me. Is this the right bus to the town hall?)
– *Evet, 8 numaralı otobüs. (Yes, number 8.)*
– Belediyeye bir kişi lütfen.
(One to the town hall, please.)
– *Yüz otuz bin lira lütfen. (That's 130,000 lira.)*
– İneceğim yeri söyler misiniz?
(Could you tell me when to get off?)
Buradan dört durak sonra. (It's four stops from here.)

NUMBERS ➤ 216; DIRECTIONS ➤ 94

Subway [Metro] Metro

A limited subway service has recently begun operating in Ankara. Istanbul's badly needed subway system is still under construction, although a subterranean funicular dating from the 1890s runs between Tünel and Karaköy.

General inquiries Genel sorular

Where's the nearest subway [metro] station?	**En yakın metro istasyonu nerede?** *en ya<u>ke</u>rn metro is<u>tas</u>yon-oo neredeh*
Where can I buy a ticket?	**Nereden bilet alabilirim?** *nereh-den bee<u>let</u> ala-<u>bee</u>leerim*
Could I have a map of the subway [metro], please?	**Bir metro planı verir misiniz lütfen?** *beer metro plan-er ve<u>reer</u> miseeniz <u>lewt</u>-fen*

Traveling Yolculuk etmek

Which line should I take for …?	**… için hangi hattı kullanmam gerekiyor?** *… it<u>chin</u> hangee <u>hat</u>-ter koo<u>llan</u>-mam gereke<u>e</u>-yor*
Is this the right train for …?	**Bu tren … -e gidiyor mu?** *boo tren … eh gi<u>dee</u>-yor moo*
Which stop is it for …?	**… için hangi durakta inmem gerekiyor?** *… it<u>chin</u> hangee doo<u>rak</u>ta <u>een</u>mem gereke<u>e</u>-yor*
How many stops is it to …?	**… -e kaç durak var?** *… eh katch doo<u>rak</u> var*
Is the next stop …?	**Bir sonraki durak … mı?** *beer son<u>rak</u>ee doo<u>rak</u> … mer*
Where are we?	**Neredeyiz?** *nereh-<u>day</u>-yerz*
Where do I change for …?	**… -e gitmek için nerede tren değiştirmeliyim?** *… eh geetmek it<u>chin</u> neredeh tren day-eesh-<u>teer</u>-maylee-yim*
What time is the last train to …?	**… -e giden en son tren saat kaçta?** *… eh geeden en son tren sa-art katch-ta*

> **DİĞER HATLARA**   to other lines/transfer

NUMBERS ➤ 216; BUYING TICKETS ➤ 73, 79

Ferry Vapur

For coastal services and cruises, reserve ahead of time through the Turkish Maritime Lines, which have agents at the docks in all Turkish ports. TML's head office is at Rıhtım Caddesi, Karaköy, Istanbul ☎ (0212) 249 9222.

In Istanbul there is a (pay) ferry to cross the city from the European side to the Asian side.

When is the … (car) ferry to Yalova?	**Yalova'ya … (araba) vapur(u) saat kaçta?** Yalova'yah … (arabah) va-_poor_(-oo) sa-art katch-ta
first/next/last	**ilk/bir sonraki/en son** eelk/beer son_ra_kee/en son
hovercraft	**"hovercraft"/emi** "hovercraft"/gemee
A round-trip [return] ticket for …	**… için gidiş dönüs bir bilet.** … itch_in_ gid_eesh_ dur_newsh_ beer bee_let_
one car and one trailer [caravan]	**bir araba ve bir karavan** beer arabah veh beer kara_van_
two adults and three children	**iki yetişkin ve üç çocuk** ikee yet-ish_kin_ veh ewch cho_jook_
I want to reserve a … cabin.	**… bir kamara ayırtmak istiyorum.** … beer kamarah eye-_yert_-mak is_tee_-yorum
single/double	**tek kişilik/iki kişilik** tek kee_sheel_ik/ikee kee_sheel_ik

CAN YELEĞİ	life preserver [life belt]
CANKURTARA SANDALI	lifeboat
ROLE YERLERİ?	muster station
GİRİLMEZ	no access

Boat trips Tekne gezileri

Is there a …?	**… var mı?** … var mer
boat trip/river cruise	**tekne gezisi** tekneh ge_zee_-see
What time does it leave?	**Ne zaman kalkıyor?** neh za_man_ _kalker_-yor
What time does it return?	**Ne zaman dönüyor?** neh za_man_ _durnew_-yor
Where can we buy tickets?	**Nereden bilet alabiliriz?** nereh-den bee_let_ ala-_beel_eeriz

TIME ➤ 220; BUYING TICKETS ➤ 73, 79

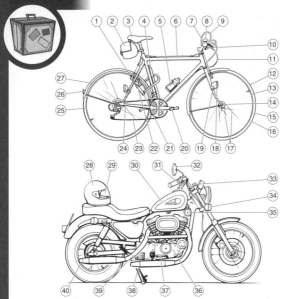

1 brake pad **fren**
2 bicycle bag **bisiklet çantası**
3 saddle **sele**
4 pump **pompa**
5 water bottle **su şişesi**
6 frame **kasa**
7 handlebars **gidon**
8 bell **zil**
9 brake cable **fren teli**
10 gear shift [lever] **vites**
11 gear control cable **vites teli**
12 inner tube **iç lastik**
13 front/back wheel **ön/arka tekerlek**
14 axle **dingil**
15 tire [tyre] **lastik**
16 wheel **tekerlek**
17 spokes **tekerlek çubukları**
18 bulb **lamba**
19 headlamp **far**
20 pedal **pedal**
21 lock **kilit**

22 generator [dynamo] **dinamo**
23 chain **zincir**
24 rear light **arka far**
25 rim **jant**
26 reflectors **reflektörler**
27 fender [mudguard] **çamurluk**
28 helmet **başlık**
29 visor **güneşlik**
30 fuel tank **yakıt deposu**
31 clutch lever **kavrama kolu**
32 mirror **ayna**
33 ignition switch **kontak anahtarı**
34 turn signal [indicator] **gösterge**
35 horn **korna**
36 engine **motor**
37 gear shift [lever] **vites kolu**
38 kick stand [main stand] **kaldırma ayağı**
39 exhaust pipe **egzoz borusu**
40 chain guard **zincir koruyucu**

82

REPAIRS ➤ 89

Bicycle/Motorbike
Bisiklet/Motorsiklet

One of the best places to rent a bicycle, as distances are small and traffic light, is Cappadocia. Mopeds and motorcycles can be rented from resorts; you will need a driver's license for smaller models, and a motorcycle license for larger ones. Check that the quoted rates include insurance and tax, and wear a helmet – it is the law and absolutely essential given the poor condition of many roads.

I'd like to rent [hire] a …	**Bir … kiralamak istiyorum.** beer … kee-_ralamak istee_-yorum
3-/10-speed bicycle	**3/10 vitesli bisiklet** ewch/on vee_tes_-lee beeseek_let_
moped/motorbike	**mopet/motorsiklet** mo-pet/mo-torseek_let_
How much does it cost per day/week?	**Günlüğü/haftalığı ne kadar?** gewn_lew_-ew/_haf_taler-er neh kaddar
Do you require a deposit?	**Ön ödeme istiyor musunuz?** urn _ur_demeh i_stee_-yor musoonuz
The brakes don't work.	**Frenler çalışmıyor.** fren-lair cha_lersh_-mer-yor
There is/are no lights.	**Farları yok.** farlar-er yok
The front/rear tire [tyre] has a flat [puncture].	**Ön/arka lastikte patlak var.** urn/arka las_teek_-teh pat_lak_ var

Hitchhiking Otostop yapmak

People do hitchhike around the country, but it is not recommended, particularly for women by themselves.

Where are you heading?	**Nereye gidiyorsunuz?** nereyeh gi_dee_-yorsoonuz
Is that on the way to …?	**… yolunda mı?** … yol_oon_da mer
Could you drop me off …?	**Beni … bırakır mısınız?** benee … ber-ak_ker_ mersernerz
here/downtown	**burada/kent merkezinde** boorada/kent mer_keze_endeh
at the … exit	**… çıkışında** … cher_kersh_ernda
Thanks for giving me a lift.	**Beni getirdiğiniz için teşekkürler.** benee getirdee-_eeneez_ itch_in_ teshek-_kewr_-lair

Taxi Taksi

Taxis can be hailed in the street and are metered. Have the address written down to avoid struggling to explain directions to drivers, who usually only speak Turkish. At night, you will be honked at by one taxi after another; it is their way of indicating that they are free. Tipping is up to you, but as rates are low and drivers usually helpful, you can always round up the fare.

Where can I get a taxi?	**Nerede taksi bulabilirim?** *neredeh taksee bull-ah-beeleerim*
Do you have the number for a taxi?	**Taksi için telefon numarası var mı?** *taksee itchin telefon noomara-ser var mer*
I'd like a taxi ...	**... bir taksi istiyorum.** *... beer taksee istee-yorum*
now	**şimdi** *shimdee*
in an hour	**bir saat sonrası için** *beer sa-art sonraser itchin*
for tomorrow at 9:00 a.m.	**yarın saat 9.00'da** *yarern sa-art dokooz-da*
The address is .... I'm going to ...	**Adres .... Ben ...-e gidiyorum.** *adress ... . Ben ... eh gidee-yorum*

◎	**BOŞ**	for hire	◎

Please take me to (the) ...	**Beni ... götürür müsünüz lütfen .** *benee ... gur-tewr-rewr mewsewnewz lewt-fen*
airport	**havaalanına** *havah-alarnernah*
train station	**tren garına** *tren gar-ernah*
this address	**bu adrese** *boo adress-eh*
How much will it cost?	**Ne kadar tutar?** *neh kaddar tootar*
Keep the change.	**Üstü kalsın.** *ewstew kalsern*

> – Beni istasyona götürür müsünüz lütfen?
> (Take me to the train station, please.)
> – Elbette (Certainly.)
> – Ne kadar tutar? (How much will it cost?)
> – Üç milyon. ... İşte burası.
> (Three million lira. ... Here we are.)
> – Teşekkür ederim. Üstü kalsın.
> (Thank you. Keep the change.)

NUMBERS ➤ 216; DIRECTIONS ➤ 94

Car/Automobile Araba

To bring your own car into Turkey you will need: a valid
driver's license; car registration papers, an international
insurance certificate, and a valid passport stamped with a
Turkish visa. Carry two reflector warning triangles and a
first-aid kit, and display a nationality plate or sticker. Find out about
the regulations of the countries you drive through to reach Turkey
from your local automobile association and insurance company.

Apart from the major cities and resorts, driving in Turkey is often a joy,
with mile after mile of open road and fabulous scenery. However, traffic in
Istanbul and Ankara is nightmarish. Dozens of overloaded buses clog
some of the highways, and the Turks have a justifiable reputation for being
dangerous drivers, taking absurd risks and driving at dangerous speeds.
Particularly lethal are three-lane highways, with a shared passing lane in
the middle. Use it only if you can see the way is clear. Driving after dark
can be very hazardous as roads can be inadequately lit, and drivers often
fail to lower their lights.

Main roads are well-maintained, but minor roads can be full of potholes,
and the tarmac can peter out altogether. By contrast, new highways with
inexpensive tolls between Istanbul and Edirne and Ankara and around
İzmir are fast and virtually deserted.

Drinking and driving is strictly forbidden. Insurance coverage for a rental
car involved in an accident may well depend on taking an alcohol test to
confirm whether or not you had been drinking.

Conversion chart

km	1	10	20	30	40	50	60	70	80	90	100	110	120	130
miles	0.62	6	12	19	25	31	37	44	50	56	62	68	74	81

Road network

Turkish motorists drive on the right, and seat belts are mandatory. Speed
limits are 50 kmph (30 mph) in urban areas, 90 kmph (50 mph) on the
open road, and 130 kmph (80 mph) on highways.

Traffic joining a road from the right has priority unless signs indicate
otherwise.

Car rental Araba kiralama

International and local car rental agencies have offices in the major cities, resorts and main airports. The driver must have a valid national or international driver's license. The minimum age is normally 21 for an economy car, but for a larger vehicle you may need to be 25 or even 30. A significant deposit is required unless you pay by credit card. If there is a second driver, you will need to say so.

Renting a car can be easier and less expensive if you make arrangements through international car rental companies or agents in your home country. Tour operators also sell competitive fly-drive deals. Jeeps are popular, but are about twice as expensive as economy cars.

Since public transportation is very inexpensive and reasonably good, consider forgetting the luxury of having your own car.

Where can I rent a car?	**Nereden bir araba kiralayabilirim?** *nereh-den beer arabah kee-ralaya-beeleerim*
I'd like to rent a(n) …	**Bir … kiralamak istiyorum.** *beer … kee-ralamak istee-yorum*
2-/4-door car	**2/4 kapılı araba** *ikee/durrt kaper-ler arabah*
an automatic	**otomatik** *otomateek*
car with 4-wheel drive	**4 çekişli araba** *durrt chekeesh-lee arabah*
car with air conditioning	**havalandırmalı araba** *havah-landerma-ler arabah*
I'd like it for a day/week.	**Bir gün/hafta için istiyorum.** *beer gewn/hafta itchin istee-yorum*
How much does it cost per day/week?	**Günlüğü/haftalığı ne kadar?** *gewnlew-ew/haftaler-er neh kaddar*
Is insurance included?	**Sigorta dahil mi?** *seegortah dah-heel mee*
Can I return the car at …?	**Arabayı … -de bırakabilir miyim?** *ara-by-yer … deh ber-akah-beeleer meeyim*
What sort of fuel does it take?	**Ne tür yakıtla çalışıyor?** *neh tewr yakert-la cha-lersher-yor*
Where is the high [full]/low [dipped] beam?	**Kısa far/uzun far kolu nerede?** *kersah far/oozun far koloo neredeh*
Could I have full insurance?	**Tam sigorta alabilir miyim?** *tam seegortah ala-beeleer meeyim*

Gas [Petrol] station Benzin istasyonu

Where's the next gas [petrol] station, please?
Bir sonraki benzin istasyonu nerede? *beer sonrakee benzeen istasyonoo neredeh*

Is it self-service?
Kendimiz mi dolduruyoruz? *kendeemiz mee doldooru-yoruz*

Fill it up, please.
Depoyu doldurun lütfen. *depo-yoo doldoorun lewt-fen*

… liters, please.
… litre lütfen. *… leet-tre lewt-fen*

premium [super]
süper *soo-pair*

regular
normal *nor-mal*

lead-free
kurşunsuz *kurshun-sooz*

diesel
dizel *dee-zel*

I'm at pump number …
Ben … numaralı pompadayım. *ben … noomara-ler pompa-dyeyerm*

Where is the air pump/water?
Hava pompası/su nerede? *havah pompa-ser/soo neredeh*

LİTRE FİYATI	price per liter

Parking Park etme

If you park illegally you are likely to be given a ticket – and run the real risk of having your car towed away. Watch out for parking signs.

Is there a parking lot [car park] nearby?
Yakında park yeri var mı? *yakernda park yair-ee var mer*

What's the charge per hour/day?
Saatlik/günlük ücreti nedir? *sa-art-lerk/gewnlewk ewjret-ee neh-deer*

Do you have some change for the parking meter?
Parkometre için bozuk paranız var mı? *parko-met-tre itchin bozook paranerz var mer*

My car has been booted [clamped]. Who do I call?
Arabam kelepcelenmiş. Kimi aramam gerekiyor? *arabam kelep-jeh-len-mish. kimee aramam gerekee-yor*

Breakdown Arıza

If you break down in a rental car, phone the 24-hour emergency line you should have been given. If traveling in your own car, contact the Turkish Touring and Automobile Club (**TTOK**), which is affiliated with automobile associations abroad. Its breakdown phone number is (0212) 278 6214. For tire repairs, look for a sign saying **lastikçi**.

Where's the nearest garage?	**En yakın araba tamirhanesi nerede?** en ya<u>kern</u> arabah ta-<u>meer</u>-harnesee neredeh
My car broke down.	**Arabam bozuldu.** ara<u>bam</u> boz<u>oo</u>ldu
Can you send a mechanic/ tow [breakdown] truck?	**Tamirci/çekici gönderebilir misiniz?** ta-<u>meer</u>-jee/chekee-jee gurn-dair-eh-beeler miseeniz
I'm a member of …	**… üyesiyim.** … ew<u>yeh</u>-seeyim
My license plate number is …	**Plaka numaram …** pla<u>ka</u> noo<u>mar</u>am…
The car is …	**Araba …** arabah …
on the highway [motorway]	**otoyolda** oto-yolda
2 km from …	**… -den 2 km uzakta** … den iki kilomet-<u>reh</u> oozak<u>ta</u>
How long will you be?	**Ne kadar sonra burada olursunuz?** neh kaddar sonrah boorada ol<u>oo</u>rsoonuz
What's wrong?	**Sorun ne?**
My car won't start.	**Araba çalışmıyor.** arabah chal<u>er</u>shmer-yor
The battery is dead.	**Akü bitmiş.** <u>a</u>kew beetmish
I've run out of gas [petrol].	**Benzin bitti.** <u>ben</u>zeen beetti
I have a flat [puncture].	**Lastik patladı.** las<u>teek</u> pat<u>la</u>-der
There is something wrong with …	**… -de bir sorun var.** … deh beer soroon var
I've locked the keys in the car.	**Anahtarları arabada unuttum.** anah-<u>tar</u>-lar-er arabada oo<u>nut</u>-tum

Repairs Onarım

Do you do repairs?

Onarım yapıyor musunuz?
onarerm yaper-yor
musoonuz

Can you repair it?

Onarabilir misiniz?
onar-ah-beeleer miseniz

Please make only
essential repairs.

Yalnızca gerekli onarımları yapın.
yalnerz-jah gerek-lee onarerm-lar-er
yapern

Can I wait for it?

Bekleyebilir miyim?
bek-lay-eh-beeleer meeyim

Can you repair it today?

Bugün onarabilir misiniz?
boo-gewn onar-ah-beeleer miseeniz

When will it be ready?

Ne zaman hazır olur?
neh zaman hazz-er oloor

How much will it cost?

Ne kadar tutar?
neh kaddar tootar

That's outrageous!

Çok pahalı! chok pahal-ler

Can I have a receipt for
my insurance?

Sigorta için fatura clabilir miyim?
seegortah itchin fatoorah ala-beeleer
meeyim

... çalışmıyor.	The ... isn't working.
Gerekli parçalar yok.	I don't have the necessary parts.
Parçaları ısmarlamam gerek.	I will have to order the parts.
Yalnızca geçici olarak onarabilirim.	I can only repair it temporarily.
Arabanızı onarmaya olanak yok.	Your car is beyond repair.
Onarılamaz.	It can't be repaired.
... -de hazır olacak.	It will be ready ...
bugün daha sonra	later today
yarın	tomorrow
... gün içinde	in ... days

DAYS OF THE WEEK ➤ 218; NUMBERS ➤ 216

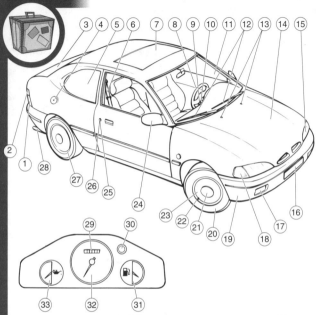

1 taillights [back lights] **arka farlar**
2 brakelights **fren lambaları**
3 trunk [boot] **bagaj**
4 gas tank door [petrol cap] **benzin deposu kapağı**
5 window **cam**
6 seat belt **emniyet kemeri**
7 sunroof **açılır tavan**
8 steering wheel **direksiyon**
9 ignition **kontak**
10 ignition key **kontak anahtarı**
11 windshield [windscreen] **ön cam**
12 windshield [windscreen] wipers **ön cam silecekleri**
13 windshield [windscreen] washer **ön cam yıkayıcı**
14 hood [bonnet] **kaput**
15 headlights **farlar**

16 license [number] plate **plaka**
17 fog lights **sis farları**
18 turn signals [indicators] **sinyal lambaları**
19 bumper **tampon**
20 tires [tyres] **lastikler**
21 hubcap **jant kapağı**
22 valve **sübap**
23 wheels **tekerlekler**
24 outside [wing] mirror **yan ayna**
25 automatic locks **merkezi kilitleme**
26 lock **kilit**
27 wheel rim **jant**
28 exhaust pipe **egzoz borusu**
29 odometer [milometer] **kilometre sayacı**
30 warning light **uyarı lambası**
31 fuel gauge **akaryakıt göstergesi**

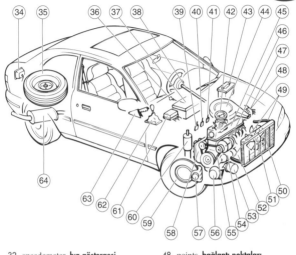

32 speedometer **hız göstergesi**
33 oil gauge **yağ göstergesi**
34 backup [reversing] lights
   geri lambaları
35 spare [spare wheel] **yedek lastik**
36 choke **tıkaç**
37 heater **ısıtıcı**
38 steering column
   direksiyon çubuğu
39 accelerator **gaz pedalı**
40 pedal **pedal**
41 clutch **debriyaj**
42 carburetor **karbüratör**
43 battery **akü**
44 air filter **filtresi**
45 camshaft **kam mili**
46 alternator **alternatör**
47 distributor **distribütör**

48 points **bağlantı noktaları**
49 radiator hose (top/bottom)
   radyatör hortumu (üst/alt)
50 radiator **radyatör**
51 fan **vantilatör**
52 engine **motor**
53 oil filter **yağ filtresi**
54 starter motor **starter motoru**
55 fan belt **vantilatör kayışı**
56 horn **korna**
57 brake pads **fren yastığı**
58 transmission [gearbox] **vites kutusu**
59 brakes **frenler**
60 shock absorbers **amortisör**
61 fuses **sigortalar**
62 gear shift [lever] **vites kolu**
63 emergency [hand] brake **el freni**
64 muffler [silencer] **susturucu**

Accidents Kazalar

In case of an accident ask the locals to help. Alternatively, you can dial the emergency services (➤ 224).

There has been an accident.	**Kaza oldu.** *kazzah oldoo*
It's …	**… -dir.** *… deer*
on the highway [motorway]	**otoyolda** *oto-yolda*
near …	**… yakınında** *… yakern-ernda*
Where's the nearest telephone?	**En yakın telefon nerede?** *en yakern telefon neredeh*
Call …	**… çağırın.** *… char-er-ern*
an ambulance	**ambülans** *ambewlans*
a doctor	**doktor** *dok-tor*
the fire department [brigade]	**itfaiye** *eet-fa-eeye*
the police	**polis** *polees*
Can you help me, please?	**Bana yardım eder misiniz lütfen?** *bana yarderm edair miseeniz lewt-fen*

Injuries Yaralanmalar

There are people injured.	**Yaralı insanlar var.** *ya-rar-ler insanlar var*
No one is hurt.	**Yaralı yok.** *ya-rar-ler yok*
He's seriously injured.	**Ciddi yaralı.** *jeed-dee ya-rar-ler*
She's unconscious.	**Kendinde değil.** *kendeendeh day-eel*
He can't breathe.	**Nefes alamıyor.** *nefes alamer-yor*
He can't move.	**Hareket edemiyor.** *hareh-ket edemee-yor*
Don't move him.	**Hareket ettirmeyin.** *hareh-ket et-teer-mayeen*

INJURIES ➤ 162; DIRECTIONS ➤ 94

Legal matters Yasal konular

What's your insurance company?	**Sigorta şirketiniz hangisi?** *seegortah sheerket-eeniz hangeesee*
What's your name and address?	**Ad ve adresiniz nedir?** *ad veh adres-seeniz neh-deer*
The car ran into me.	**Araba bana çarptı.** *arabah bana charpter*
The car was going too fast.	**Araba çok hızlı gidiyordu.** *arabah chok herzler gidee-yordu*
The car was driving too close.	**Araba çok yakın seyrediyordu.** *arabah chok yakern say-red-eeyordu*
I had the right of way.	**Yol önceliği benimdi.** *yol urnjeh-leeyee benimdee*
I was (only) driving … kmph.	**Ben (yalnızca) saatte … km ile gidiyordum.** *ben (yalnerzjah) sa-art-teh … keelomet-tre eeleh gidee-yordum*
I'd like an interpreter.	**Tercüman istiyorum.** *tair-jew-man istee-yorum*
I didn't see the sign.	**İşareti görmedim.** *eesharet-ee gurmedim*
This person saw it happen.	**Bu kişi olayı gördü.** *boo keeshee oly-yer gurdew*
The license plate number was …	**Plaka numarası …** *plaka noomara-ser*

… görebilir miyim lütfen?	May I see your …, please?
ehliyetinizi	driver's license
sigorta kartınızı	insurance card
ruhsatınızı	vehicle registration document
Saat kaçta oldu?	What time did it happen?
Nerede oldu?	Where did it happen?
Olaya başka birisi karıştı mı?	Was anyone else involved?
Tanık var mı?	Are there any witnesses?
Hızlı gidiyordunuz.	You were speeding.
Işıklarınız çalışmıyor.	Your lights aren't working.
Bir ceza ödemeniz gerekiyor.	You'll have to pay a fine (on the spot).
Karakolda ifade almamız gerek.	We need to take a statement from you at the station.

TIME ➤ 220

Asking directions Yol sormak

Excuse me.	**Afedersiniz.** *af-edair-seeniz*
How do I get to …?	**… -e nasıl gidebilirim?** *… eh nassirl gid-ehbeeleerim*
Where is …?	**… nerede?** *… neredeh*
Can you show me on the map where I am?	**Haritada nerede olduğumu gösterebilir misiniz?** *hareeta-da neredeh oldoo-oomu go-stair-eh-beeleer miseeniz*
I've lost my way.	**Yolumu kaybettim.** *yoloomu ky-bettim*
Can you repeat that, please?	**Tekrar eder misiniz, lütfen?** *tekrar edair miseeniz lewt-fen*
More slowly, please.	**Daha yavaş, lütfen.** *dah-ha yavash lewt-fen*
Thanks for your help.	**Yardımınız için teşekkürler.** *yarderm-ernerz itchin teshekkewr-lair*

Traveling by car Araba ile yolculuk

Is this the right road for …?	**Bu … yolu mu?** *boo … yol-oo moo*
Is it far?	**Uzak mı?** *oozak mer*
How far is it to … from here?	**… buradan ne kadar uzakta?** *… booradan neh kaddar oozaktah*
Where does this road lead?	**Bu yol nereye çıkıyor?** *boo yol nereyeh cherker-yor*
How do I get onto the highway [motorway]?	**Otoyola nasıl çıkabilirim?** *oto-yolah nassirl cherk-ah-beeleerim*
What's the next town called?	**Bir sonraki kentin adı nedir?** *beer sonrakee kentin add-er neh-deer*
How long does it take by car?	**Araba ile ne kadar sürer?** *arabah eeleh neh kaddar sew-rair*

– Afedersiniz. Tren garına nasıl gidebilirim?
(Excuse me. How do I get to the train station?)
– Üçüncü yoldan sağa dönün tam önünüzde.
(Take the third right, then go straight ahead.)
– Üçüncü yoldan sağa. Uzak mı?
(Third right. Is it far?)
– Yürüyerek on dakika. (It's ten minutes on foot.)
– Yardımınız için teşekkürler. (Thanks for your help.)
– Bir şey değil. (You're welcome.)

COMMUNICATION DIFFICULTIES ➤ 11

Location Yer

... -dir.	It's ...
doğru ilerde	straight ahead
solda	on the left
sağda	on the right
sokağın sonunda	at the end of the street
köşede	on the corner
köşeyi dönünce	around the corner
... yönünde	in the direction of ...
... karşısında/... arkasında	opposite .../behind ...
... yanında/... sonra	next to .../after ...
... -den aşağı doğru gidin.	Go down the ...
ara sokak/ana sokak	side street/main street
... -i geçin.	Cross the ...
meydan/köprü	square/bridge
Üçüncü yoldan sağa dönün.	Take the third right.
... sola dönün.	Turn left ...
ilk trafik ışıklarından sonra	after the first traffic light
ikinci kavşakta	at the second intersection [crossroad]

By car Araba ile

Buranın ... -de.	It's ... of here.
kuzey/güney	north/south
doğu/batı	east/west
... yolundan gidin.	Take the road for ...
Yanlış yoldasınız.	You're on the wrong road.
... -e geri gitmelisiniz.	You'll have to go back to ...
... işaretlerini izleyin.	Follow the signs for ...

How far? Ne kadar uzakta?

...-dir.	It's ...
yakın/uzak	close/a long way
yürüyerek 5 dakika	5 minutes on foot
araba ile 10 dakika	10 minutes by car
100 metre ilerde	about 100 meters down the road
10 kilometre uzakta	about 10 kilometers away

TIME ➤ 220; NUMBERS ➤ 216

Road signs Trafik işaretleri

YOL DEĞİŞTİRME	detour [diversion]
TEK YÖN	one-way street
KAPALI YOL	road closed
OKUL	school zone [path]
DUR	stop
SOLLAMA YASAK	no passing [overtaking]
YAVAŞ SÜRÜNÜZ	drive slowly
FARLARI YAKINIZ	use headlights

Town plans Kent planları

ana cadde	main [high] street
banka	bank
buradasınız	you are here
danışma bürosu	information office
hastane	hospital
havaalanı	airport
kilise	church
mağaza	department store
metro istasyonu	subway [metro] station
okul	school
otobüs durağı	bus stop
otobüs yolu	bus route
otopark	parking lot [car park]
park	park
polis karakolu	police station
postane	post office
sinema	movie theater [cinema]
spor alanı	playing field [sports ground]
stadyum	stadium
taksi durağı	taxi stand [rank]
tiyatro	theater
tren garı	train station
yaya bölgesi	pedestrian zone [precinct]
yaya geçidi	pedestrian crossing

Sightseeing

Tourist information office

Turist danışma bürosu

In Turkey, tourist offices are everywhere, but rarely have much useful information. However, they are often worth visiting to pick up a map of the city or resort. Travel agents are usually far more helpful.

In resorts and towns, tourist offices are usually located in the main square or near the harbor.

Where's the tourist office?	**Turist danışma bürosu nerede?** *tooreest danersh-ma bewro-soo neredeh*
What are the main points of interest?	**Başlıca ilginç yerler nelerdir?** *bashler-jah eelgeench yerler neh-lair-deer*
We're here for …	**Buraya … için geldik.** *booraya … itchin geldik*
a few hours	**birkaç saat** *beerkatch sa-art*
a day	**bir gün** *beer gewn*
a week	**bir hafta** *beer hafta*
Can you recommend …?	**… önerebilir misiniz?** *… owe-nair-eh-beeleer miseeniz*
a sightseeing tour	**bir tur** *beer toor*
an excursion	**bir gezinti** *beer gezintee*
a boat trip	**bir gemi gezisi** *beer gemee gezee-see*
Do you have any information on …?	**… hakkında bir bilginiz var mı?** *… hak-kernda beer beelgeeniz var mer*
Are there any trips to …?	**… -e tur var mı?** *… eh toor var mer*

DAYS OF THE WEEK ➤ 218; DIRECTIONS ➤ 94

Excursions Gezintiler

How much does the tour cost?
Gezi ne kadar?
ge<u>zee</u> neh kaddar

Is lunch included?
Öğle yemeği dahil mi?
owe-leh ye-<u>may</u>-ee dah-<u>heel</u> mee

Where do we leave from?
Nereden hareket ediyoruz?
nereh-den hareh-<u>ket</u> edee-yoruz

What time does the tour start?
Tur ne zaman başlıyor?
toor neh za<u>man</u> <u>bash</u>ler-yor

What time do we get back?
Ne zaman geri dönüyoruz?
neh za<u>man</u> geree <u>durn</u>ew-yoruz

Do we have free time in …?
… -de serbest zamanımız olacak mı?
… deh sair-<u>best</u> za<u>man</u>-ernerz olah-jak mer

Is there an English-speaking guide?
İngilizce konuşan rehber olacak mı?
eengee<u>leez</u>-jeh kon<u>oo</u>shan reh-bair olah-jak mer

On tour Turda

Are we going to see …?
… -i görecek miyiz?
… ee <u>gurr</u>eh-jek meeyiz

We'd like to have a look at the …
… -e bir bakmak istiyoruz.
… eh bak-mak i<u>stee</u>-yoruz

Can we stop here …?
Burada … durabilir miyiz?
boorada … doorah-bee<u>leer</u> meeyiz

to take photographs
fotoğraf çekmek için
foto-<u>raf</u> chek-mek it<u>chin</u>

to buy souvenirs
hediyelik eşya satın almak için
he<u>deeye</u>-lik esh-ya <u>satern</u> almak it<u>chin</u>

to use the bathrooms [toilets]
tuvalete gitmek için
too-<u>va</u>-let-eh geetmek it<u>chin</u>

Would you take a photo of us, please?
Fotoğrafımızı çekebilir misiniz lütfen?
foto-<u>rafer</u>-merz-er chek-eh-bee<u>leer</u> miseeniz <u>lewt</u>-fen

How long do we have here/in …?
Burada/… -de ne kadar zamanımız var? *boorada/… deh neh kaddar za<u>man</u>er-merz var*

Wait! … isn't back yet.
Bekleyin! … daha dönmedi˘
bek<u>lay</u>een … dah-ha <u>durn</u>-medee

Sights Gezi yerleri

The Ministry of Tourism provides a free road map of the country, as well as detailed maps of parts of Istanbul, Ankara, İzmir, and Antalya. If you are planning to drive a lot, get a good map before you leave your home country.

Where is the …?	**… nerede?** … neredeh
art gallery	**sanat galerisi** sa<u>nat</u> gal-<u>air</u>-eesee
battle site	**savaş meydanı** sa<u>vash</u> may-<u>dan</u>-er
botanical garden	**botanik bahçesi** botan-<u>eek</u> bah-che-see
castle	**kale** ka-leh
cathedral	**katedral** ka-teh-<u>dral</u>
cemetery	**mezarlık** me<u>zar</u>-lerk
church	**kilise** kee-<u>lee</u>seh
downtown area	**kent merkezi** kent mairkez-ee
fountain	**çeşme** chesh-meh
historic site	**tarihi yer** taree-<u>hee</u> yair
market	**pazar** pa<u>zar</u>
(war) memorial	**anıt** an-ert
monastery	**manastır** mana<u>ster</u>
museum	**müze** mew-zeh
old town	**eski kent** eskee kent
opera house	**opera binası** opair-ah bee<u>na</u>-ser
palace	**saray** sa-<u>rye</u>
park	**park** park
parliament building	**parlamento binası** parla-<u>mento</u> bee<u>na</u>-ser
ruins	**harabeler** hara<u>be</u>ler
shopping area	**alışveriş merkezi** alirsh-ver<u>eesh</u> mair-kez-ee
statue	**heykel** hay-kel
theater	**tiyatro** tee-<u>yat</u>-tro
tower	**kule** kooleh
town hall	**belediye binası** beleh-<u>dee</u>-yesee bee<u>na</u>-ser
viewpoint	**manzara** <u>manzarah</u>
Can you show me on the map?	**Bana haritada gösterebilir misniz?** bana <u>hareeta</u>-da go-stair-eh-bee<u>leer</u> miseeniz

DIRECTIONS ➤ 94

Admission Giriş

As a tourist, you need to pay for almost every museum and gallery. However, there are discounts for groups and families.

Is the ... open to the public?	**... halka açık mı?** ... hal-kah acherk mer
May we look around?	**Çevreye bakabilir miyiz?** chev-ray-eh bakah-beeleer meeyiz
What are the hours?	**Açılış saatleri nedir?** acherl-ersh sa-art-lairee neh-deer
When does it close?	**Ne zaman kapanıyor?** neh zaman kapaner-yor
Is ... open on Sundays?	**... pazar günleri açık mı?** ... pazar gewn-lairee acherk mer
When's the next guided tour?	**Bir sonraki rehberli tur ne zaman?** beer sonrakee reh-bair-lee toor ne zaman
Do you have you a guidebook (in English)?	**(İngilizce) Rehber kitabınız var mı?** (eengeeleez-jeh) reh-bair keetab-ernerz var mer
May I take photos?	**Fotoğraf çekebilir miyim?** foto-raf chekeh-beeleer meeyim
Is there access for the disabled?	**Özürlüler girebilir mi?** urzewr-lew-lair geereh-beeleer mee
Is there an audioguide in English?	**İngilizce teybe alınmış rehber var mı?** eengeeleez-jeh taybeh alernmersh reh-bair var mer

Paying / Tickets Ödeme/Biletler

... tickets, please.	**... biletler lütfen.** ... beelet-lair lewt-fen
How much is the entrance fee?	**Giriş ücreti ne kadar?** geerish ewjret-ee neh kaddar
Are there any discounts for ...?	**... için indirim var mı?** ... itchin eendeerim var mer
children/groups	**çocuklar/gruplar** chojook-lar groop-lar
senior citizens	**emekliler** emeklee-lair
students	**öğrenciler** ur-ren-jee-lair
the disabled	**özürlüler** urzewr-lew-lair
One adult and two children, please.	**Bir yetişkin, iki çocuk lütfen** beer yeteesh-kin ikee chojook lewt-fen
I lost my ticket.	**Biletimi kaybettim.** beelet-imee ky-bettim

TIME ➤ 220

○	**GİRİŞ SERBEST**	free admission
	KAPALI	closed
	HEDİYELİK EŞYA DÜKKANI	gift shop
	EN SON GİRİŞ SAATİ 17.00	latest entry at 5 p.m.
	BİR SONRAKİ TUR ...	next tour at ...
	GİRİLMEZ	no entry
	FLAŞLA FOTOĞRAF ÇEKİLMEZ	no flash photography
	FOTOĞRAF ÇEKİLMEZ	no photography
	AÇIK	open
○	**ZİYARET SAATLERİ**	visiting hours	○

Impressions İzlenimler

It's ...	**... -dir.** *... deer*
amazing	**hayret verici** *hi-ret veree-jee*
beautiful	**güzel** *gewzel*
bizarre	**garip** *gareep*
boring	**sıkıcı** *ser-ker-jer*
breathtaking	**nefes kesici** *nefess kesee-jee*
incredible	**inanılmaz** *eenan-erlmaz*
interesting	**ilginç** *eelginch*
lots of fun	**çok eğlendirici** *chok ay-lendeer-eejee*
magnificent	**muhteşem** *mooh-teh-shem*
romantic	**romantik** *romanteek*
strange	**şaşırtıcı** *sha-sher-ter-jer*
stunning	**çarpıcı** *charper-jer*
superb	**mükemmel** *mew-kemmel*
terrible	**berbat** *bair-bat*
ugly	**çirkin** *cheerkin*
It's a good value.	**Değer.** *day-air*
It's a rip-off.	**Çok kazık.** *chok kazerk*
I like it.	**Beğendim.** *bay-endim*
I don't like it.	**Beğenmedim.** *bay-enmeh-dim*

101

altın gold(en)
avlu courtyard
ayrıntı detail
başka bir müzeden on loan
balık sırtı herringbone
balmumu waxwork
bina building
branda canvas
çatı roof
çizim drawing
demir işi ironwork
deniz manzarası seascape
dönemi reign
döşemelik tapestry
duvar wall
duvar nakışı frieze
duvarda oluk ağzı gargoyle
duvar resmi mural
düzenlenmiş bahçe formal garden
fresk fresco
fuaye foyer
geçici sergi temporary exhibit
girinti alcove
gölge shadow
gömüt tomb
gümüş silver
gümüş takımlar silverware
güzel sanatlar fine arts
hamam Turkish baths
hendek drawbridge
heykel sculpture
imparatoriçe empress
iş works
kale çukuru moat
kalıp molding

kamara stateroom
kanat wing (*of building*)
kapı door/gate
kapı aralığı doorway
kapı aynası paneling
kil clay
kilise avlusu churchyard
kilisenin doğu ucu apse
kilisenin orta kesimi nave
kiriş beam
köşe taşı cornerstone
konferans lecture
koro (bölmesi) choir (stall)
kral king
kraliçe queen
kule tower
kule külahı spire
kütüphane library
mahzen crypt
manzara landscape
mazgallı siper battlement
merdiven staircase
merdivenler stairs
mermer marble
metal oyma etching
metal para coin
mezar grave
mezar taşı headstone
mine enamel
mobilya furniture
model model
mücevher gemstone
mücevherat jewelry
odun kömürü charcoal
ölçek 1:100 scale 1:100
ölü doğa still life

org organ
oyma engraving
payanda buttress
pencere window
pişmiş toprak terra-cotta
resim painting/picture
resim levhası panel
ressam painter
ressamı ... painted by ...
saat clock
sahne stage
sarkma overhanging
sergi exhibition
sergi muhafazası display cabinet
sergilenen şey exhibit
silah weapon
sulu boya watercolor
sunak altar(piece)
sütun pillar
tablo painting
taç crown
tahta wood
tasarım design
taslak sketch
taş stone
tavan ceiling
tonoz vault
türbe tomb
tuğla brick
ufak kule turret
usta master
ustalık işi masterpiece
üçgen alınlık pediment
vaftiz kurnası font
vaiz kürsüsü pulpit
vitray cam stained-glass
  window
yağlı boya oils

yaldızlı gilded
yan duvarın çatıyla
  birleştiği yer gable
yarı keresteli half-
  timbered
yaşanmış lived
yeşillik foliage
yontma carving
yükseklik height
yüzyıl century
zanaat crafts
zırh armory

Other useful terms:

... -de başlandı started in ...
... -de bulunmuş
  discovered in ...
... -de dikilmiş erected in ...
... -de doğmuş born in ...
... -de inşa edilmiş built in ...
... -de kurulmuş founded in ...
... -de ölmüş died in ...
... -de restore edildi restored in ...
... -de tamamlanmış
  completed in ...
... -de yeniden inşa edildi
  rebuilt in ...
... ekolü school of ...
... ile by ... (*person*)
... -in bağışı donated by ...
... tarafından sipariş edilmiş
  commissioned by ...
... tarafından tasarlanmış
  designed by ...
... tarafından yok edilmiş
  destroyed by ...
... üslubunda in the style of ...

103

Who? / What? / When?
Kim? / Ne? / Ne zaman?

What's that building?	**Bu bina nedir?**	*boo beenah neh-deer*
When was it built?	**Ne zaman inşa edilmiş?**	
	neh zaman eenshah edeelmish	
Who was the artist/architect?	**Sanatçı/mimar kim?**	
	sanat-cher meemar kim	
What style is that?	**Ne üslubunda?**	*neh ewslooboonda*
Which period is that?	**Hangi dönem?**	*hangee durnem*

Architectural style Üslubunda

Bizans *beezans*
Byzantine architecture. Influenced by Greek and Roman architecture but has a special character of its own. Particularly distinctive are churches built in the shape of a cross with a dome at each point, such as St. Sophia in Istanbul.

Selçuk *selchook*
The Seljuk style. Characterized by cylindrical mausoleums with conical roofs and mosques with elaborate minarets, such as the "Fluted Minaret" (Yivli Minare) in Antalya.

Osmanlı *os-mahn-ler*
Ottoman architecture. Best exemplified by the magnificent mosques, whose domes and minarets still largely dominate the Istanbul skyline.

Rulers Hükümdarlar

Tarih Öncesi   8,500–2000 B.C.
Neolithic civilization. Artifacts found at Çatalhöyük, the most important neolithic site, can be viewed at the Museum of Anatolian Civilizations in Ankara.

Hitit Dönemi   2000–1200 B.C.
The most impressive ruins from the Hittite period are at Hattuşaş, the ancient Hittite capital, some 80 miles north of Ankara.

Yunan Dönemi   1000–350 B.C.
The Ancient Greeks who colonized Turkey founded a number of states and flourished until crushed by the Persian King Cyrus. The most famous ruins they left behind are those of the city of Ephesus on the Aegean coast.

Roma Dönemi   190 B.C.–A.D. 330
The Romans invaded Turkey in the second century B.C. and turned it into a province of their empire.

Bizans Dönemi   330–1453

The Byzantine Empire came into being when the Emperor Constantine moved the Roman capital to Byzantium, built where Istanbul now stands, and renamed it Constantinople after himself. Remains of the impressive achievements of Byzantine civilization are still to be found in this city, the conquest of which by the Ottomans in 1453 brought the empire to an end.

Selçuk Dönemi   1071–1243

The Seljuks defeated the Byzantine Emperor Romanos IV at the Battle of Malazgirit and reigned over central and southern Anatolia until they themselves were defeated by Genghis Khan in 1243.

Osmanlı Dönemi   1299–1923

Having come to power after the collapse of the Seljuk Empire, the Ottomans enjoyed a meteoric rise, going on to conquer all the rest of Turkey and much of the Middle East, North Africa, and Eastern Europe. Under Süleyman the Magnificent (1495–1566), the Ottoman Empire was the superpower of its day. Although traces of Ottoman civilization are present everywhere in Turkey, visiting the Topkapi Palace Museum in Istanbul gives you a good idea of the wealth and power the sultans once had at their disposal.

Çağdaş Türkiye   1923–

Modern Turkey, which rose out of the ashes of the Ottoman Empire after World War I, is the creation of Kemal Atatürk (1881–1938) whose statues and portraits the visitor will see everywhere. Atatürk turned Turkey into a republic, and westernized its legal system and lifestyle. Since then Turkish history has occasionally been turbulent, but today the country has a parliamentary democracy and is relatively stable and prosperous (although Islamic fundamentalism remains a consideration).

Places of worship İbadet yerleri

The national religion is Islam, though, as Turkey is a secular state, complete freedom of worship is granted to non-Muslims, who make up a small percentage of the population. You should be respectful of local customs when visiting a mosque: wear suitable clothing and take off your shoes.

mosque	**cami** _jahmee_
Catholic/Protestant church	**Katolik/Protestan kilisesi** _katoleek/protestan keeleesesee_
synagogue/temple	**havra/tapınak** _havrah/tapernak_
What are the prayer times?	**İdadet saatleri ne zaman?** _eebadet sa-atlairee neh zaman_

In the countryside Kırda

I'd like a map of ...	**... haritası istiyorum.** ... _hareeta-ser_ _istee_-yorum
this region	**bu bölge** _boo burlgeh_
walking routes	**yürüyüş yolları** _yew-rew-_yewsh_ yol-lar-er_
cycle routes	**bisiklet yolları** _beesee-_klet_ yol-lar-er_
How far is it to ...?	**... ne kadar uzakta?** ... _neh kaddar oo_zakta_
Is there a right of way?	**Geçiş hakkı var mı?** _ge_cheesh_ hak-ker var mer_
Is there a trail/scenic route to ...?	**... -e giden yol/manzaralı yol var mı?** ... _eh geeden yol/_manzara_-ler yol var mer_
Can you show me on the map?	**Bana haritada gösterebilir misiniz?** _bana _hareeta_-da go-stair-eh-bee_leer_ miseeniz_
I'm lost.	**Kayboldum.** _ky-_boldoom_

Organized walks Organize yürüyüşler

When does the guided walk start?	**Rehberli yürüyüş ne zaman başlıyor?** _reh-bair-lee yew-rew-_yewsh_ neh za_man_ _bash_ler-yor_
When will we return?	**Ne zaman geri döneceğiz?** _neh za_man_ geree durneh-_jay_iz_
Is it a hard course?	**Zorlu bir yol mu?** _zor-loo beer yol moo_
gentle/medium/tough	**rahat/orta/güç** _ra_hat_/or_tah_/gewch_
I'm exhausted.	**Çok yoruldum.** _chok yo_rool_-dum_
How long are we resting here?	**Burada ne kadar dinleneceğiz?** _boorada neh kaddar deen_len_-eh-jayiz_
What kind of ... is that?	**Bu ne tür bir ...?** _boo neh tewr beer_
animal/bird	**hayvan/kuş** _hi-_van_/koosh_
flower/tree	**çiçek/ağaç** _chee_chek_/aa-arch_

Geographic features
Coğrafi özellikler

beach	**plaj** *plazh*
bridge	**köprü** *kurprew*
canal	**kanal** *ka-nal*
cave	**mağara** *ma-aarah*
cliff	**uçurum** *oochoorum*
farm	**çiftlik** *chift-lik*
field	**tarla** *tarlah*
footpath	**patika** *pateeka*
forest	**orman** *orman*
hill	**tepe** *tepeh*
lake	**göl** *gurl*
mountain	**dağ** *daa*
mountain pass	**dağ geçidi** *daa getchee-dee*
mountain range	**sıra dağ** *ser-ra daa*
nature reserve	**milli park** *meel-lee park*
panorama	**manzara** *manzara*
park	**park** *park*
peak	**tepe** *tepeh*
picnic area	**piknik alanı** *peeknik alan-er*
pond	**gölcük** *gurl-jewk*
rapids	**ivinti yeri** *eevintee yair-ee*
river	**ırmak** *er-mak*
sea	**deniz** *deneez*
stream	**dere** *dereh*
valley	**vadi** *var-dee*
viewpoint	**manzara seyretme yeri** *manzara seyretmeh yeree*
village	**köy** *kur-y*
vineyard/winery	**bağ/saraphane** *baa/sharap-haneh*
waterfall	**şelale** *shelar-leh*
wood	**fundalık** *foonda-lerk*

Leisure

Events Etkinlikler

Publications giving listings for leisure activities are hard to come by, although festival programs can usually be obtained from tourist offices. If you are staying in a small resort, ear-piercing Western music will quickly lead you to the hottest night spot. If staying in a major city, consult your friendly hotel receptionist.

Do you have a program of events?	**Etkinlik programı var mı?** *etkinlik pro-ram-er var mer*
Can you recommend a ...?	**Bir ... önerebilir misiniz?** *beer ... owe-nair-eh-beeleer miseeniz*
ballet	**bale** *ba-leh*
concert	**konser** *kon-sair*
movie [film]	**film** *feelm*
opera	**opera** *opair-ah*
play	**tiyatro oyunu** *teeyat-tro oyoonu*

Availability Yer var mı?

When does it start?	**Ne zaman başlıyor?** *neh zaman bashler-yor*
When does it end?	**Ne zaman bitiyor?** *neh zaman beetee-yor*
Are there any seats for tonight?	**Bu gece için yer var mı?** *boo geh-jeh itchin yair var mer*
Where can I get tickets?	**Nereden bilet alabilirim?** *nereh-den beelet ala-beeleerim*
There are ... of us.	**... kişiyiz.** *... keeshee-yiz*

Tickets Biletler

How much are the seats?	**Biletler ne kadar?**
	beelet-lair neh kaddar
Do you have anything cheaper?	**Daha ucuz yer var mı?**
	dah-ha oojooz yair var mer
I'd like two tickets for tonight's concert.	**Bu geceki konser için iki bilet lütfen.**
	boo geh-jeh-kee kon-sair itchin ikee beelet lewt-fen
I'd like to reserve …	**… ayırtmak istiyorum.**
	… eye-yertmak istee-yorum
three tickets for Sunday evening	**Pazar gecesi için üç bilet**
	pazar geh-jeh-see itchin ewch beelet

Kredi kartınızın … nedir?	What's your credit card …?
numarası	number
türü	type
geçerlilik süresi sonu	expiration [expiry] date
Burasını imzalar mısınız lütfen?	Can you sign here, please?
Lütfen biletleri … alınız.	Please pick up the tickets …
saat … -e kadar alınız.	by … p.m.
yer ayırtma masasından	at the reservation desk

| Can I pay by credit card? | **Kredi kartı ile ödeyebilir miyim?** *kredee kart-er eeleh urday-eh-beeleer meeyim* |
| May I have a program, please? | **Bir program alabilir miyim lütfen?** *beer pro-ram ala-beeleer meeyim lewt-fen* |

– Yardımcı olabilir miyim? (Can I help you?)
– Bu geceki konser için iki bilet lütfen.
(I'd like two tickets for tonight's concert, please.)
– Elbette. (Certainly.)
– Kredi kartı ile ödeyebilir miyim?
(Can I pay by credit card?)
– Evet. (Yes.)
– O zaman Visa ile ödeyeceğim.
(In that case, I'll pay by Visa.)
– Teşekkür ederim … Burasını imzalar mısınız lütfen?
(Thank you … Can you sign here, please?)

| **BİLETLER BİTTİ** | sold out |
| **YER AYIRTMA** | advance reservations |

NUMBERS ➤ 216

Movies [Cinema] Sinema

Movies are reasonably cheap in Turkey. During the summer months you will find open-air theaters in the Princess Islands in Istanbul and in smaller cities. Films are not up-to-date with the rest of the continent. They arrive in Turkey a few months after they are released in Europe or the U.S. Most films are in their original language with Turkish subtitles.

Is there a multiplex theater [cinema] near here?	**Buraya yakın çok salonlu sinema var mı?** *booraya ya<u>kern</u> chok salon-loo <u>seen</u>ema var mer*
What's playing at the movies [on at the cinema] tonight?	**Bu gece hangi filmler oynuyor?** *boo geh-jeh hangee feelm-lair <u>oy</u>nu-yor*
Is the film dubbed?	**Film seslendirmeli mi?** *feelm ses-len<u>deer</u>me-lee mee*
Is the film subtitled?	**Film alt yazılı mı?** *feelm alt <u>yaz</u>er-ler mer*
Is the film in the original English?	**Film İngilizce mi?** *feelm eengee<u>leez</u>-jeh mee*
A …, please.	**Bir … lütfen.** *beer … <u>lewt</u>-fen*
box [carton] of popcorn	**kutu patlamış mısır** *<u>koo</u>-too <u>patla</u>-mersh mer-ser*
chocolate ice cream [choc-ice]	**çikolatalı dondurma** *cheeko-<u>lata</u> don<u>doorma</u>*
hot dog	**sosisli sandöviç** *so<u>sees</u>-lee <u>sandur</u>-veech*
soft drink	**alkolsüz içecek** *alkol-sewz itcheh-jek*
small/regular/large	**küçük/normal/büyük** *kew<u>chewk</u>/nor-mal/bew<u>yewk</u>*

Theater Tiyatro

What's playing at the State Theater?	**Devlet Tiyatrosu'nda ne oynuyor?** *dev<u>let</u> tee<u>yat</u>-trosoonda neh <u>oy</u>nu-yor*
Who's the playwright?	**Oyun yazarı kim?** *o<u>yoon</u> yaz<u>ar</u>-er kim*
Do you think I'd enjoy it?	**Sizce beğenir miyim?** *seez-<u>jeh</u> bay-en<u>eer</u> meeyim*
I don't know much Turkish.	**Fazla Türkçe bilmiyorum.** *fazlah <u>tewrk</u>-che <u>beel</u>mee-yorum*

Opera/Ballet/Dance
Opera/Bale/Dans

Your stay ought to include at least one visit to a nightclub with belly dancing. The best and most expensive performers are found at the top nightspots. You could also enjoy some traditional folk dancing, like the "Spoon Dance" or "Sword and Shield Dance" of Bursa. If you feel energetic you can join in with the folk dancing at your local taverna.

Where's the theater?	**Tiyatro nerede?** teeyat-tro neredeh
Who's dancing?	**Dansçılar kim?** _dans_-cher-lar kim
Who's the composer/soloist?	**Besteci/soloist kim?** besteh-_jee_/soloist kim
Is formal dress required?	**Takım elbise gerekli mi?** takerm el_bee_seh _gerek_-lee mee
I'm interested in belly dancing.	**Göbek dansı ilgimi çekiyor.** gur_bek_ dan_ser_ ilgeemee cheke_eyor_

Music/Concerts Müzik/Konserler

Where's the concert hall?	**Konser salonu nerede?** kon-sair salon-oo neredeh
Which orchestra/band is playing?	**Hangi orkestra/grup çalıyor?** hangee or_kestra_/groop _chaler_-yor
What are they playing?	**Ne çalacaklar?** neh _chalah_-jak-lar
Who's the conductor/soloist?	**Orkestra şefi/solo kim?** or_kestra_ shefee/solo kim
Who's the support band?	**Destek grubu hangisi?** des_tek_ groob-oo _hangee_-see
I really like …	**… severim.** … se_vairim_
folk music/country music	**halk müziği/country müziği** halk mew_zee_-yee/kuntree mew_zee_-yee
jazz	**caz** jaz
music of the sixties	**'60'ların müziğini** _al_tmersh-larern mew_zee_-yeenee
pop/rock music	**pop/rock müziği** pop/rock mew_zee_-yee
soul music	**soul müziği** soul mew_zee_-yee
Have you ever heard of her/him/them?	**Hiç onu/onları duydunuz mu?** hitch onoo/onlar-er _doydoo_-nooz moo
Are they popular?	**Burada beğeniliyor mu?** boorada bay-e_neel_-ee-yor moo

Nightlife Gece hayatı

What is there to do in the evenings?	**Geceleri ne yapılır?** *geh-jeh-lairee neh yaperl-er*
Can you recommend a …?	**… önerebilir misiniz?** *… owe-nair-eh-beeleer miseeniz*
Is there a …?	**… var mı?** *… var mer*
bar/restaurant	**bar/lokanta** *bar/lokanta*
cabaret/casino	**kabare/kumarhane** *kabareh/koomarharneh*
discotheque	**diskotek** *deesko-tek*
gay club	**eşcinsel klübü** *esh-jeen-sel klewb-ew*
nightclub	**gece klübü** *geh-jeh klewb-ew*
What type of music do they play?	**Ne tür müzik çalıyorlar?** *neh tewr mewzeek chaler-yor-lar*
How do I get there?	**Oraya nasıl gidebilirim?** *oraya nassirl geedeh-beeleerim*
Is there an admission charge?	**Giriş ücreti var mı?** *gireesh ewjret-ee var mer*

Admission Giriş

What time does the show start?	**Gösteri ne zaman başlıyor?** *go-stair-ee neh zaman bashler-yor*
Is there a cover charge?	**Masa ücreti var mı?** *massah ewjret-ee var mer*
Is a reservation necessary?	**Yer ayırtmak gerekiyor mu?** *yair eye-yertmak gerekee-yor moo*
Do we need to be members?	**Üye olmak gerekiyor mu?** *ew-yeh olmak gerekee-yor moo*
Can you have dinner there?	**Orada akşam yemeği veriyorlar mı?** *orada aksham ye-may-yee veree-yor-lar mer*
How long will we have to stand in line [queue]?	**Ne kadar sırada beklemek gerekecek?** *neh kaddar ser-rah-da bekleh-mek gerek-eh-jek*
I'd like a good table.	**İyi bir masa istiyorum.** *eeyee beer massah istee-yorum*

TIME ➤ 220; TAXI ➤ 84

Children Çocuklar

Can you recommend something for the children?
Çocuklar için bir şeyler önerebilir misiniz? *chojook-lar itchin beer shay-lair owe-nair-eh-beeleer miseniz*

Are there changing facilities here for babies?
Bebeğin altını değiştirecek bir yer var mı? *be-bay-yin altern-er day-eeshteer-eh-jek beer yair var mer*

Where are the bathrooms [toilets]?
Tuvalet nerede? *too-va-let neredeh*

amusement arcade
oyun salonu *oyoon salon-oo*

fairground
lunapark *loonah-park*

kiddie [paddling] pool
çocuk havuzu *chojook havooz-oo*

playground
çocuk parkı *chojook park-er*

play group
oyun grubu *oyoon groob-oo*

zoo
hayvanat bahçesi *hi-vanat bah-che-see*

Baby-sitting Çocuk bakıcılığı

Can you recommend a reliable baby-sitter?
Güvenilir bir bebek çocuk önerebilir misiniz? *gewven-eeleer beer bebek chojook owe-nair-eh-beeleer miseniz*

Is there constant supervision?
Sürekli nezaret var mı? *sew-rek-lee naza-ret var mer*

Is the staff properly trained?
Personel yeterince eğitimli mi? *pair-sonnel yetair-eenjeh ay-eetim-lee mee*

When can I bring them?
Ne zaman getirebilirim? *neh zaman geteer-eh-beeleerim*

I'll pick them up at …
… -de alacağım. *… deh ala-jy-yerm*

We'll be back by …
… -e kadar geri döneriz. *… eh kaddar geree durnaireez*

She's 3, and he's 18 months.
Kız 3 yaşında, erkek 18 aylık. *kerz ewch yashernda air-kek on sekeez eye-lerk*

Sports Spor

Soccer is the national game in Turkey. In fact it is the addiction of Turkish men. Tickets to games are reasonably cheap, and the stadiums are quite organized. You will find the locals frequently talking to you about the soccer clubs in Europe.

Summer sports are available in holiday resorts. Ask at your hotel or resort for further information and prices.

Spectator İzleme

Is there a soccer [football] game [match] this Saturday?	**Bu cumartesi futbol maçı var mı?** *boo jew-marteh-see footbol match-er var mer*
Which teams are playing?	**Hangi takımlar oynuyor?** *hangee takerm-lar oynu-yor*
Can you get me a ticket?	**Bana bir bilet alabilir misiniz?** *bana beer beelet ala-beeleer miseeniz*
What's the admission charge?	**Giriş ücreti ne kadar?** *gireesh ewjret-ee neh kaddar*
Where's the racetrack [racecourse]?	**Hipodrom nerede?** *heepo-drom neredeh*
Where can I place a bet?	**Nerede bahis oynayabilirim?** *neredeh bahees oyn-eye-yabeeleerim*
American football	**Amerikan futbolu** *Amereekan footbol-oo*
angling	**olta ile balık avlama** *olta eeleh balerk avlama*
archery	**okçuluk** *ok-chooluk*
athletics	**atletizm** *atlet-eezm*
badminton	**badminton** *badmeen-ton*
baseball	**beyzbol** *bayz-bol*
basketball	**basketbol** *basketbol*
boxing	**boks** *boks*
canoeing	**kano** *ka-no*
cycling	**bisiklet** *beesee-klet*
gliding	**planörcülük** *plan-urjew-lewk*
golf	**golf** *golf*

greyhound racing	**köpek yarışı**
	kurpek yarersh-er
horse racing	**at yarışı** *at yarersh-er*
ice hockey	**buz hokeyi** *booz ho-kay-ee*
judo	**judo** *joo-do*
mountaineering	**dağcılık** *daa-jerlerk*
pool [billiards]	**bilardo** *beelardo*
rapelling [abseiling]	**iple iniş** *eep-leh eenish*
rock climbing	**kayaya tırmanma** *ky-eye-ya termanma*
rowing	**kürekçilik** *kewrek-cheelik*
rugby	**ragbi** *ragbee*
soccer [football]	**futbol** *footbol*
squash	**skuaş** *skooash*
swimming	**yüzme** *yewz-meh*
table tennis	**masa tenisi** *massah teneesee*
tennis	**tenis** *tenees*
volleyball	**voleybol** *vo-laybol*

Participating Oynamak

Is there a ... nearby?	**Yakında ... var mı?** *yakernda ... var mer*
golf course	**golf sahası** *golf saha-ser*
sports club	**spor klübü** *spor klewb-ew*
Are there any tennis courts?	**Tenis kortları var mı?**
	tenees kortlar-er var mer
What's the charge per ...?	**... ücreti nedir?** *... ewjret-ee neh-deer*
day/round/hour	**günlük/bir tur/saatlik**
	gewnlewk/beer toor/sa-artlerk
Do I need to be a member?	**Üye olmam gerekiyor mu?**
	ew-yeh olmam geretee-yor moo
Where can I rent ...?	**Nerede bir ... kiralayabilirim?**
	neredeh beer ... keer-al-eye-yabeeleerim
boots	**çizme** *cheezmeh*
clubs	**sopa** *so-pah*
equipment	**donanım** *donanerm*
a racket	**raket** *ra-ket*

Can I get lessons?	**Ders alabilir miyim?** *dairs ala-beeleer meeyim*
Do you have a fitness room?	**Jimnastik salonunuz var mı?** *zheemnasteek salon-oonuz var mer*
May I join in?	**Girebilir miyim?** *geer-eh-beeleer meeyim*

Özür dilerim, doluyuz.	I'm sorry. We're booked.
… ön ödeme var.	There is a deposit of …
Bedeniniz kaç?	What size are you?
Vesikalık fotoğraf gerek.	You need a passport-size photo.

At the beach Plajda

Beach safety is usually the individual's responsibility as few beaches have lifeguards. Avoid too much sun and use sunblock whenever you are out in the sun.

Is the beach pebbly/ sandy?	**Plaj çakıllı/kumlu mu?** *plazh chakerl-ler/koomlu moo*
Is there a … here?	**Burada … var mı?** *boorada … var mer*
children's pool	**çocuk havuzu** *chojook havooz-oo*
swimming pool	**yüzme havuzu** *yewz-meh havooz-oo*
indoor/open-air	**kapalı/açık** *kapal-er/atcherk*
Is it safe to swim/dive here?	**Burada yüzmek/dalmak güvenli mi?** *boorada yewzmek/dal-mak gewvenlee mee*
Is it safe for children?	**Çocuklar için güvenli mi?** *chojook-lar itchin gewvenlee mee*
Is there a lifeguard?	**Cankurtaran var mı?** *jan-koortar-ran var mer*
I want to rent a/some …	**… kiralamak istiyorum.** *… keerah-lamak istee-yorum*
deck chair	**katlanabilir koltuk** *katlan-ah-beeleer koltook*
jet-ski	**jet ski** *jet skee*

motorboat	**motorlu tekne**
	mo-torloo tekneh
diving equipment	**dalış donanımı**
	dalersh donanermer
umbrella [sunshade]	**şemsiye** _shemsee-yeh_
surfboard	**surf tahtası** surf _tahta-ser_
water skis	**su kayağı** soo ky-_yar_-er
For … hours.	**… saat için.** … sa-art itch_in_

Skiing Kayak

The main ski area is in Bursa, Ulu Dağ. It is only open during the winter months. There are hotels, bed and breakfasts, and motels available.

What's the snow like?	**Kar nasıl?** kar _nassirl_
heavy/icy	**ağır/buzlu** aa-yer/boozloo
powdery/wet	**yumuşak/ıslak** yoomu_shak_/ers_lak_
I'd like to rent some …	**… kiralamak istiyorum.**
	… keerah-lamak _istee_-yorum
poles	**kayak sopası** ky-_yak_ so-pa-ser
skates	**paten** paten
ski boots	**kayak çizmesi** ky-_yak_ _cheez_meh-see
skis	**kayak** ky-_yak_
These are too big/small.	**Bunlar çok büyük/küçük.**
	boonlar chok bew_yewk_/kew_chewk_
They're uncomfortable.	**Rahatsız.** ra_hat_-serz
A lift pass for a day/five days.	**Bir/beş günlük teleferik pasosu lütfen.**
	beer/besh gewnlewk tele-_fair_-eek
	passo-soo _lewt_-fen
I'd like to join the ski school.	**Kayak okuluna girmek istiyorum.**
	ky-_yak_ o_kool_unah geermek _istee_-yorum
I'm a beginner.	**Yeni başlıyorum.** yenee _bash_ler-yorum
I'm experienced.	**Deneyimliyim.** de-nay-_eem_lee-yim

TELEFERİK	cable car/gondola
KOLTUKLU TELEFERİK	chair lift
ÇEKİCİ TELEFERİK	drag lift

117

Making friends Tanıştırma

Surnames were introduced in Turkey only in the 1920s and are still seldom used even in formal modes of address. Ali Demir, for instance, should be addressed not as "Demir Bay" (Mr. Demir) but as "Ali Bey," and his wife, Ayşe, should be addressed as "Ayşe Hanım."

Turkish has a formal and an informal "you." Strangers use the formal "you" (**siz**) in conversation until they get to know each other better. These days, however, it isn't unusual for young people to dispense with formalities and start using the informal version (**sen**) right away. (➤ 169 for more details.)

Regardless of the mode of address employed, most people will shake hands when first introduced.

Hello. We haven't met.	**Merhaba. Tanışmadık.** *mer-habah. <u>ta</u>nershma-derk*
My name is …	**Adım …** *aderm*
May I introduce …?	**… -i tanıştırabilir miyim?** *… ee tanershter-ah-bee<u>leer</u> meeyim*
Pleased to meet you.	**Tanıştığımıza memnun oldum.** *tanersh-<u>ter</u>-ermerz-ah memnoon <u>ol</u>doom*
What's your name?	**Adınız nedir?** *adern-erz neh-deer*
How are you?	**Nasılsınız?** *<u>na</u>ssirl-sernerz*
Fine, thanks. And you?	**İyiyim, teşekkürler. Siz?** *eeyee-yim teshek-<u>kewr</u>-lair. seez*

– *Merhaba, nasılsınız?*
(Hello, how are you?)

– *İyiyim, teşekkürler. Siz?*
(Fine, thanks. And you?)

– *İyiyim, teşekkürler.*
(Fine, thanks.)

Where are you from? Nerelisisiniz?

Where are you from?	**Nerelisiniz?** *nereh-leesee-neez*
Where were you born?	**Nerede doğdunuz?** *neredeh doh-doonuz*
I'm from …	**… -denim.** *… denim*
Australia	**Avustralya** *aus-tral-yah*
Britain	**Britanya** *breetan-yah*
Canada	**Kanada** *kanadah*
England	**İngiltere** *eengeel-tair-eh*
Ireland	**İrlanda** *eer-landah*
Scotland	**İskoçya** *eeskotch-yah*
the U.S.	**ABD** *ah-beh-deh*
Wales	**Galler Ülkesi** *gal-lair ewlkeh-see*
Where do you live?	**Nerede oturuyor sunuz?** *neredeh otooru-yorsoonuz*
What part of Turkey are you from?	**Türkiye'nin neresindensiniz?** *tewrk-eeyeh-nin nereh-sinden-seeniz*
Cyprus	**Kıbrıs** *kerbrers*
We come here every year.	**Buraya her yıl geliriz.** *booraya hair yerl geleeriz*
It's my/our first visit.	**Benim/bizim ilk ziyaretim/iz.** *benim/beezim eelk zeeyar-reteem/iz*
Have you ever been to …?	**… -e hiç gittiniz mi?** *… eh hitch gitteeniz mee*
the U.K./U.S.	**Birleşik Krallık/ABD** *beerleshik kral-lerk/ah-beh-deh*
Do you like it here?	**Burayı beğendiniz mi?** *boora-yer bayen-dineez mee*
What do you think of the …?	**… hakkında ne düşünüyorsunuz?** *… hak-kernda neh dew-shewn-ew-yorsoonuz*
I love the … here.	**Burada … -i çok beğendim.** *boorada … ee chok bay-endim*
I don't really like the … here.	**Burada … -i hiç beğenmedim.** *boorada … ee hitch bay-enmedim*
food/people	**yemekler/insanlar** *yemek-lair/eensan-lar*

Who are you with? Kiminlesiniz?

Who are you with?	**Kiminlesiniz?**	*kimeen-leh-seeniz*
I'm on my own.	**Tek başımayım.**	*tek basherm-my-yerm*
I'm with a friend.	**Bir arkadaş ile birlikteyiz.**	
	beer arkadash eeleh beerlikte-yeez	
I'm with my …	**… ile birlikteyim.**	*… eeleh beerlikte-yeem*
husband/wife	**kocam/karım**	*ko-jam/ka-rerm*
family	**ailem**	*eye-lem*
children/parents	**çocuklar/ana baba**	
	chojook-lar/anna babah	
boyfriend/girlfriend	**erkek arkadaşım/kız arkadaşım**	
	air-kek arkadasherm/kerz arkadasherm	
father/son	**babam/oğlum**	*babam/o-loom*
mother/daughter	**annem/kızım**	*an-nem/ker-zerm*
brother/uncle	**erkek kardeşim/amcam**	
	air-kek kardeshim/am-jam	
sister/aunt	**kız kardeşim/teyzem**	
	kerz kardeshim/tay-zem	
What's your son's/ wife's name?	**Oğlunuzun/karınızın adı nedir?**	
	o-loonoozun/kar-ernerzern ad-er neh-deer	
Are you married?	**Evli misiniz?**	*ev-lee miseeniz*
I'm …	**… -im.**	*… -eem*
married/single	**evli/bekar**	*ev-lee/be-kar*
divorced/separated	**boşanmış/ayrı**	*boshanmersh/eye-rer*
engaged	**nişanlı**	*neeshan-ler*
We live together.	**Beraber yaşıyoruz.**	
	bera-bair yasher-yoruz	
Do you have any children?	**Çocuğunuz var mı?**	
	chojoo-yoonuz var mer	
We have two boys and a girl.	**İki oğlumuz ve bir kızımız var.**	*ikee o-loomuz veh beer kerzermerz var*
How old are they?	**Kaç yaşındalar?**	*katch yashernda-lar*
They're 10 and 12.	**On ve oniki.**	*on veh on ikee*

What do you do? Ne iş yapıyorsunuz?

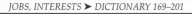

What do you do?	**Ne iş yapıyorsunuz?** *neh eesh yaper-yorsoonuz*
What are you studying?	**Ne okuyorsunuz?** *neh okoo-yorsoonuz*
I'm studying …	**… okuyorum.** *… okoo-yorum*
I'm in …	**… -deyim.** *… day-yim*
business	**iş idaresi** *eesh eedareh-see*
engineering	**mühendislik** *mewhendees-lik*
sales	**satış** *satersh*
Who do you work for …?	**Kimin için çalışıyorsunuz?** *kimeen itchin chalersher-yorsoonuz*
I work for …	**… için çalışıyorum.** *… itchin chalersher-yorsoonuz*
I'm (a/an) …	**… -im.** *… eem*
accountant	**muhasebeci** *moohaseh-bejee*
housewife	**ev kadını** *ev kadern-er*
student	**öğrenci** *ur-ren-jee*
retired	**emekli** *emek-lee*
self-employed	**kendi işim var** *kendee eeshim var*
between jobs	**işten yeni ayrıldım** *eeshten yenee eye-rerldim*
What are your interests/ hobbies?	**Nelere ilgi duyarsınız?** *nelereh eelgee doyar-sernerz*
I like …	**… severim.** *… sevairim*
music	**müzik** *mewzeek*
reading	**okumak** *okoomak*
sports	**spor** *spor*
I play …	**… oynarım.** *… oynarerm*
Would you like to play …?	**… oynamak ister misiniz?** *… oynamak eestair miseeniz*
cards	**kağıt** *ky-yert*
chess	**satranç** *satranch*

JOBS, INTERESTS ➤ DICTIONARY 169–201

What weather! Havaya bak!

What a lovely day!	**Ne güzel bir gün!** *neh gew_zel_ beer gewn*
What terrible weather!	**Hava ne berbat!** *havah neh ber_bat_*
It's hot/cold today!	**Bugün hava sıcak/soğuk!** *boogewn havah ser_jak_/so-_ook_*
Is it usually this warm?	**Genellikle bu kadar ılık mıdır?** *genel-_likleh_ boo kaddar erlerk merder*
Do you think it's going to … tomorrow?	**Sizce yarın … olacak mı?** *seez-jeh _yar_-ern … olah-jak mer*
be a nice day	**güzel bir gün** *gew_zel_ beer gewn*
rain	**yağmur** *_yaa_-moor*
snow	**kar** *kar*
What is the weather forecast for tomorrow?	**Yarın için hava tahmini nasıl?** *_yar_-ern itch_in_ havah _tah_mee-nee _nas_sirl*
It's …	**… -dir.** *… deer*
cloudy	**bulutlu** *boo_loot_-loo*
foggy	**sisli** *_sees_-lee*
icy	**buzlu** *_booz_-loo*
stormy	**fırtınalı** *_fer_-terna-ler*
windy	**rüzgarlı** *rewz-_gar_-ler*
It's raining.	**Yağmur yağıyor.** *_yaa_-moor _yaa_-er-yor*
It's snowing.	**Kar yağıyor.** *kar _yaa_-er-yor*
It's sunny.	**Güneşli.** *gew_nesh_-lee*
Has the weather been like this for long?	**Hava uzun zamandır böyle mi?** *havah oo_zoon_ za_mander_ bow-leh mee*
What's the pollen count?	**Çiçek tozu ölçümü nedir?** *chee-_chek_ toz-oo url_chewm_-ew neh-deer*
high/medium/low	**yüksek/orta/düşük** *yewk_sek_/ortah/dew_shewk_*

HAVA DURUMU	weather forecast

122

Enjoying your trip?
Gezinizden memnun musunuz?

Tatilde misiniz?	Are you on vacation?
Buraya nasıl geldiniz/ yolculuk ettiniz?	How did you get/ travel here?
Nerede kalıyorsunuz?	Where are you staying?
Ne kadar zamandır buradasınız?	How long have you been here?
Ne kadar kalacaksınız?	How long are you staying?
Bu güne kadar neler yaptınız?	What have you done so far?
Bundan sonra nereye gideceksiniz?	Where are you going next?
Tatilinizden memnun musunuz?	Are you enjoying your vacation?

I'm here on …	**… amacıyla buradayım.** *… amajer-eelah boora-dye-yerm*
business/vacation [holiday]	**iş/tatil** *eesh/tateel*
We came by …	**… ile geldik.** *… eeleh geldik*
train/bus/plane	**tren/otobüs/uçak** *tren/oto-bews/oochak*
car/ferry	**araba/vapur** *arabah/vapoor*
I have a rental [hire] car.	**Araba kiraladım.** *arabah keerah-laderm*
We're staying in/at …	**… -de kalıyoruz.** *… deh kaler-yoruz*
a campsite	**kamp yeri** *kamp yair-ee*
a guesthouse	**misafirhane** *meesaf-fer-harneh*
a hotel	**otel** *oh-tel*
a youth hostel	**gençlik yurdu** *genchlik yoordu*
with friends	**arkadaşlar ile** *arkadashlar eeleh*
Can you suggest …?	**… önerebilir misiniz?** *… owe-nair-eh-beeleer miseeniz*
things to do	**yapılacak şeyler** *yaperl-ajak shay-lair*
places to eat	**yemek yenilecek yerler** *yemek yeneel-eh-jek yair-lair*
places to visit	**görülecek yerler** *gur-rewl-eh-jek yair-lair*
We're having a great time.	**Çok eğleniyoruz.** *chok ay-lenee-yoruz*
We're having a terrible time.	**Berbat geçiyor.** *bair-bat getchee-yor*

Invitations Davetler

Would you like to have dinner with us on …?	**Bizimle … -de akşam yemeği yemek ister misiniz?** *beezim-leh … deh aksham ye-may-yee yemek istair miseeniz*
May I invite you to lunch?	**Sizi öğle yemeğine davet edebilir miyim?** *seezi owe-leh ye-may-yeeneh da-vet edeh-beeleer meeyim*
Can you come for a drink this evening?	**Bu gece bir içki içmek için gelir misiniz?** *boo geh-jeh beer itchkee itchmek itchin geleer miseeniz*
We are having a party. Can you come?	**Parti veriyoruz. Gelebilir misiniz?** *partee veree-yoruz. gel-eh-beeleer miseeniz*
May we join you?	**Size katlabilir miyiz?** *seez-eh katerl-ah-beeleer meeyiz*
Would you like to join us?	**Bize katılmak ister misiniz?** *beez-eh katerlmak istair miseeniz*

Going out Dışarı çıkmak

What are your plans for …?	**… için planınız ne?** *… itchin planernerz neh*
today/tonight	**bugün/bu gece** *boo-gewn/boo geh-jeh*
tomorrow	**yarın** *yar-ern*
Are you free this evening?	**Bu gece boş musunuz?** *boo geh-jeh bosh musoonuz*
Would you like to …?	**… ister misiniz?** *… istair miseeniz*
go dancing	**dansa gitmek** *dans-ah geetmek*
go for a drink	**içki içmeye gitmek** *itchkee itch-may-eh geetmek*
go out for a meal	**yemeğe çıkmak** *ye-may-yeh cherkmak*
go for a walk	**yürüyüşe çıkmak** *yew-rew-yewsh-eh cherkmak*
go shopping	**alışverişe çıkmak** *alersh-vereesh-eh cherkmak*
I'd like to go to …	**… -e gitmek isterim.** *… eh geetmek istairim*
I'd like to see …	**… -i görmek isterim.** *… ee gurmek istairim*
Do you enjoy …?	**… -den menun musunuz?** *… den memnoon musoonuz*

124

Accepting/Declining
Kabul etmek/Reddetmek

As a tourist in Turkey you will come across two very distinct cultures. At international resorts, topless bathing is acceptable and Western music blasts from bars into the late hours. By comparison, in parts of the main cities and in the interior, Turkey is markedly conservative. Behave and dress with restraint to avoid being very conspicuous. For example, public displays of affection between members of the opposite sex are frowned upon.

Thank you. I'd love to.	**Teşekkür ederim. Sevinirim.**
	teshek-kewr ederim. sevin-eerim
Thank you, but I'm busy.	**Teşekkür ederim ama meşgulum.**
	teshek-kewr ederim amah meshgool-um
May I bring a friend?	**Bir arkadaşımı getirebilir miyim?** *beer*
	arkadasherm-er geteer-eh-beeleer meeyim
Where shall we meet?	**Nerede buluşalım?** *neredeh bullooshalerm*
I'll meet you …	**Sizinle … -de buluşalım.**
	seezin-leh … deh bullooshalerm
in front of your hotel	**otelinizin önünde**
	oh-teleeneez-in owe-newndeh
I'll call for you at 8.	**8'de sizi alacağım.**
	sekeez-deh seez-ee ala-jy-yerm
Could we make it a bit later/earlier?	**Biraz daha geç/erken yapabilir miyiz?**
	beeraz dah-ha getch/air-ken yapah-beeleer meeyiz
How about another day?	**Başka bir güne ne dersiniz?**
	bashkah beer gewn-eh neh dair-seniz
That will be fine.	**Tamam.** *tamam*

Dining out/in Dışarda/evde yemek

If you are invited to dine at someone's home, bring a small gift. Also, you may be asked to take your shoes off.

Let me buy you a drink.	**Size bir içki ısmarlayayım.**
	seez-eh beer itchkee ersmar-ly-yay-yerm
Do you like …?	**… ister misiniz?** *… istair miseeniz*
What are you going to have?	**Ne istersiniz?** *neh istairseeniz*
That was a lovely meal.	**Ne güzel bir yemekti.**
	neh gewzel beer yemek-tee

TIME ➤ 220

Encounters Karşılaşma

Do you mind if …?	**… sizce bir sakıncası var mı?** *… seez-jeh beer sakern-ja-ser ver mer*
I sit here/I smoke	**buraya oturmamın/sigara içmemin** *booraya otoormamern/seegarah itchme-meen*
Can I get you a drink?	**Size bir içki alabilir miyim?** *seez-eh beer itchkee ala-beeleer meeyim*
I'd love to have some company.	**Birinin arkadaşlığından çok memnun olurum.** *beeree-nin arkadashler-erndan chok memnoon oloorum*
What's so funny?	**Komik olan nedir?** *komeek olan neh-deer*
Is my Turkish that bad?	**Türkçem o kadar kötü mü?** *tewrk-chem oh kaddar kurtew mew*
Shall we go somewhere quieter?	**Daha sakin bir yere gidelim mi?** *dah-ha sakeen beer yair-eh geedeleem mee*
Leave me alone, please!	**Beni yalnız bırakın lütfen!** *benee yalnerz berakern lewt-fen*
You look great!	**Çok iyi görünüyorsunuz!** *chok eeyee gur-ewn-ew-yor-soonuz*
Would you like to come home with me?	**Benimle eve gelmek ister misiniz?** *beneem-leh eveh gelmek istair miseeniz*
I'm not ready for that.	**Buna hazır değilim.** *boonah hazzer day-eelim*
I'm afraid we have to leave now.	**Korkarım şimdi gitmemiz gerek.** *korkarerm shimdee geetme-miz gerek*
Thanks for the evening.	**Gece için teşekkürler.** *geh-jeh itchin teshek-kewr-lair*
It was great.	**Çok güzeldi.** *chok gewzel-dee*
Can I see you again tomorrow?	**Sizi yarın yine görebilir miyim?** *seez-ee yarern yeeneh gur-eh-beeleer meeyim*
See you soon.	**Görüşmek üzere.** *gurewshmek ewzair-eh*
May I have your address?	**Adresinizi verir misiniz?** *adreeseeniz-ee vereer miseeniz*

Telephoning Telefon etmek

If you make a call from your hotel room, you may pay a significant surcharge. You can make calls from phone booths or PTT offices with metal tokens (**jeton**) or phone cards (**telefon kartı**); at PTT offices you can also make metered calls. For international calls use the meter or a phone card. At major resorts, there can be lines to use the telephone facilities during the evening. Fax facilities are also available at PTT offices.

To make an international call, dial 00, then dial the country code (1 for the U.S. and Canada, 44 for the U.K., 353 for Ireland), and the number, including the full area code without the initial 0.

For intercity calls within Turkey, dial 0, then the area code and the seven-digit local number. All local numbers in Istanbul, Ankara, İzmir, Adana, and Bursa are seven digits. The ringing tone is a long single tone. Calling is slightly cheaper after 8 p.m. and on Sundays.

Can I have your telephone number?	**Telefon numaranızı öğrenebilir miyim?** *telefon numara nerzer ureneh beeleer meeyim*
Here's my number.	**İşte numaram.** *eeshteh noomaram*
Please call me.	**Lütfen beni arayın.** *lewt-fen benee ah-rye-yern*
I'll give you a call.	**Sizi arayacağim.** *seez-ee ah-rye-ya-jy-yerm*
Where's the nearest telephone booth?	**En yakın telefon kulübesi nerede?** *en yakern tele-fon koolewbeh-see neredeh*
May I use your phone?	**Telefonunuzu kullanbilir miyim?** *tele-fonoonuz kool-lan-ah-beeleer meeyim*
It's an emergency.	**Acil bir durum.** *ajeel beer doorum*
I'd like to call someone in England.	**İngiltere'den birini aramak istiyorum.** *eengeeltair-eh-den beereenee aramak istee-yorum*
What's the area [dialling] code for …?	**… için alan kodu nedir?** *… itchin alan ko-doo neh-deer*
I'd like a phone card, please.	**Bir telefon kartı lütfen.** *beer tele-fon kart-er lewt-fen*
What's the number for Information [Directory Enquiries]?	**Bilinmeyen Numaralar kaç?** *beelin-may-yen noomara-lar katch*
I'd like the number for …	**… -in numarasını istiyorum.** *… een noomara-serner istee-yorum*
I'd like to call collect [reverse the charges].	**Görüşme parasını karşı tarafın ödemesini istiyorum.** *gur-rewsh-meh para-serner karsher tarafern urdeme-see istee-yorum*

Speaking Konuşmak

Hello. This is …	**Merhaba. Ben …** *mer-habah. ben*
I'd like to speak to …	**… ile konuşmak istiyorum.** *… eeleh kon<u>oo</u>shmak i<u>stee</u>-yorum*
Extension …	**dahili hattı …** *dah-<u>heel</u>-ee hat-ter*
Can you speak louder, please?	**Daha yüksek sesle konuşur musunuz lütfen?** *dah-ha yewk<u>sek</u> ses-leh kon<u>oo</u>shoor musoonuz <u>lewt</u>-fen*
Can you speak more slowly, please?	**Daha yavaş konuşur musunuz lütfen?** *dah-ha ya<u>vash</u> ses-leh kon<u>oo</u>shoor musoonuz <u>lewt</u>-fen*
Could you repeat that, please?	**Tekrar eder misiniz lütfen?** *tek-rar e<u>dair</u> miseeniz <u>lewt</u>-fen*
I'm afraid he/she's not in.	**Korkarım kendisi burada değil.** *kor<u>ka</u>rerm kendee-see boorada <u>day</u>-eel*
You have the wrong number.	**Yanlış numara.** *<u>yan</u>lersh noo<u>mara</u>h*
Just a moment, please.	**Bir dakika lütfen.** *beer da<u>kee</u>kah <u>lewt</u>-fen*
Hold on, please.	**Bir dakika lütfen.** *beer da<u>kee</u>kah <u>lewt</u>-fen*
When will he/she be back?	**Ne zaman geri gelecek?** *neh za<u>man</u> geree <u>gel</u>-eh-jek*
Will you tell him/her that I called?	**Aradığımı söyler misiniz?** *arah-<u>der</u>-er-mer sow-<u>lair</u> miseeniz*
My name is …	**Adım …** *aderm*
Would you ask him/her to call me?	**Beni aramasını söyler misiniz?** *beneem arah-<u>der</u>-er-mer sow-<u>lair</u> miseeniz*
I must go now.	**Şimdilik bu kadar.** *<u>sheem</u>deelik boo kaddar*
Thank you for calling.	**Aradığınız için teşekkür ederim.** *arah-<u>der</u>-er-nerz itchin teshek-<u>kewr</u> ederim*
I'll be in touch.	**Sizi arayacağım.** *seez-ee ah-rye-ya-<u>jy</u>-yerm*
Bye.	**Güle güle.** *gew-leh gew-leh*

128

Stores & Services

Stores normally open from 9 or 9:30 a.m. to 7 p.m., Monday through Saturday. Some establishments are closed during the afternoon in the summer, but this does not apply to enterprises dealing with tourists. Often small shops in tourist areas will stay open later, and be open on Sundays.

ESSENTIAL

I'd like …	**… istiyorum.** … _istee_-yorum
Do you have …?	**… var mı?** … var mer
How much is that?	**Bu ne kadar?** boo neh kaddar
Thank you.	**Teşekkür ederim.** teshek-_kewr_ ederim

AÇIK	open
KAPALI	closed
İNDİRİM	clearance

129

Stores and services
Dükkanlar ve hizmetler
Where is …? … nerede?

Where's the nearest …?	**En yakın … nerede?** *en yakern … neredeh*
Is there a good …?	**İyi bir … var mı?** *eeyee beer … var mer*
Where's the main shopping mall [centre]?	**Ana alışveriş merkezi nerede?** *anna alersh-vereesh merkez-ee neredeh*
Is it far from here?	**Buradan uzakta mı?** *boorah-dan oozakta mer*
How do I get there?	**Oraya nasıl gidebilirim?** *oraya nassirl geed-eh-beeleerim*

Stores Dükkanlar

bakery	**fırın** *fer-ern*
bank	**banka** *bankah*
bookstore	**kitapçı** *keetap-chee*
butcher	**kasap** *kasap*
camera store	**fotoğraf malzemeleri dükkanı** *foto-raf malzemeh-lair-ee dewk-kan-er*
clothing store [clothes shop]	**elbise mağazası** *elbeeseh ma-aazer-ser*
convenience store	**bakkal** *bak-kal*
department store	**mağaza** *ma-aazah*
drugstore	**eczane** *ej-zarne*
fish store [fishmonger]	**balıkçı dükkanı** *balerk-cher dewk-kan-er*
florist	**çiçekçi dükkanı** *chee-chek-chee dewk-kan-er*
gift store	**hediyelik eşya dükkanı** *hedee-yeh-lik esh-yah dewk-kan-er*

health food store	**sağlıklı yiyecekler dükkanı** *saa-lerk-ler yee-yeh-jek-lair dewk-kan-er*
jeweler	**kuyumcu** *koy-oomjoo*
liquor store [off-licence]	**tekel bayii** *te-kel by-yee*
music store	**müzik dükkanı** *mewzeek dewk-kan-er*
newsstand [newsagent]	**gazete bayii** *gazeteh bayee-ee*
pastry shop	**pastane** *pastarne*
pharmacy [chemist]	**eczane** *ej-zarne*
produce store	**manav** *ma-nav*
shoe store	**ayakkabıcı** *eye-yakka-ber-jer*
souvenir store	**hediyelik eşya dükkanı** *hedee-yeh-lik esh-yah dewk-kan-er*
sporting goods store	**spor malzemeleri dükkanı** *spor malzemeh-lair-ee dewk-kan-er*
supermarket	**süpermarket** *sew-pair-mar-ket*
tobacconist	**tütüncü** *twetwen-jew*
toy store	**oyuncakçı** *oyoonjak-cher*

Services Hizmetler

clinic	**klinik** *klineek*
dentist	**diş doktoru** *deesh dok-tor-oo*
doctor	**doktor** *dok-tor*
dry cleaner	**kuru temizleyici** *kooroo temeez-lay-eejee*
hairdresser/barber	**kuaför/berber** *kooa-furr/bair-bair*
hospital	**hastane** *hastarne*
laundromat	**çamaşırhane** *chamasher-harne*
optician	**gözlükçü** *gurz-lewk-chew*
police station	**polis karakolu** *polees karakol-oo*
post office	**postane** *postarne*
travel agency	**seyahat acentası** *say-ah-hat ajenta-ser*

Opening hours Çalışma saatleri

In cities, stores usually open from 9 a.m. to 7 p.m. Monday
through Saturday. In resorts many stores are open as late as
midnight and operate seven days a week.

When does the ... open/close?	**... ne zaman açılıyor/kapanıyor?** *... neh zaman atcherler-yor/kapaner-yor*
Are you open in the evening?	**Geceleri açık mısınız?** *geh-jeh-lair-ee acherk mersernerz*
Where is the ...	**... nerede?** *... neredeh*
cashier [cash desk]	**kasa** *kassah*
escalator	**yürüyen merdiven** *yew-rew-yen mair-dee-ven*
elevator [lift]	**asansör** *assan-sur*
store guide	**mağaza rehberi** *ma-aazah reh-bair-ee*
first [ground (U.K.)] floor	**zemin kat** *zemeen kat*
second [first (U.K.)] floor	**birinci kat** *beereen-jee kat*
Where's the ... department?	**... reyonu nerede?** *... rayo-noo neredeh*

ÇALIŞMA SAATLERİ	business hours
GİRİŞ	entrance
YÜRÜYEN MERDİVEN	escalator
ÇIKIŞ	exit
ACİL/YANGIN ÇIKIŞI	emergency/fire exit
ASANSÖR	elevator [lift]
MERDİVEN	stairs
TUVALET	restroom

Service Hizmet

Can you help me?	**Yardımcı olur musunuz?** _yarderm-jer oloor musoonuz_
I'm looking for ...	**... -i arıyorum.** _... ee arer-yorum_
I'm just browsing.	**Yalnızca bakıyorum.** _yalnerzjah baker-yorum_
It's my turn.	**Sıra benim.** _ser-rah beneem_
Do you have any ...?	**... var mı?** _var mer_
I'd like to buy ...	**... satın almak istiyorum.** _satern almak istee-yorum_
Could you show me ...?	**Bana ... -i gösterebilir misniz?** _bana ... ee go-stair-eh-beeleer miseeniz_
How much is this / that?	**Bu/şu ne kadar?** _boo/shoo neh kaddar_
That's all, thanks.	**Bu kadar, teşekkürler.** _boo kaddar teshek-kewr-lair_

Günaydın/iyi günler efendim.	Good morning / afternoon, ma'am / sir.
Yardımcı olabilir miyim?	Can I help you?
Hepsi bu kadar mı?	Is that everything?
Başka bir şey?	Anything else?

– _Yardımcı olabilir miyim?_ (Can I help you?)
– _Hayır teşekkürler. Yalnızca bakıyorum._
(No, thanks. I'm just browsing.)
– _Peki._ (Fine.)

– _Afedersiniz._ (Excuse me.)
– _Evet, yardımcı olabilir miyim?_
(Yes, can I help you?)
– _Bu ne kadar?_ (How much is this?)
– _Bir bakayım. ... Beş milyon._
(Um, I'll just check. ... That's five million lira.)

SELF SERVİS	self-service

Preferences Tercih

I want something …	**… bir şeyler istiyorum.**
	… beer shay-lair istee-yorum
It must be …	**… olmalı.** *… olma-ler*
big/small	**büyük/küçük** *bewyewk/kewchewk*
cheap/expensive	**ucuz/pahalı** *oojooz/pahal-ler*
dark/light (color)	**koyu/açık** *koy-yoo/atcherk*
light/heavy	**hafif/ağır** *hafeef/aa-er*
oval/round/square	**oval/yuvarlak/kare**
	o-val/yoovarlak/kareh
genuine/imitation	**gerçek/taklit** *gerchek/takleet*
I don't want anything too expensive.	**Çok pahalı bir şey istemiyorum.**
	chok pahal-ler beer shay istemee-yorum
In the region of … lira.	**… lira civarında.** *… leerah jeevar-ernda*

Ne … istersiniz?	What … would you like?
renk/biçim	color/shape
nitelik/nicelik	quality/quantity
Kaç tane istersiniz?	How many would you like?
Ne tür istersiniz?	What sort would you like?
Ne kadardan ne kadara bir fiyat düşünüyorsunuz?	What price range are you thinking of?

Do you have anything …?	**… bir şey var mı?** *… beer shay var mer*
larger/smaller	**daha büyük/daha küçük**
	dah-ha bewyewk/dah-ha kewchewk
better quality	**daha iyi kalite** *dah-ha eeyee kalee-teh*
cheaper	**daha ucuz** *dah-ha oojooz*
Can you show me …?	**… gösterebilir misiniz?**
	… go-stair-eh-beeleer miseeniz
this one/these	**bunu/bunları** *boon-oo/boonlar-er*
that one/those	**şunu/şunları** *shoon-oo/shoonlar-er*
the one in the window/ display case	**vitrindekini**
	veetreen-dekeenee
some others	**başkalarını** *bashkah-lahrer-ner*

COLOR ➤ 143

Conditions of purchase
Satın alma koşulları

Is there a guarantee?

Garantisi var mı?
garantee-see var mer

Are there any instructions with it?

Kullanım talimatları var mı?
koollanerm taleem-atlah-rer var mer

Out of stock Tükendi

Özür dilerim, kalmadı.	I'm sorry. We don't have any.
Tükendi.	We're out of stock.
Size başka bir şey/farklı bir şey gösterebilir miyim?	Can I show you something else/a different kind?
Sizin için sipariş verelim mi?	Shall we order it for you?

Can you order it for me?

Benim için sipariş verir misiniz?
beneem ichin siparish vereermee-siniz

How long will it take?

Ne kadar sürer?
ne kaddar sewrer

Is there another store that sells ...?

... satan başka bir mağaza var mı?
... satan bashka ma-aazer var mer

Decisions Karar verme

That's not quite what I want.

Bu tam istediğim gibi değil.
boo tam istay-dee-yeemee gibee day-eel

No, I don't like it.

Hayır, beğenmedim.
hi-yer bay-yen-medim

That's too expensive.

Çok pahalı. *chok pahal-ler*

I'd like to think about it.

Biraz düşünmek istiyorum.
beeraz dewshewn-mek istee-yorum

I'll take it.

Alıyorum. *aler-yorum*

> – Günaydın. Bir "sweatshirt" arıyorum.
> (Good morning. I'm looking for a sweatshirt.)
> – Elbette. Ne renk istersiniz?
> (Certainly. What color would you like?)
> – Portakal rengi lütfen. Ve büyük bir şey istiyorum.
> (Orange, please. And I want something large.)
> – Buyrun. Beş milyon lira. (Here you are. That's 5 million lira.)
> – Bu tam istediğim gibi değil. Teşekkür ederim.
> (Hmm, that's not quite what I want. Thank you.)

Paying Ödeme

There is sales tax [VAT] – known as KDV – on every item you buy. The rate is currently 15 percent.

Where do I pay?	**Nereye ödeyeceğim?** *nereh-yeh ur-day-ye-jayim*
How much is that?	**Ne kadar?** *neh kaddar*
Could you write it down, please?	**Yazar mısınız lütfen?** *yazar mersernerz lewt-fen*
Do you accept traveler's checks [cheques]?	**Seyahat çeki kabul ediyor musunuz?** *say-ya-hat chek-ee kabool edee-yor musoonuz*
I'll pay by …	**… ile ödeyeceğim.** *… eeleh ur-day-eh-jayim*
cash	**nakit** *nakeet*
credit card	**kredi kartı** *kredee kart-er*
I don't have any smaller change.	**Bozuğum yok.** *bozoo-oom yok*
Sorry, I don't have enough money.	**Afedersiniz. Yeterli param yok.** *aff-edair-seniz. yet-air-lee param yok*

Nasıl ödeyeceksiniz?	How are you paying?
İşlem onaylanmadı/kabul edilmedi.	This transaction has not been approved/accepted.
Kart geçerli değil.	This card is not valid.
Kimlik kartınızı görebilir miyim?	May I have additional identification?
Bozuğunuz yok mu?	Do you have any smaller change?

Could I have a receipt, please?	**Fiş alabilir miyim lütfen?** *fish ala-beeleer meeyim lewt-fen*
I think you've given me the wrong change.	**Sanırım yanlış para üstü verdiniz.** *saner-rerm yanlersh parah ewstew verdeeniz*

KASA	cashier

136

Complaints Şikayetler

This doesn't work.	**Bu çalışmıyor.** *boo chalershmer-yor*
Can you exchange this, please?	**Bunu değiştirebilir misiniz lütfen?** *boon-oo day-eeshteer-eh-beeleer miseeniz*
I'd like a refund.	**Paramı geri istiyorum.** *param-er geree istee-yorum*
Here's the receipt.	**İşte fiş.** *eeshteh fish*
I don't have the receipt.	**Fiş almadım.** *fish almaderm*
I'd like to see the manager.	**Müdürü görmek istiyorum.** *mewdewr-ew gurmek istee-yorum*

Repairs/Cleaning Onarım/Temizleme

This is broken. Can you fix it?	**Bu bozuldu. Onarabilir misiniz?** *boo bozooldu. owe-nar-ah-beeleer miseeniz*
Do you have ... for this?	**Bunun için ... var mı?** *boonun itchin ... var mer*
a battery	**pil** *peel*
replacement parts	**yedek parça** *yedek parchah*
There's something wrong with ...	**... -de bir gariplik var.** *... deh beer gareeplik var*
Can you ... this?	**Bunu ... misiniz?** *boon-oo ... miseeniz*
clean	**temizleyebilir** *temeez-lay-eh-beeleer*
press	**ütüleyebilir** *ew-tewleh-ye-beeleer*
patch	**yamalayabilir** *yamalah-ya-beeleer*
Could you alter this?	**Bunu değiştirebilir misiniz?** *boon-oo day-eeshteer-eh-beeleer miseeniz*
When will it be ready?	**Ne zaman hazır olacak?** *neh zaman haz-zer olah-jak*
This isn't mine.	**Bu benim değil.** *boo beneem day-eel*
There's ... missing.	**... eksik.** *ekseek*

TIME ➤ 220; DATES ➤ 218

Bank/Currency exchange
Banka/Döviz bozdurma

Hotels have by far the worst exchange rates. Next worst are banks. Away from the resorts, some branches cannot cope with the administrative hassles of dealing with traveler's checks. The best rates of exchange can be found at the ubiquitous dedicated currency exchange outlets (**döviz bürosu**). Some only deal with cash, others accept traveler's checks too. Cash machines are common, allowing you to withdraw currency in Turkish lira.

You will always get the best exchange rate in Turkey, so arrive with just a small amount of Turkish lira. Moreover, as inflation is running at such a high rate, acquire only a small amount of Turkish lira at a time. You will get a better exchange rate for cash than for traveler's checks. Keep your exchange slips. You may be asked to show these when leaving the country.

Where's the nearest …?	**En yakın … nerede?** en ya<u>kern</u> … neredeh
bank	**banka** bankah
currency exchange office [bureau de change]	**döviz bürosu** dur-<u>veez</u> bewro-soo

Changing money Para bozdurma

KAMBİYO	currency exchange
AÇIK/KAPALI	open/closed
VEZNE	cashiers

Can I exchange foreign currency here?	**Burada döviz bozdurabilir miyim?** boorada dur-<u>veez</u> boz-door-ah-bee<u>leer</u> meeyim
I'd like to change some dollars/pounds into Turkish lira.	**Dolar/İngiliz sterlini bozdurmak istiyorum.** do-lar/eengee<u>leez</u> sterlee-nee boz<u>door</u>mak istee-yorum
I want to cash some traveler's checks [cheques].	**Seyahat çeki bozdurmak istiyorum.** say-ya-<u>hat</u> chek-ee boz<u>door</u>mak istee-yorum
What's the exchange rate?	**Döviz kuru nedir?** dur-<u>veez</u> kooru neh-deer
How much commission do you charge?	**Ne kadar komisyon alıyorsunuz?** neh kaddar ko<u>mees</u>-yon al<u>er</u>-yorsoonuz
Could I have some small change, please?	**Biraz bozuk verir misiniz lütfen?** beeraz bo<u>zook</u> ve<u>reer</u> miseeniz <u>lewt</u>-fen
I've lost my traveler's checks. These are the numbers.	**Seyahat çeklerimi kaybettim. Numaraları burada.** say-ya-<u>hat</u> chek-laireemee ky-<u>bet</u>tim. noo<u>mara</u>-larer boorada

Security Güvenlik

... görebilir miyim?	Could I see ...?
pasaportunuzu	your passport
kimlik	some identification
banka kartınızı	your bank card
Adresiniz nedir?	What's your address?
Nerede kalıyorsunuz?	Where are you staying?
Bu formu doldurun lütfen.	Fill out this form, please.
Burasını imzalayınız.	Please sign here.

ATMs [Cash machines] Paramatik

Can I withdraw money on my credit card here?

Buradan kredi kartımla para çekebilir miyim? *booradan kredee kart-ermlah parah chek-eh-beeleer meeyim*

Where are the ATMs [cash machines]?

Paramatikler nerede? *paramateek-lair neredeh*

Can I use my ... card in the cash machine?

Paramatikte ... kartımı kullanabilir miyim? *paramateek-teh ... kart-ermer kool-lan-ah-beeleer meeyim*

The cash machine has eaten my card.

Paramatik kartımı yuttu. *paramateek kart-ermer yoot-tu*

PARAMATİK	ATM [cash machine]

Pharmacy Eczane

Pharmacies are open during normal shopping hours. Every town also has at least one all-night pharmacy (**nöbetçi eczane**). The address is posted in the windows of all other pharmacies.

Where's the nearest (all-night) pharmacy?	**En yakın nöbetçi eczane nerede?** *en ya_kern_ nur_bet_-chee ej-_zarne_ neredeh*
What time does the pharmacy open/close?	**Eczane ne zaman açılıyor/kapanıyor?** *ej-_zarne_ neh za_man_ atcherler-yor/ kapaner-yor*
Can you make up this prescription for me?	**Bana bu reçeteyi hazırlar mısınız?** *bana boo re_chete_-yee haz-zer-_lar_ mersernerz*
Shall I wait?	**Bekleyeyim mi?** *bek-_lay_-yeeyim mee*
I'll come back for it.	**Geri geleceğim.** *geree geleh-_jay_-yim*

Dosage instructions Kullanma miktarı

How much should I take?	**Ne kadar almalıyım?** *neh kaddar _al_-maler-yerm*
How many times a day should I take it?	**Günde kaç defa almalıyım?** *gewndeh katch defah _al_-maler-yerm*
Is it suitable for children?	**Çocuklar için uygun mu?** *cho_jook_-lar itch_in_ oygoon moo*

Take …	**… alın.**
… tablets/… teaspoons	**… tablet/… çay kaşığı**
before/after meals	**yemeklerden önce/sonra**
with water	**su ile**
whole	**tam**
in the morning/at night	**sabahları/akşamları**
for … days	**… gün**

İÇİLMEZ	for external use only
İLACI İÇTİKTEN SONRA	do not drive after taking
ARABA KULLANMAYINIZ.	medication

Asking advice Danışmak

I'd like some medicine for …?	… için bir ilaç istiyorum.
	… itchin beer eelatch istee-yorum
a cold	soğuk algınlığı so-ook algern-ler-er
a cough	öksürük urk-sewr-ewk
diarrhea	ishal eeshal
a hangover	akşamdan kalmalık
	akshamdan kalma-lerk
hay fever	saman nezlesi saman nezleh-see
insect bites	böcek sokması bur-jek sokmah-ser
a sore throat	boğaz ağrısı bo-aaz aa-rer-ser
sunburn	güneş yanığı gewnesh yaner-er
motion [travel] sickness	yol tutması yol tootmah-ser
an upset stomach	mide bozukluğu meedeh bozookloo-oo
Can I get it without a prescription?	Reçetesiz alabilir miyim?
	recheteh-seez ala-beeleer meeyim
Can I have some …?	Biraz … alabilir miyim?
	beeraz … ala-beeleer meeyim
antiseptic cream	antiseptik krem antee-septeek krem
aspirin	aspirin aspeerin
bandaid® [plasters]	yara bandı yarah band-er
condoms	prezervatif pre-zervateef
cotton [cotton wool]	pamuk pamook
gauze [bandages]	bandaj bandazh
insect repellent	böcek kovucu bur-jek kovoo-joo
painkillers	ağrı kesici aa-rer kesee-jee
vitamins	vitamin veetameen

141

Toiletries Güzellik malzemeleri

I'd like some …	**… istiyorum.** … _istee_-yorum
after-shave	**after shave** _aff_-ter shayve
after-sun lotion	**güneş banyosu sonrası kremi** _gewnesh_ ban-yo-soo _sonrah_-ser krem-ee
deodorant	**deodorant** day-odor-_ant_
razor blades	**jilet** zhee_let_
sanitary napkins [towels]	**kadın bağı** ka_dern_ _baa_-er
soap	**sabun** sa_boon_
sun block	**güneş geçirmez krem** gewnesh gecheer_mez_ krem
sunscreen lotion	**güneş kremi** gew_nesh_ krem-ee
factor …	**… faktör** … fak_tur_
tampons	**tampon** tampon
tissues	**kağıt mendil** ka-_ert_ men_deel_
toilet paper	**tuvalet kağıdı** too-_va_-let ka-_erd_-er
toothpaste	**diş macunu** deesh ma_joo_nu

Haircare Saç bakımı

comb	**tarak** ta_rak_
conditioner	**saç kremi** satch krem-ee
hair mousse	**saç jölesi** satch _zhurleh_-see
hair spray	**saç spreyi** satch spray-ee
shampoo	**şampuan** sham_pooan_

For the baby Bebek için

baby food	**bebek maması** bebek _mama_-ser
baby wipes	**bebek mendili** bebek men_deel_-ee
diapers [nappies]	**bebek bezi** bebek bez-ee
sterilizing solution	**sterilize solüsyonu** stair-ee_leez_eh so_lews_-yonoo

Clothing Giyim

On the Aegean and Mediterranean coasts you will spend summer days dressed in swimsuit, T-shirt, and shorts. Pack something a bit fancier for the evening and bring a sturdy pair of shoes and a sun hat for visiting archaeological sites. In the spring and fall, you will need a sweater on some evenings; in winter, warm clothes and a raincoat. In Central Anatolia you will need something warm for the evenings, even in summer, and to bundle up seriously in winter.

In Istanbul, modest dress, such as trousers for men and a long dress/skirt for women, is most appropriate, and women should pack a shawl for visiting mosques.

General Genel

I'd like …	**… istiyorum.** … _istee_-yorum
Do you have any …?	**… var mı?** … var mer

BAYAN GİYİMİ	ladieswear
ERKEK GİYİMİ	menswear
ÇOCUK GİYİMİ	childrenswear

Color Renkler

I'm looking for something in …	**… bir şeyler arıyorum.** … beer shay-lair _arer_-yoroom
beige	**bej** bezh
black	**siyah** see-_yah_
blue	**mavi** _mavee_
brown	**kahverengi** _kahveh_-rengee
green	**yeşil** ye_sheel_
gray	**gri** gree
orange	**portakal rengi** porta_kal_ rengee
pink	**pembe** pembeh
purple	**mor** mor
red	**kırmızı** ker-_merzer_
white	**beyaz** bay-_yaz_
yellow	**sarı** _sar_-er
dark …/light …	**koyu …/açık …** koy-_oo_/at_cherk_
I want a darker/lighter shade.	**Daha koyu/açık tonunu istiyorum.** dah-ha koy-_oo_/at_cherk_ ton_oo_noo _istee_-yorum

Clothes and accessories
Elbise ve aksesuarlar

belt	**kemer** kem-_air_
bikini	**bikini** bik_eenee_
blouse	**bluz** blooz
bra	**sütyen** _sewt_-yen
briefs	**külot** _kew_-lot
cap	**kep** kep
coat	**palto** pal-to
dress	**elbise** el_beeseh_
handbag	**el çantası** el _chantah_-ser
hat	**şapka** shap-kah
jacket	**ceket** je_ket_
jeans	**kot pantalon** kot pantal_on_
leggings	**leging** leh-ging
pants (U.S.)	**pantolon** pant_olon_
pantyhose [tights]	**tayt** tye-t
raincoat	**yağmurluk** _yaa_-moorluk
scarf	**eşarp** esh_arp_
shirt (men's)	**gömlek** gurm-_lek_
shorts	**şort** short
skirt	**etek** et_ek_
socks	**çorap** cho-rap
stockings	**kadın çorabı** _kadern_ cho-_rab_-er
suit	**takım elbise** takerm el_beeseh_
sweater	**süveter** sew-_vet_-er
sweatshirt	**sweatshirt** "sweatshirt"
swimming trunks	**mayo** _my_-yo
swimsuit	**mayo** _my_-yo
T-shirt	**tişört** tee-shurt
tie	**kravat** kra_vat_
trousers	**pantolon** pantal_on_
underpants	**külot** _kew_-lot
with long/short sleeves	**uzun/kısa kollu** oo_zoon_/ker_sah_ kol-loo
with a V-/round neck	**V yaka/bisiklet yaka** veh _yaka_/beesee-_klet_ yaka

Shoes Ayakkabı

boots	**bot** *bot*
flip-flops	**sandalet** *san<u>da</u>-let*
running [training] shoes	**koşu ayakkabısı** *ko<u>shoo</u> eye-<u>yaka</u>ber-ser*
sandals	**sandalet** *san<u>da</u>-let*
shoes	**ayakkabı** *eye-<u>yaka</u>bah*
slippers	**terlik** *<u>tair</u>lik*

Walking/Hiking gear Yürüyüş donanımı

knapsack	**sırt çantası** *sert <u>chanta</u>-ser*
walking boots	**yürüyüş çizmeleri** *yew-rew-<u>yewsh</u> <u>cheez</u>meh-lair-ee*
waterproof jacket [anorak]	**anorak** *<u>ano</u>rak*
windbreaker [cagoule]	**başlıklı yağmurluk** *<u>bashlerk</u>-ler <u>yaa</u>-moorluk*

Fabric Kumaş

I want something in …	**… bir şeyler istiyorum.** *… beer shay-lair i<u>stee</u>-yorum*
cotton	**pamuklu** *pa<u>mook</u>-loo*
denim	**kot kumaşı** *kot koo<u>mash</u>-er*
lace	**dantel** *dan<u>tel</u>*
leather	**deri** *deree*
linen	**keten** *ke-ten*
wool	**yün** *yewn*
Is this …?	**Bu … mi?** *boo … mee*
pure cotton	**saf pamuk** *saf pa<u>mook</u>*
synthetic	**sentetik** *sen<u>teteek</u>*
Is it hand/machine washable?	**Elde/makinede yıkanabilir mi?** *eldeh/ma<u>kee</u>ne-deh yer-kan-ah-bee<u>leer</u> mee*

YALNIZCA KURU TEMİZLEME	dry clean only
YALNIZCA ELDE YIKAYIN	handwash only
ÜTÜLEMEYİNİZ	do not iron
KURU TEMİZLEME YAPTIRMAYINIZ	do not dry clean

Does it fit? Oldu mu?

Can I try this on?	**Bunu deneyebilir miyim?** *boon-oo den-nay-yeh-bee<u>leer</u> meeyim*
Where's the fitting room?	**Soyunma odası nerede?** *soy<u>oo</u>nma odda-ser neredeh*
It fits well. I'll take it.	**İyi oldu. Alıyorum.** *eeyee <u>ol</u>doo <u>a</u>ler-yorum*
It doesn't fit.	**Olmadı.** *<u>oy</u>ma-der*
It's too ...	**Çok ...** *chok*
short/long	**kısa/uzun** *ker<u>sah</u>/oo<u>zoon</u>*
tight/loose	**sıkı/bol** *ser<u>ker</u>/bol*
Do you have this in size ...?	**Bunun ... bedeni var mı?** *boonun ... be<u>den</u>-ee var mer*
What size is this?	**Bunun bedeni nedir?** *boonun be<u>den</u>-ee neh-deer*
Could you measure me, please?	**Bedenimi ölçebilir misiniz?** *be<u>den</u>eemee url-che-bee<u>leer</u> miseeniz*
I don't know Turkish sizes.	**Türk beden numaralarını bilmiyorum.** *tewrk be<u>den</u> noo<u>ma</u>ra-larern-er <u>beel</u>mee-yorum*

Size Beden

All Turkish clothing and shoe sizes are the same as Continental sizes.

Dresses/Suits						Women's shoes			
American	8	10	12	14	16	18	6	7	8	9
British	10	12	14	16	18	20	$4^{1/2}$	$5^{1/2}$	$6^{1/2}$	$7^{1/2}$
Continental	36	38	40	42	44	46	37	38	40	41

Shirts				Men's shoes							
American } British	15	16	17	18	5	6	7	8	$8^{1/2}$	9	$9^{1/2}$	10	11
Continental	38	41	43	45	38	39	41	42	43	43	44	44	45

ÇOK BÜYÜK	extra large (XL)
BÜYÜK	large (L)
ORTA	medium (M)
KÜÇÜK	small (S)

1 centimeter (cm.) = 0.39 in. 1 inch = 2.54 cm.
1 meter (m.) = 39.37 in. 1 foot = 30.5 cm.
10 meters = 32.81 ft. 1 yard = 0.91 m.

Health and beauty
Sağlık ve güzellik

I'd like a …	**… istiyorum.** … _istee_-yorum
facial	**yüz bakımı** yewz baker_mer_
manicure	**manikür** manee-_kewr_
massage	**masaj** ma_sazh_
waxing	**ağda** _aa_-da

Hairdresser Kuaför

Hairdressers are reasonably cheap in Turkey and they give a very friendly service. Tips should be 20 percent of the bill.

I'd like to make an appointment for …	**… için bir randevu istiyorum.** … itch_in_ beer ran-_day_-voo istee-yorum
Can you make it a bit earlier/later?	**Biraz daha erken/geç olabilir mi?** beeraz dah-ha air_ken_/getch olah-bee_leer_ mee
I'd like a …	**… istiyorum.** … _istee_-yorum
cut and blow-dry	**kesme ve kurutma** kesmeh veh kur_oo_tma
shampoo and set	**şampuanla yıkama** sham_poo_an-lah _yer_kama
trim	**uçlarından alma** _ooch_lar-erndan _alma_
I'd like my hair …	**Saçımı … istiyorum.** _satch_-ermer … _istee_-yorum
highlighted	**rengini açmak** rengee_nee_ atchmak
permed	**perma yapmak** _pair_-ma yapmak
Don't cut it too short.	**Çok kısa kesmeyin.** chok ker_sah_ _kes_-may-yin
A little more off the …	**… -den birazcık daha.** … den bee_raz_-jirk dah-ha
back/front	**arka/ön** arka/urn
neck/sides	**ense/yanlar** en_seh_/_yan_lar
top	**üst** ewst
That's fine, thanks.	**Bu iyi, teşekkürler.** boo eeyee teshek-_kewr_-lair

Household articles Ev eşyaları

I'd like a(n)/	... istiyorum.
some ...	... *istee-yorum*
adapter	**adaptör** *adap-tur*
alumin(i)um foil	**alimünyum kağıt** *aleemewn-yoom ka-ert*
bottle opener	**şişe açacağı** *sheesheh atcha-jy-yer*
can [tin] opener	**konserve açacağı** *kon-sair-veh atcha-jy-yer*
clothes pins [pegs]	**mandal** *mandal*
corkscrew	**şarap açacağı** *sharap atcha-jy-yer*
light bulb	**ampul** *ampool*
matches	**kibrit** *kibreet*
paper napkins	**kağıt peçete** *ka-ert peche-teh*
plastic wrap [cling film]	**plastik ambalaj kağıdı** *plasteek ambalazh ka-erd-er*
plug (electric)	**elektrik fişi** *elektreek fish-ee*
scissors	**makas** *ma-kas*
screwdriver	**tornavida** *torna-veeda*

Cleaning items Temizlik maddeleri

bleach	**çamaşır suyu** *chamasher soo-yoo*
dishcloth	**bulaşık bezi** *boolasherk bez-ee*
dishwashing [washing-up] liquid	**bulaşık deterjanı** *boola-sherk detair-jan-er*
garbage [refuse] bags	**çöp torbası** *churp torba-ser*
detergent [washing powder]	**deterjan** *detair-jan*
sponge	**sünger** *sewn-gair*

Dishes/Utensils Tabak çanak/Çatal bıçak

bowls	**çanak** *chanak*
cups	**fincan** *fernjan*
forks	**çatal** *cha-tal*
glasses	**bardak** *bar-dak*
knives	**bıçak** *ber-chak*
mugs	**kupa** *koopah*
plates	**tabak** *tabak*
spoons	**kaşık** *kasherk*
teaspoons	**çay kaşığı** *chy kasher-er*

Jeweler Kuyumcu

Could I see ...?
... görebilir miyim?
... gur-eh-beeleer meeyim

this / that
bunu / şunu
boon-oo / shoon-oo

It's in the window / display cabinet.
Vitrinde.
vitreendeh

alarm clock
çalar saat *chalar sa-art*

battery
pil *peel*

bracelet
bilezik *beelezik*

brooch
broş *brosh*

chain
zincir *zinjeer*

clock
saat *sa-art*

earrings
küpe *kewpeh*

necklace
kolye *kol-yeh*

ring
yüzük *yewzewk*

watch
kol saati *kol sa-art-ee*

Materials Maddeler

Is this real silver / gold?
Bu gerçek gümüş mü / altın mı?
boo gair-chek gewmewsh mew / altern mer

Is there a certificate for it?
Belgesi var mı? *belgesee var mer*

Do you have anything in ...?
... bir şeyler var mı?
... beer shay-lair var mer

copper
bakır *bak-er*

crystal (quartz)
kuartz *koo-artz*

cut glass
cam *jam*

diamond
elmas *el-mas*

enamel
mine *meeneh*

gold
altın *altern*

gold plate
altın kaplama *altern kaplama*

pearl
inci *een-jee*

pewter
kurşun kalay alaşımı
koorshun ka-lye alash-ermer

platinum
platin *pla-teen*

silver
gümüş *gewmewsh*

silver plate
gümüş kaplama *gewmewsh kaplama*

stainless steel
paslanmaz çelik *paslan-maz cheleek*

149

Newsstand [Newsagent]/
Tobacconist Gazete bayii/Tütüncü

Do you sell English-language books/newspapers?	**İngilizce kitap/gazete satıyor musunuz?** *ingeeleez-jeh keetap/gazeteh sateryor moosunuz*
I'd like a(n)/some ...	**... istiyorum.** *... iste-yorum*
book	**kitap** *keetap*
candy [sweets]	**şeker** *she-kair*
chewing gum	**sakız** *sakerz*
chocolate bar	**çikolata** *cheekolat-ah*
cigarettes (pack of)	**sigara** *seegarah*
cigars	**puro** *pu-ro*
dictionary	**sözlük** *surz-lewk*
English–Turkish	**İngilizce-Türkçe** *eengeeleez-jeh-tewrk-che*
envelopes	**zarf** *zarf*
guidebook of ...	**... kılavuzu** *... keelavooz-oo*
lighter	**çakmak** *chak-mak*
magazine	**dergi** *dair-gee*
map	**harita** *hareetah*
map of the town	**kent planı** *kent plan-er*
matches	**kibrit** *kibreet*
newspaper	**gazete** *gazeteh*
American/English	**Amerikan/İngiliz** *ameree-kan/eengeeleez*
pen	**kalem** *kalem*
road map of ...	**... -in yol haritası** *... een yol hareeta-ser*
stamps	**pul** *pool*
tobacco	**tütün** *tewtewn*
writing paper	**mektup kağıdı** *mektoop ka-erd-er*

Photography Fotoğrafçılık

I'm looking for a/an … camera. | **… bir fotoğraf makinesi arıyorum.** … *beer foto-raf makeenesee arer-yorum*

automatic	**otomatik** *otoma-teek*
compact	**küçük** *kewchewk*
disposable	**tek kullanımlık** *tek koollan-ermlerk*
SLR (single lens reflex)	**SLR** *se-leh-re*
I'd like a(n) …	**… istiyorum.** … *istee-yorum*
battery	**pil** *peel*
camera case	**makine kılıfı** *makeeneh ker-ler-fer*
electronic flash	**elektronik flaş** *elektron-eek flash*
filter	**filtre** *feel-tray*
lens	**objektif** *objek-teef*
lens cap	**objektif kapağı** *objek-teef ka-py-yer*

Film/Processing Film/Banyo

I'd like … film.	**… bir film istiyorum.** … *beer feelm istee-yorum*
black and white	**siyah beyaz** *seeyah bay-yaz*
color	**renkli** *renk-lee*
24/36 exposures	**24/36 pozluk** *yirmee durrt/otooz alter poz-look*
I'd like this film developed, please.	**Bu filmi banyo ettirmek istiyorum lütfen.** *boo feelm ban-yo et-teer-mek istee-yorum lewt-fen*
Would you enlarge this, please?	**Bunu büyütebilir misiniz lütfen?** *boon-oo bew-yewt-eh-beeleer miseeniz lewt-fen*
How much do … exposures cost?	**… poz ne kadar?** … *poz neh kaddar*
When will the photos be ready?	**Fotoğraflar ne zaman hazır olur?** *foto-raf-lar neh zaman haz-zer oloor*
I'd like to collect my photos.	**Fotoğraflarımı almaya geldim.** *foto-raf-larerm-er al-my-ya geldim*
Here's the receipt.	**İşte fiş.** *eeshteh fish*

Post office Postane

Post offices can be identified by the letters PTT in black on a yellow background. City post offices, and those in many towns, are open 24 hours a day, weekends included, for telephoning, and sometimes sending telegrams and changing money. For other services they may remain open until 8 p.m. Smaller post offices are open Monday through Saturday until 5 or 6 p.m. only, and may close for lunch.

It is advisable to send all foreign mail by air.

General inqueries Genel sorular

Where is the post office?	**Postane nerede?** *postarne* neredeh
What time does the post office open/close?	**Postane ne zaman açılıyor/kapanıyor?** *postarne* neh za*man* at*cher*ler-yor/ka*paner*-yor
Does it close for lunch?	**Öğle yemeği için kapanıyor mu?** owe-leh ye-*may*-yee itch*in* ka*paner*-yor moo
Where's the mailbox [postbox]?	**Posta kutusu nerede?** postah ku*too*soo neredeh
Is there any mail for me?	**Bana mektup geldi mi?** bana mek*toop* *gel*dee mee

Buying stamps Pul almak

I'd like to send these postcards to …	**Bu kartpostalları … -e göndermek istiyorum.** boo kartpos*tal*-larer … eh gurn-*dair*mek is*tee*-yorum
A stamp for this postcard/letter, please.	**Bu kartpostal/mektup için pul lütfen.** boo kartpos*tal*/mek*toop* itch*in* pool *lewt*-fen
A … lira stamp, please.	**… liralık bir pul lütfen.** … *leera*-lerk beer pool *lewt*-fen
What's the postage for a letter to …?	**… -e mektup kaça** … eh mek*toop* kachah

---

– Merhaba, bu kartpostalları ABD'ye göndermek istiyorum.
(Hello, I'd like to send these postcards to the U.S.)

– Kaç tane? (How many?)

– Dokuz, lütfen. (Nine, please.)

– Dokuz çarpı 150,000 lira: bir milyon üç yüz elli bin lira lütfen.
(That's 150,000 lira times nine: 1,350,000 lira, please.)

Sending packages Paket göndermek

I want to send this package [parcel] by ...	**Bu paketi ... ile göndermek istiyorum.** *boo pa<u>ket</u>-ee ... eeleh gurn-<u>dair</u>mek istee-yorum*
airmail	**uçak ile** *oo<u>chak</u> eeleh*
special delivery [express]	**özel ulak** *ur<u>zel</u> oolak*
registered mail	**taahhütlü** *ta-ah-<u>hewt</u>-lew*
It contains ...	**İçinde ... var.** *itch<u>in</u>-deh ... var*

Lütfen gümrük beyanını doldurunuz.	Please fill out the customs declaration form.
Değeri nedir?	What's the value?
İçinde ne var?	What's inside?

Telecommunications Telekomünikasyon

I'd like a phone card, please.	**Bir telefon kartı lütfen.** *beer tele-fon kart-er <u>lewt</u>-fen*
30/60/100 units	**30/60/100 kredilik** *otooz/<u>alt</u>mersh/yewz <u>kredee</u>-lik*
Do you have a photocopier?	**Fotokopi makinesi var mı?** *foto<u>kop</u>-ee ma<u>keene</u>-see var mer*
I'd like to send a message ...	**... ile bir mesaj göndermek istiyorum.** *... eeleh beer me<u>saj</u> gurn-<u>dair</u>mek <u>istee</u>-yorum*
by e-mail/fax	**e-posta/faks** *eh-<u>postah</u>/faks*
What's your e-mail address?	**e-posta adresiniz nedir?** *eh-<u>postah</u> a<u>dres</u>eeneez neh-deer*
Can I access the Internet here?	**Buradan Internete erişebilir miyim?** *boorah-dan intair-net-eh eresh-eh-bee<u>leer</u> beeyim*
What are the charges per hour?	**Saatlik ücreti nedir?** *sa-art-lerk ewj-<u>ret</u>-ee neh-deer*
How do I log on?	**Nasıl gireceğim?** *<u>nass</u>irl geereh-<u>jay</u>-yim*

PUL	stamps
PAKET/KOLİ	packages
BOŞALTMA SAATİ ...	next collection ...

153

Souvenirs Hediyelik eşya

One of the most fascinating shopping experiences in Turkey is the bazaar. Some bazaars are immense labyrinths where you will find everything from shoelaces to gold earrings, from potatoes to fine Bursa silk. The most famous bazaar is probably Kapalı Çarşı (Covered Bazaar) in Istanbul, followed by the nearby Mısır Çarşısı (Spice Bazaar).

Generally, you will have to be ready to haggle for many items, although fixed prices are becoming more common. When you do bargain, bargain with firmness. If you are offered tea or coffee during the process, accept it as a perfectly sincere gesture.

dolls	**bebek**	bebek
lace	**dantel**	dan_tel_
perfume	**parfüm**	par-_fewm_
porcelain	**porselen**	porse_len_
pottery	**çömlek**	churm_lek_
leather goods	**deri eşyalar**	deree esh-yah-lar
jewelry	**mücevher**	mew_jev_-hair
carpets	**halı**	_hal_-ler
rugs	**kilim**	kee_leem_
silk garments	**ipek eşya**	_ee_pek esh-yah

Gifts Armağan

bottle of wine	**şarap**	sharap
box of chocolates	**kutu çikolata**	ku_too_ cheeko-_lat_ah
calendar	**takvim**	tak_veem_
key ring	**anahtarlık**	anah-_tar_-lerk
postcards	**kartpostal**	kartpos_tal_
scarf	**eşarp**	e_sharp_
souvenir guide	**hediyelik eşya rehberi**	he_dee_eye-lik esh-yah reh-_bair_-ee
tea towel	**kurulama bezi**	ku_roo_lama bez-ee
T-shirt	**tişört**	tee-shurt

Music Müzik

I'd like a …	**… istiyorum.** … *istee-yorum*
cassette	**kaset** *ka-set*
compact disc	**disk** *deesk*
record	**plak** *plak*
video cassette	**video kaseti** *vee-deo ka-set-ee*
Who are the popular native singers/bands?	**Sevilen yerel şarkıcılar/gruplar hangileri?** *seveelen yair-el shark-erjer-lar/groop-lar hangee-lair-ee*

Toys and games Oyuncak ve oyunlar

I'd like a toy/game …	**… bir oyuncak/oyun istiyorum.** … *beer oyoon-jak/oyoon istee-yorum*
for a boy	**erkek çocuk için** *air-kek chojook itchin*
for a 5-year-old girl	**5 yaşında bir kız çocuk için** *besh yashernda beer kerz chojook itchin*
ball	**top** *top*
chess set	**satranç seti** *satranch set-ee*
doll	**bebek** *bebek*
electronic game	**elektronik oyun** *elektron-eek oyoon*
teddy bear	**oyuncak ayı** *oyoonjak eye-yer*
pail and shovel [bucket and spade]	**kova ve kürek** *ko-vah veh kewrek*

Antiques Antika eşyalar

How old is this?	**Bu ne kadar eski?** *boo neh kaddar eskee*
Do you have anything of the … era?	**… döneminden bir şey var mı?** … *durnemeen-den beer shay var mer*
Can you send it to me?	**Bana gönderebilir misiniz?** *bana gurn-dair-eh-beeleer miseeniz*
Will I have problems with customs?	**Gümrükte sorun çıkar mı?** *gewm-rewk-teh soroon cher-kar mer*
Is there a certificate of authenticity?	**Hakikilik belgesi var mı?** *hakeekeelik belge-see var mer*

RULERS ➤ 104

Supermarket/Minimart
Süpermarket/Bakkal

Turkish supermarkets are similar to their Western counterparts. However, they are often more expensive than smaller, local markets. The most famous and the largest supermarket chain is *Migros*, which can be found all over Istanbul, Ankara, and İzmir. Smaller towns and cities will have at least one or two supermarkets. Convenience stores are known as **bakkal**. They are open from the early hours of the morning to late at night. They are usually very small shops.

At the supermarket Süpermarkette

Excuse me. Where can I find …?	**Afedersiniz. Nerede … bulabilirim?** *aff-edair-seeniz. neredeh … bull-ah-beeleerim*
Do I pay for this here?	**Bunu burada mı ödeyeceğim?** *boon-oo boorada mer ur-day-eh-jayim*
Where are the carts [trolleys]/baskets?	**El arabaları/sepetler nerede?** *el araba-lar-er/sepet-lair neredeh*
Is there a … here?	**Burada bir … var mı?** *booradah beer … var mer*
pharmacy	**eczane** *ej-zarne*
delicatessen	**şarküteri** *sharkew-tair-ee*

KONSERVELER	canned foods
SÜT ÜRÜNLERİ	dairy products
TAZE BALIK	fresh fish
TAZE ET	fresh meat
TAZE ÜRÜNLER	fresh produce
DONDURULMUŞ GIDA	frozen foods
EV EŞYALARI	household goods
KÜMES HAYVANLARI	poultry
ŞARAP VE ALKOLLÜ İÇKİLER	wines and spirits
EKMEK VE KEKLER	bread and cakes

Weights and measures
- 1 kilogram or kilo (kg.) = 1000 grams (g.); 100 g. = 3.5 oz.; **1 kg.** = 2.2 lb 1 oz. = **28.35 g.**; 1 lb. = **453.60 g.**
- 1 liter (l.) = 0.88 imp. quart or 1.06 U.S. quart 1 imp. quart = **1.14 l.** 1 U.S. quart = **0.951 l.** 1 imp. gallon = **4.55 l.** 1 U.S. gallon = **3.8 l.**

Food hygiene Gıda sağlığı

AÇTIKTAN SONRA ... GÜN İÇİNDE TÜKETİNİZ	eat within ... days of opening
BUZDOLABINDA SAKLAYINIZ	keep refrigerated
MİKRODALGA FIRINA KONULABİLİR	microwaveable
VEJETARYENLER İÇİN UYGUNDUR	suitable for vegetarians
SON KULLANMA TARİHİ ...	use by ...

At the minimart Bakkalda

I'd like some of that/those. **Şundan/şunlardan biraz istiyorum.**
shoondan/shoonlardan beeraz istee-yorum

this one/that one **bu/şu** *boo/shoo*

these/those **bunlar/şunlar** *boonlar/shoonlar*

to the left/right **solda/sağda** *sol-da/saa-da*

over there/here **orada/burada** *orada/boorada*

Where is/are the ...? **... nerede?** *... neredeh*

I'd like some ...? **Biraz ... istiyorum.** *beeraz ... istee-yorum*

a kilo (of)/half a kilo (of) **bir kilo/yarım kilo** *beer keelo/yarerm keelo*

a liter (of)/half a liter (of) **bir litre/yarım litre**
beer lee-tray/yarerm lee-tray

apples **elma** *elmah*

beer **bira** *beerah*

bread **ekmek** *ek-mek*

cheese **peynir** *payneer*

coffee **kahve** *kah-veh*

cookies [biscuits] **bisküvi** *bis-kew-vee*

eggs **yumurta** *yumoortah*

ham **jambon** *dzhambon*

jam **reçel** *rechel*

milk **süt** *sewt*

potato chips [crisps] **patates cipsi** *patat-es jeeps-ee*

soft drinks **alkolsüz içecekler** *al-kol-sewz itch-ejeklair*

tomatoes **domates** *domartes*

That's all, thanks. **Bu kadar, teşekkürler.**
boo kaddar teshe-kewr-lair

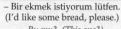

– Bir ekmek istiyorum lütfen.
(I'd like some bread, please.)
– Bu mu? *(This one?)*
– Evet, o. *(Yes, that one.)*
– Elbette. … Bu kadar mı? *(Certainly. … Is that all?)*
– Birkaç tane de yumurta. *(And some eggs.)*
– Buyrun. *(Here you are.)*

Provisions/Picnic Erzak/Piknik

Traditional Turkish bread is crusty, white, and very tasty. You will find traditional bread as well as another type called **pide,** which is flat. In restaurants, bread is often served warm.

Bakeries are called **fırın,** but are not common in tourist areas. If you would like to buy bread straight from the oven, you will need to go outside the tourist areas. Otherwise, even the smaller shops sell commercially produced bread.

beer	**bira**	*beerah*
butter	**tereyağı**	*tair-eh-yaa-er*
cakes	**kek**	*kek*
cheese	**peynir**	*payneer*
cooked meats	**pişmiş et**	*peeshmeesh et*
cookies [biscuits]	**bisküvi**	*bis-kew-vee*
grapes	**üzüm**	*ewzewm*
instant coffee	**neskafe**	*neskafeh*
lemonade	**limonata**	*leemonatah*
margarine	**margarin**	*margareen*
oranges	**portakal**	*portakal*
rolls	**küçük yuvarlak ekmek**	*kewchewk yoovarlak ek-mek*
sausages	**sosis**	*sosees*
tea bags	**poşet çay**	*poshet chy*
wine	**şarap**	*sharap*
yogurt	**yoğurt**	*yo-oort*

MEAT ➤ 45; VEGETABLES ➤ 46

Police Polis

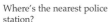

The police are everywhere in Turkey, in various guises.
Regular police wear blue uniforms. Treat them with respect
and they are likely to reciprocate. In an emergency, ☎ 155.

Where's the nearest police station?	**En yakın polis karakolu nerede?** *en ya_kern_ poleess kara_kol_-oo neredeh*
Does anyone here speak English?	**Burada İngilizce konuşan biri var mı?** *boorada eengee_leez_-jeh kon_oo_shan beeree var mer*
I want to report a(n) …	**Bir … haber vermek istiyorum.** *beer … ha-_bair_ vermek iss_tee_-yorum*
accident/attack	**kaza/saldırı** *kaz-zah/_salder_-er*
mugging/rape	**hırsızlık/tecavüz** *_her_-serzlerk/teh-_ja_-vewz*
My child is missing.	**Çocuğum kayıp.** *cho_joo_-oom ky-_yerp_*
Here's a photo of him/her.	**İşte fotoğrafı.** *eeshteh foto-_raf_-er*
Someone's following me.	**Birisi beni izliyor.** *beeree-see benee iz_lee_-yor*
I need an English-speaking lawyer.	**İngilizce konuşan bir avukata ihtiyacım var.** *eengee_leez_-jeh kon_oo_shan beer _avoo_kat-ah eehtee-_yar_-jerm var*
I need to make a phone call.	**Bir telefon görüşmesi yapmam gerekiyor.** *beer tele-fon gur-_rewsh_-mesee yapmam gerek_ee_-yor*
I need to contact the … Consulate.	**… Konsolosluğunu aramalıyım.** *… konsolos-loo-oo-noo ara_maler_-yerm*
American/British	**Amerika/İngiliz** *ameree-_kan_/eengee_leez_*

Onu tarif eder misiniz?	Can you describe him/her?
erkek/kadın	male/female
sarışın/kumral	blond(e)/brunette
kızıl saçlı/kır	red-headed/gray-haired
uzun/kısa saçlı/kel	long/short hair/balding
yaklaşık boyu …	approximate height …
yaşı (yaklaşık) …	age (approximate) …
… giyiyordu.	He/She was wearing …

CLOTHES ➤ 144; COLOR ➤ 143

Lost property / Theft Kayıp eşya/Hırsızlık

I want to report a theft.	**Bir hırsızlığı haber vermek istiyorum.** *beer herserz-ler-er ha-bair vermek istee-yorum*
My bag was snatched.	**Çantamı çaldılar.** *chantam-er chalern-der*
My … has been stolen from my car.	**Arabamdan … çalındı.** *arabamdan … chalern-der*
I've been robbed / mugged.	**Soyuldum.** *soyooldum*
I've lost my …	**… kaybettim.** *… ky-bettim*
My … has been stolen.	**… çalındı.** *… chalern-der*
bicycle	**bisikletim** *beesee-klet-im*
camera	**fotoğraf makinem** *foto-raf makeenem*
car	**arabam** *arabam*
credit cards	**kredi kartlarım** *kredee kart-larerm*
handbag	**el çantam** *el chantam*
money	**param** *param*
passport	**pasaportum** *pasaportoom*
purse	**cüzdanım** *jewzdan-erm*
rental car	**kiralık arabam** *keerah-lerk arabam*
ticket	**biletim** *beeletim*
wallet	**cüzdanım** *jewzdan-erm*
watch	**saatim** *sa-arteem*
What should I do?	**Ne yapmalıyım?** *neh yapmarler-yerm*
I need a police report for my insurance claim.	**Sigortadan para almak için polis raporu gerekiyor.** *seegortah-dan para almak itchin polees rapooru gerekee-yor*

Ne kayıp?	What's missing?
Ne alındı?	What's been taken?
Ne çalındı?	What's been stolen?
Ne zaman oldu?	When did it happen?
Nerede kalıyorsunuz?	Where are you staying?
Nereden alındı?	Where was it taken from?
O sırada siz neredeydiniz?	Where were you at the time?
Sizin için bir tercüman getirtiyoruz.	We're getting an interpreter for you.
Olayla ilgileneceğiz.	We'll look into the matter.
Lütfen bu formu doldurun.	Please fill out this form.

Health

No mandatory vaccinations are required to enter Turkey, but vaccinations against polio, tetanus, typhoid, and hepatitis A are recommended. You are advised to take anti-malarial tablets if traveling in Southeast Turkey east of Antalya, especially around Adana. Make sure your travel insurance provides adequate health coverage.

The most likely ailment to hit you in Turkey is diarrhea. In restaurants, hygiene standards vary enormously: eat where you can see that the prepared dishes, such as cold appetizers, are refrigerated and the hot food is freshly cooked. Be wary about eating unwashed salads and fruit, and food from street stalls. Drink bottled water. Beware of shellfish from the polluted waters around Istanbul.

Doctor (general) Doktor (genel)

Where can I find a hospital/dentist? [surgery]	**Nerede bir hastane/diş kliniği bulabilirim?** neredeh beer hastarneh/deesh klinee-yee bull-ah-beeleerim
Where's there a doctor/dentist who speaks English?	**İngilizce konuşan bir doktor/diş doktoru var mı?** eengeeleez-jah konoo<u>shan</u> beer dok-tor/deesh dok-toroo var mer
Could the doctor come to see me here?	**Doktor beni gelip burada görebilir mi?** dok-tor benee geleep boorada gur-eh-bee<u>leer</u> mee
Can I make an appointment for …?	**… için randevu alabilir miyim?** … itch<u>in</u> ran-day-voo ala-bee<u>leer</u> meeyim
today/tomorrow	**bugün/yarın** boo-gewn/yar<u>ern</u>
as soon as possible	**en yakın zaman** en yak<u>ern</u> zaman
It's urgent.	**Acil.** aj<u>eel</u>
I have an appointment with Doctor …	**Doktor … ile randevum var.** doctor … eeleh ran-day-voom var

Accident and injury Kaza ve yaralanma

My … is hurt/injured.	**… incindi/yaralandı.**
	… eenjeen-dee/yararlan-der
husband/wife	**kocam/karım** *ko-jam/kar-erm*
son/daughter	**oğlum/kızım** *o-loom/ker-zerm*
friend	**arkadaşım** *arkadasherm*
child	**çocuğum** *chojoo-oom*
He/She is	**O …** *oh*
unconscious	**baygın** *by-gern*
(seriously) injured	**(ciddi biçimde) yaralandı**
	(jeed-dee beechim-deh) yararlan-der
bleeding (heavily)	**kanaması var (ağır)** *kana-masser var*
I have a(n) …	**Bir … var.** *beer … var*
blister	**su toplanması** *soo toplanma-ser*
boil	**çıban** *cherban*
bruise	**çürük** *chewrewk*
burn	**yanık** *yanerk*
cut	**kesik** *keseek*
graze	**sıyrık** *suy-rerk*
insect bite/sting	**böcek sokması** *burjek sokma-ser*
lump	**şiş** *sheesh*
rash	**kaşıntı** *kashernter*
strained muscle	**kas kasılması** *kas kaserlma-ser*
swelling	**şişlik** *sheesh-lik*
My … hurts.	**… acıyor.** *… ajer-yor*

Symptoms Belirtiler

I've been feeling ill for … days.	**… gündür kendimi hasta hissediyorum.** *… gewn-dewr kendimee hasta hiss<u>edee</u>-yorum*
I feel faint.	**Bayılacak gibiyim.** *by-<u>yerl</u>-ajak gibee-yim*
I have a fever.	**Ateşim var.** *at<u>esh</u>im var*
I've been vomiting.	**Kusuyorum.** *<u>koo</u>soo-yorum*
I have diarrhea.	**İshalim var.** *<u>ees</u>-halim var*
It hurts here.	**Burası acıyor.** *boora-ser a<u>jer</u>-yor*
I have (a/an) …	**… var.** *… var*
backache	**sırt ağrım** *sert aa-rerm*
cold	**soğuk algınlığım** *so-<u>ook</u> al<u>gern</u>ler-erm*
cramps	**kramp** *kramp*
earache	**kulak ağrım** *koo<u>lak</u> aa-rerm*
headache	**baş ağrım** *bash aa-rerm*
sore throat	**boğaz ağrım** *bo-az aa-rerm*
stomachache	**mide ağrım** *meedeh aa-rerm*
sunstroke	**güneş çarpması** *gew<u>nesh</u> <u>charp</u>ma-ser*

Conditions Sağlık durumu

I have arthritis.	**Arteritim var.** *arteh-ree-<u>teem</u> var*
I have asthma.	**Astımım.** *aster-<u>merm</u>*
I am …	**Ben …** *ben*
deaf	**sağırım** *saa-er-erm*
diabetic	**şeker hastasıyım** *she-kair hasta-<u>ser</u>-erm*
epileptic	**sara hastasıyım** *sarah hasta-<u>ser</u>-erm*
handicapped	**özürlüyüm** *urzwr-<u>lew</u>-yewm*
(… months) pregnant	**(… aylık) hamileyim** *(… eye-lerk) ha<u>mee</u>-layim*
I have a heart condition.	**Kalp hastasıyım.** *kalp hasta-<u>ser</u>-erm*
I have high/low blood pressure.	**Tansiyonum yüksek/düşük.** *Tansee <u>yo</u>noom yew<u>ksek</u>/dew<u>shewk</u>*
I had a heart attack … years ago.	**… yıl önce kalp krizi geçirdim.** *… yerl urn<u>jeh</u> kalp kreezee get<u>cheer</u>dim*

163

Doctor's inquiries Doktorun sorulari

Ne kadar zamandır kendinizi böyle hissediyorsunuz?	How long have you been feeling like this?
İlk defa mı oluyor bu?	Is this the first time you've had this?
Başka ilaç alıyor musunuz?	Are you taking any other medication?
Herhangi bir şeye alerjiniz var mı?	Are you allergic to anything?
Tetanos aşısı oldunuz mu?	Have you been vaccinated against tetanus?
İştahınız iyi mi?	Is your appetite okay?

Examination Muayene

Ateşinizi/tansiyonunuzu ölçeceğim.	I ll take your temperature/ blood pressure.
Kolunuzu sıyırın lütfen.	Roll up your sleeve, please.
Belden yukarı soyunun.	Please undress to the waist.
Lütfen uzanın.	Please lie down.
Ağzınızı açın.	Open your mouth.
Derin nefes alın.	Breathe deeply.
Öksürün lütfen.	Cough, please.
Neresi acıyor?	Where does it hurt?
Burası acıyor mu?	Does it hurt here?

Diagnosis Teşhis

Röntgen çektirmenizi istiyorum.	I want you to have an X-ray.
Kan/dışkı/idrar örneği almam lazım.	I want a blood/stool/urine specimen.
Bir uzman doktor görmenizi istiyorum.	I want you to see a specialist.
Hastaneye gitmenizi istiyorum.	I want you to go to a hospital.
Kırılmış/burkulmuş.	It's broken/sprained.
Çıkmış/yırtılmış.	It's dislocated/torn.

... var.	You have (a/an) ...
akciğer iltihabı	pneumonia
apandisitiniz	appendicitis
bademcik	tonsilitis
basur	hemorrhoids
bulaşıcı cinsel hastalık	venereal disease
fıtık	hernia
gastrit	gastritis
kemik çatlaması	fracture
kızamık	measles
nezleniz	cold
sistitiniz	cystitis
siyatik	sciatica
tümör	tumor
... iltihab	inflammation of ...
yemek zehirlenmesi	food poisoning
İltihaplı.	It's infected.
Bulaşıcı.	It's contagious.

Treatment Tedavi

Size bir ... veriyorum.	I'll give you ...
antiseptik	an antiseptic
ağrı kesici	some painkillers
... için reçete yazacağım.	I'm going to prescribe ...
antibiyotik kürü	a course of antibiotics
fitil	some suppositories
Herhangi bir ilaca karşı alerjiniz var mı?	Are you allergic to any medication?
... bir tane alın	Take one ...
her ... saatte bir	every ... hours
günde ... kere	... times a day
her yemekten önce/sonra	before/after each meal
ağrırsa	in case of pain
... gün için	for ... days
Ülkenize dönünce bir doktora başvurun.	Consult a doctor when you get home.

Parts of the body
Vücudun bölümleri

appendix	**apandisit**	apan-dee-<u>seet</u>
arm	**kol**	kol
back	**sırt**	sert
bladder	**idrar torbası**	ee<u>drar</u> torba-ser
bone	**kemik**	kemeek
breast	**meme**	memeh
chest	**göğüs**	gur-<u>ews</u>
ear	**kulak**	<u>koo</u>lak
eye	**göz**	gurz
face	**yüz**	yewz
finger	**parmak**	parmak
foot	**ayak**	eye-yak
gland	**salgı bezesi**	sal-ger beze-see
hand	**el**	el
head	**baş**	bash
heart	**kalp**	kalp
jaw	**çene**	cheneh
joint	**eklem**	ek-lem
kidney	**böbrek**	bur-brek
knee	**diz**	deez
leg	**bacak**	bajak
lip	**dudak**	doodak
liver	**ciğer**	jee-air
mouth	**ağız**	aa-erz
muscle	**kas**	kas
neck	**boyun**	boy-oon
nose	**burun**	bur-oon
rib	**kaburga**	kaboorga
shoulder	**omuz**	omooz
skin	**deri**	deree
stomach	**mide**	meedeh
thigh	**but**	boot
throat	**boğaz**	bo-az
thumb	**baş parmak**	bash parmak
toe	**ayak parmağı**	eye-yak par-my-yer
tongue	**dil**	deel
tonsils	**bademcik**	ba-dem-jeek
vein	**damar**	damar

Gynecologist
Kadın hastalıkları uzmanı

I have …   **… var.** … var

abdominal pains   **karın ağrım** karern aa-rerm

period pains   **aybaşı ağrım** eye-bash-er aa-rerm

a vaginal infection   **vajina iltihaplanması**
                                  vajeena eelteehaplanma-ser

I haven't had my period   **… aydan beri aybaşı olmuyor.**
for … months.   … eye-dan bair-ee eye-bash-erm olmu-yor

I'm on the Pill.   **Doğum kontrol hapı kullanıyorum.**
                                  do-oom hap-er kool-lan-er-yorum

Hospital Hastane

Please notify my family.   **Lütfen aileme bildirin.**
                                  lewt-fen eye-lemeh bildeerin

I'm in pain.   **Acı içindeyim.** ajer itchin-dayim

I can't eat/sleep.   **Yemek yiyemiyorum/uyuyamıyorum.**
                                  yemek yee-yemee-yorum/
                                  oyoo-yam-er-yorum

When will the doctor come?   **Doktor ne zaman gelecek?**
                                  dok-tor neh zaman gel-ejek

Which ward is … in?   **… hangi koğuşta?** … hangee ko-ooshta

I'm visiting …   **… -i ziyaret edeceğim.**
                                  … ee zee-yaret edeh-jay-yim

Optician Göz doktoru

I'm near [short-] sighted/   **Uzağı/yakını görme bozukluğum var.**
far [long-] sighted.   oozay-er/yakern-er gurmeh
                                  bozookloo-oom var

I've lost …   **… kaybettim.** … ky-bettim

one of my contact lenses   **kontak lenslerimden birini**
                                  kontak lens-lair-eemden beereenee

my glasses/a lens   **gözlüğümü/camını**
                                  gurzlew-ewmew/jamern-er

Could you give me a   **Yeni bir tane verebilir misiniz?** yenee
replacement?   beer tarneh vereh-beeleer miseeniz

Dentist Diş doktoru

I have a toothache.

Dişim ağrıyor.
deeshim aa-rer-yor

This tooth hurts.

Bu diş acıyor.
boo deesh ajer-yor

I've lost a filling/tooth.

Bir dolgum/dişim düstü.
beer dolgoom/deeshim dewsh-_tew_

Can you repair this denture?

Bu protezi onarabilir misiniz?
boo pro_tez_ee o_nar_ah-bee_leer_ miseeniz

I don't want it extracted.

Çekilmesini istemiyorum.
che_keel_-meseenee _iste_mee-yorum

Size iğne yapacağım/ uyuşturacağım.	I'm going to give you an injection/ an anesthetic.
Dolguya/kaplamaya ihtiyacınız var.	You need a filling/cap (crown).
Çekmem lazım.	I'll have to take it out.
Geçici olarak onarabilirim.	I can only fix it temporarily.
... saat bir şey yemeyin.	Don't eat anything for ... hours.

Payment and insurance Ödeme ve sigorta

How much do I owe you?

Borcum ne kadar?
bor_joom_ neh kaddar

I have insurance.

Sigortam var.
seegor_tam_ var

Can I have a receipt for my insurance?

Sigorta için fiş alabilir miyim?
seegor_tah_ itc_hin_ feesh ala-bee_leer_ meeyim

Would you fill out this insurance form, please?

Bu sigorta formunu doldurur musunuz lütfen? boo seegor_tah_ formoonoo doldu_roor_ musoonuz _lewt_-fen

To enable correct usage, most terms in this dictionary are either followed by an expression or cross-referenced to pages where the word appears in a phrase. The notes below provide some basic grammar guidelines.

Nouns

There is no equivalent of the English "the" (definite article) in Turkish, but "a/an" is **bir** (➤ 15).

Plurals are made by adding a suffix which can be **-ler** or **-lar**, depending on the final vowel of the singular word, following the system of vowel harmony (➤ 6). For example:

yemek meal   **yemekler** meals

kitap book   **kitaplar** books

Nouns in Turkish change their ending according to their function in a sentence. These grammatical case endings are themselves subject to change due to vowel harmony (➤ 6). At this level, it is often difficult to separate the case endings from the other suffixes added to a word and therefore it is better to learn words within a complete phrase, if possible.

Adjectives

Adjectives come before the noun and are the same for singular and plural words:

uzun yol the long road   **uzun yollar** the long roads

Verbs

Turkish verbs use a stem with suffixes to denote the tense (present, past, or future) and the person doing the action. The stem of the verb can be found by removing **mak** or **mek** from the infinitive of the verb, e.g. the stem of **gelmek** (to come) is **gel**; the stem of **açmak** (to open) is **aç**.

To put the verb into the present continuous (which can also be used for future), the suffix **-iyor** is added to the stem, followed by one of these personal suffixes:

I **um**	you (*informal*) **sun**	he/she/it (no ending required)
we **uz**	you (*formal*) **sunuz**	they **lar**

I am coming **geliyorum**   he/she/it is opening/will open **açıyor**

we are coming/will come **geliyoruz**   they are opening **açıyorlar**

The negative suffix for the present tense is an **-m** between the verb stem and the **iyor** suffix:

he isn't coming **gelmiyor**

a.m. öğleden önce

about *(approximately)* yaklaşık 15

abroad yurtdışı

accept, to kabul etmek 136

accident kaza 92, 159

accidentally kazayla 28

accompany, to eşlik etmek 65

accountant muhasebeci 121

acne sivilce

across karşı tarafta 12

acrylic akrilik

actor oyuncu

adapter adaptör 26, 148

address adres 23, 84, 93, 126

adjoining room yan yana oda 22

admission charge giriş ücreti 114

adult yetişkin 81, 100

afraid: I'm ~ *(I'm sorry)* korkarım 126

after sonra 13, 95, 165

after shave after shave 142

after-sun lotion güneş bayosu sonrası kremi 142

afternoon: in the ~ öğleden sonra 221

aged: to be ~ yaşında olmak 159

ago önce 221; **... years ago** ... yıl önce 163

agree: I don't ~ katılmıyorum

air: ~ conditioning havalandırma 22, 25; **~mattress** hava yatağı 31; **~ pump** hava pompası 87; **~ sickness bag** sıhhi torba 70

airmail uçak ile 153

airport havaalanı 84, 96

aisle seat koridor kenarı koltuk 69, 73

alarm clock çalar saat 149

alcoholic *(drink)* alkollü

all hepsi

allergic: to be ~ alerjisi olmak 164, 165

allergy alerji

allowance *(customs)* gümrüküz geçebilecek 67

almost neredeyse

alone yalnız; **leave me alone!** beni yalnız bırakın! 126

already zaten 28

also ayrıca 19

alter, to değiştirmek 137

aluminum foil alimünyum kağıt 148

always her zaman 13

am: I am ben

amazing hayret verici 101

ambassador elçi

ambulance ambülans 92

American Amerikan 150, 159

American Plan (A.P.) tam pansiyon 24

amount *(money)* tutar 42

amusement arcade oyun salonu 113

and ve 19

anesthetic: give an ~ uyuşturma 168

animal hayvan 106

another başka bir 21, 25, 125

antacid mide asidine karşı ilaç

antibiotics antibiyotik 165

antifreeze antifriz

antique *(object)* antika eşya 155

antiseptic antiseptik 165; **~ cream** antiseptik krem 141

any herhangi bir

anyone biri 67; **does ~ speak English?** İngilizce bilen kimse var mı?

anything else? başka bir şey var mı?

apartment apartman dairesi 28

beach plaj 107, 116
beam *(headlights)* far 86
beard sakal
beautiful güzel 14, 101
because çünkü 15; **~ of** yüzünden 15
bed yatak 21; **~ and breakfast** oda ve kahvaltı 24
bedding yatak takımı 29
bedroom yatak odası 29
beer bira 40, 157, 158
before önce 13, 165, 221
begin, to başlamak
beginner yeni başlayan 117
behind arkasında 95
beige bej 143
belong: this belongs to me bu bana ait
belt kemer 144
berth kuşet 73, 76, 77
best en iyisi
better daha iyi 14
between *(time)* arasında 221
bib önlük
bicycle bisiklet 74, 83, 160
bidet bidey
big büyük 14, 117, 134
bigger daha büyük 24
bikini bikini 144
bill fatura 32; *(restaurant, etc.)* hesap 42
bin liner çöp tobası
binoculars dürbün
bird kuş 106
birthday doğum günü 219
biscuits bisküvi 157, 158
bite *(insect)* sokmak
bitten: I've been bitten by a dog beni köpek ısırdı
bitter acı 41
bizarre garip 101

black siyah 143; *(coffee)* sütsüz 40; **~ and white film** *(camera)* siyah beyaz film 151
bladder idrar torbası 166
blanket battaniye 27
bleach çamaşır suyu 148
bleeding: he's ~ kanaması var 162
blind panjur 25
blister su toplanması 162
blocked, to be tıkanmak 25
blood kan 164; **~ group** kan grubu; **~ pressure** tansiyon 163, 164
blouse bluz 144
blow-dry kurutma 147
blue mavi 143
boarding card biniş kartı 70
boat trip tekne gezisi 81, 97
boil çıban 162
boiled kaynamış
boiler kazan 29
bone kemik 166
book kitap 150; **~store** kitapçı 130
booklet of tickets bilet karnesi 79
booted, to be kelepçelenmek 87
boots bot 145; *(sport)* çizme 115
boring sıkıcı 101
born: to be ~ doğmak 119; **I was ~ in ...** ...-de doğdum
borrow: may I ~ your ...? ...-inizi ödünç alabilir miyim?
botanical garden botanik bahçesi 99
bottle şişe 37, 40; **~ of wine** şarap 154; **~-opener** şişe açacağı 148
bowel bağırsak
bowls çanak 148
box kutu 110; **~ of chocolates** kutu çikolata 154
boy erkek çocuk 120, 155

can opener konserve açacağı 148
Canada Kanada 119
canal kanal 107
cancel, to iptal etmek 68
cancer *(disease)* kanser
candy şeker 150
cap *(hat)* kep 144; *(dental)* kaplama 168
car araba 30, 72, 81, 86, 88, 93, 123, 160; **~ ferry** araba vapuru 81; **~ park** otopark 26, 96; **~ rental** araba kiralama 70; **by ~** araba ile 95
car *(train compartment)* vagon 74
carafe sürahi 37, 40
caravan karavan 30
cards kağıt 121
careful: be careful! dikkat edin!
carpet *(rug)* halı
carrier bag torba
carry-cot portbebe
cart el arabası 156
carton kutu 100
case *(suitcase)* bavul 69
cash para 42; nakit 136; **~ desk** kasa 132; **~ machine** paramatik 139
cashier kasa 132
casino kumarhane 112
cassette kaset 155
castle kale 99
catch, to *(bus)* yetişmek
cathedral katedral 99
Catholic Katolik 105
cave mağara 107
CD CD; **CD-player** CD-çalar
cemetery mezarlık 99
center of town kent merkezi 21
central heating kalorifer
ceramics seramik

certificate belge 149, 155
chain zincir 149
change *(coins)* bozuk para 87, 136
change, to *(alter)* değiştirmek 39, 68; *(bus/train)* aktarma yapmak 74, 79; *(money)* bozdurmak 138
changing facilities bebeğin altını değiştirecek yer 113
charcoal odun kömürü 31
charge ücret 30, 115, 153
charter flight charter uçuşu
cheap ucuz 14, 134
cheaper daha ucuz 21, 24, 109, 134
check book çek defteri
check: ~ in check-in yaptırmak 69; **~-in desk** check-in masası 69; **~ out** *(hotel)* otelden ayrılmak 32; **please check the ...** lütfen ...-i kontrol edin
cheers! şerefe!
cheese peynir 157, 158
chemist eczane 131
cheque book çek defteri
chess satranç 121; **~ set** satranç seti 155
chest göğüs 166
chewing gum sakız 150
child çocuk 159, 162; **~ seat** çocuk sandalyesi 39; **~minder** çocuk bakıcısı
children çocuklar 22, 24, 39, 66, 74, 81, 100, 113, 116, 120, 140
chocolate *(flavor)* çikolatalı 40; **~ bar** çikolata 150; **~ ice cream** çikolatalı dondurma 110
Christmas Noel 219
church kilise 96, 99, 105
cigarettes sigara 150; **cigarette kiosk** tütüncü 130
cigars puro 150
cinema sinema 110

A-Z

destination gidilen yer

details ayrıntılar

detergent deterjan 148

develop, to *(photos)* banyo ettirmek 151

diabetes şeker hastalığı

diabetic *(person)* şeker hastası 39; **to be ~** şeker hastası olmak 163

dialling code alan kodu 127

diamond elmas 149

diapers bebek bezi 142

diarrhea ishal 141; **to have ~** ishal olmak 163; **I have ~** ishalim var

dice zar

dictionary sözlük 150

diesel dizel 87

diet: I'm on a ~ rejim yapıyorum

difficult zor 14

dining: ~ car yemekli vagon 74, 77; **~ room** yemek salonu 26

dinner: to have ~ akşam yemeği yemek 124; **~ jacket** smokin

direct *(train, etc.)* aktarmasız 74

direct, to *(to a place)* yolunu göstermek 18

direction: in the ~ of ... yönünde 95

directory *(telephone)* rehber

dirty kirli 14, 28

disabled *(person)* özürlü 22, 100

discotheque diskotek 112

discount indirim

dish *(meal)* yemek 37, 39

dishcloth bulaşık bezi 148

dishwashing liquid bulaşık deterjanı 148

dislocated, to be çıkmak 164

display cabinet vitrin 149

disposable camera tek kullanımlık fotoğraf makinesi 151

distilled water arı su

disturb: don't disturb rahatsız etmeyin

dive, to dalmak 116

diving equipment dalış donanımı 117

divorced, to be boşanmış olmak 120

dizzy: I feel ~ başım dönüyor

do, to yapmak; **what do you do?** ne iş yapıyorsunuz? 121

doctor doktor 92, 131, 161

doll bebek 155

dollar dolar 67, 138

door kapı 25, 29

double iki kişilik 81; **~ bed** iki kişilik yatak 21; **~ room** iki kişilik oda 21

downtown kent merkezi 83, 99

dozen düzine 217

draft [draught] *(beer, etc.)* fıçı 40

dress elbise 144

drink *(beverage)* içki 37, 70, 125, 126

drinking water içme suyu 30

drip, to: the faucet [tap] drips musluk damlıyor

drive, to seyretmek 93

driver sürücü; **driver's license** ehliyet 93

drop someone off, to bırakmak 83

drowning: someone is drowning birisi boğuluyor

drugstore eczane 130

drunk sarhoş

dry cleaner kuru temizleyici 131

dry-clean, to kuru temizleme yapmak

dubbed, to be seslendirmek 110

during içinde 221

dustbins çöp bidonları 30

duvet yorgan

extension dahili hat 128
extra *(additional)* daha 23
extract, to *(tooth)* çekmek 168
eye göz 166

F **fabric** kumaş 145
face yüz 166
facial yüz bakımı 147
facilities hizmetler 22, 30
faint: to feel ~ bayılacak gibi olmak 163
fairground lunapark 113
fall *(autumn)* sonbahar 219
family aile 66, 74, 120, 167
famous ünlü
fan *(air)* vantilatör 25
far uzak 95, 130; **~-sighted** yakını görme bozukluğu 167; **how far is it?** ne kadar uzakta? 72, 94, 106
farm çiftlik 107
fast *(speed)* hızlı 17, 93; *(clock)* ileri 221; **~-food restaurant** hazır yemek lokantası 35
father baba 120
faucet musluk 25
faulty: this is ~ bu arızalı
favorite favori
fax faks 22, 153; **~ machine** faks makinesi
February Şubat 218
feed, to yemek vermek 39
feeding bottle biberon
feel ill, to hasta hissetmek 163
female kadın 159
ferry vapur 81, 123
fever ateş 163
few birkaç tane 15; **a few** birkaç tanesi 15
fiancé(e) nişanlı
field tarla 107
fifth beşinci 217

fight *(brawl)* kavga
fill: ~ out *(form)* doldurmak 168; **~ up** *(car)* doldurmak 87
filling *(dental)* dolgu 168
film film 108, 110, 151
filter filtre 151
find, to bulmak 18
fine *(well)* iyi 19, 118; *(penalty)* ceza 93
finger parmak 166
fire yangın; **~ alarm** yangın alarmı; **~ department [brigade]** itfaiye 92; **~ escape** yangın merdiveni; **~ exit** yangın çıkışı 132; **~ extinguisher** yangın söndürme aleti; **there's a fire!** yangın var!
firewood odun
first ilk 68, 75, 81; **~class** birinci sınıf 68, 73
fish: ~ restaurant balık lokantası 35; **~ store [fishmonger]** balıkçı dükkânı 130
fit, to *(clothes)* olmak 146
fitting room soyunma odası 146
fix, to onarmak 168
flashlight el feneri 31
flat *(tire [tyre])* patlak 83, 88
flavor: what flavors do you have? hangi çeşitler var?
flea pire
flight uçuş 68, 70; **~ number** uçuş numarası 68
flip-flops sandalet 145
floor *(level)* kat 132
florist çiçekçi dükkânı 130
flower çiçek 106
flu grip
flush: the toilet won't flush tuvaletin sifonu akmıyor
fly *(insect)* sinek

foggy: to be ~ sisli olmak 122

folk: ~ art halk sanatı; **~ music** halk müziği 111

follow, to izlemek 95, 159

food yiyecek 39, 119; **~ poisoning** yemek zehirlenmesi 165

foot ayak 166; **~path** patika 107

football *(soccer)* futbol 114

for *(time)* için 13, 117; **~ a day** bir gün için 86; **~ a week** bir hafta için 86

foreign currency döviz 138

forest orman 107

forget, to unutmak 42

fork çatal 39, 41, 148

form form 23, 168

formal dress takım elbise 111

fortnight iki hafta

fortunately iyi ki 19

fountain çeşme 99

four-door car dört kapılı araba 86

four-wheel drive dört çekişli araba 86

fourth dördüncü 217

foyer *(hotel, theater)* fuaye

fracture kemik çatlaması 165

frame *(glasses)* çerçeve

free *(available)* boş 36, 124; *(without charge)* ücretsiz 69

freezer dondurucu 29

French fries patates kızartması 38

frequent: how frequent? ne sıklıkta? 75

frequently sık sık

fresh taze 41

Friday Cuma 218

fried kızartılmış

friend arkadaş 123, 125, 162

friendly arkadaşça

fries patates kızartması 40

frightened: to be ~ korkmak

from -den 12, 70, 72; **from ... to ...** *(time)* ... -den ... -e kadar 13, 221; **where are you from?** nerelisiniz? 119

front ön 83, 147

frosty: to be ~ dona çekmek

frying pan tava 29

fuel *(gasoline [petrol])* yakit 86

full dolu 14; **~ board** tam pansiyon 24; **~ up** *(restaurant, etc.)* dolu 36; **to be ~** dolu olmak 21

fun: to have ~ eğlenmek

funny komik 126

furniture mobilya

fuse sigorta 28; **~ box** sigorta kutusu 28

G game *(match)* maç 114; *(toy)* oyun 155

garage *(parking)* garaj 26; *(repair)* araba tamirhanesi 88

garbage bags çöp torbası 148

garden bahçe 35

gas: gaz; **~ bottle** gaz tüpü 28; **~ station** benzin istasyonu 87; **I smell gas!** gaz kokusu var!

gasoline benzin 88

gastritis gastrit 165

gate *(airport)* biniş kapısı 70

gauze bandaj 141

gay club eşcinsel klübü 112

genuine gerçek 134

get *(find)* bulmak 84; **~ back** *(return)* geri dönmek 98; **~ off** *(bus, etc.)* inmek 79; **~ to** gitmek 70, 77; **how do I get to ...?** ... -e nasıl gidebilirim? 72, 94

gift armağan 67; **~ shop** hediyelik eşya dükkanı 130

girl kız çocuk 120, 155

girlfriend kız arkadaş 120

give, to vermek 136

gland salgı bezesi 166

glass bardak 37, 39, 40, 148

glasses *(optical)* gözlük 167

glossy finish *(photos)* parlak

glove eldiven

go, to gitmek 18, 66, 93, 124; **~ for a walk** yürüyüşe çıkmak 124; **~ out for a meal** yemeğe çıkmak 124; **~ shopping** alışverişe çıkmak 124; **let's go!** gidelim!; **where does this bus go?** bu otobüs nereye gidiyor?; **go away!** git!

goggles koruyucu gözlük

gold altın 149; **~ plate** altın kaplama 149

golf golf 114; **~ course** golf sahası 115

good iyi 14, 35, 42; **~ afternoon** iyi günler 10; **~ evening** iyi akşamlar 10; **~ morning** günaydın 10; **~ night** iyi geceler 10; **~ value** değmek 101

good-bye hoşçakal; güle güle 10

grandparents büyükbaba ile büyükanne

grapes üzüm 158

grass ot

gray gri 143

graze sıyrık 162

great şahane 19

Greece Yunanistan

green yeşil 143

greengrocer manav

grilled ızgara

grocery store bakkal

ground *(earth)* zemin 31

groundcloth [groundsheet] su geçirmez yaygı 31

group grup 66, 100

guarantee garanti 135

guesthouse misafirhane 123

guide *(tour)* gezi rehberi 98; **~book** rehber kitabı 100; **guided tour** rehberli tur 100; **guided walk** rehberli yürüyüş 106

guitar gitar

gum jiklet

guy rope germe halatı 31

gynecologist kadın hastalıkları uzmanı 167

H hair saç 147; **~ mousse** saç jölesi 142; **~ spray** saç spreyi 142; **~cut** saç tıraşı; **~dresser** kuaför 131, 147

half yarım 217; **~ board** yarım pansiyon 24; **~ past** buçuk 220

ham jambon 157

hammer çekiç 31

hand el 166; **~ baggage** el çantası 69; **~ washable** elde yıkanabilir 145; **~bag** el çantası 144, 160

handicap *(golf)* handikap

handicrafts el sanatları

handkerchief mendil

hanger askı 27

hangover akşamdan kalmalık 141

happen, to olmak 93

happy: I'm not happy with the service hizmetten memnun değilim

harbor liman

hard *(solid)* sert 31; *(difficult)* zorlu 106

hat şapka 144

have, to sahip olmak 120; *(dish in restaurant)* almak 42; *(hold stock of)* olmak 133;
could I have? … isteyebilir miyim? 38;
does the hotel have …? otelde … var mı? 22;
I'll have … … istiyorum 37

hay fever saman nezlesi 141

head baş 166; **~ache** baş ağrısı 163

health: ~ food store sağlıklı yiyecekler dükkanı 130; **~ insurance** sağlık sigortası 168

hear, to duymak

hearing aid kulaklık

heart kalp 166; **~ attack** kalp krizi 163

heat [heating] ısıtıcı 25

heavy ağır 14, 69, 117, 134

height boy 159

hello merhaba 10, 118

help: can you help me? yardımcı olabilir misiniz? 18, 92, 133

hemorrhoids basur 165

her onun 16

here burada 12, 17, 31, 35, 77, 106, 119

hernia fıtık 165

hers onun 16

hi! selam! 10

high yüksek 122, 163

highlight, to *(hair)* rengini açmak 147

highway otoyol 88, 92, 94

hiking açık arazide spor yürüyüşü; **~ gear** yürüyüş donanımı

hill tepe 107

him o 16

hire kiralamak 83

his onun 16

historic site tarihi yer 99

hitchhiking otostop yapmak 83

HIV-positive HIV pozitif

hobby *(pastime)* hobi 121

hold on, to *(wait)* beklemek 128

hole *(in clothes)* delik

holiday tatil 123; **~ resort** tatil yeri; **on ~** tatil için 66

home ev 126; **we're going ~** eve dönüyoruz

homosexual *(adj.)* eşcinsel

honeymoon: we're on ~ balayındayız

hopefully umarım 19

horse at; **~ racing** at yarışı 115

hospital hastane 96, 131, 164, 167

hot sıcak 14, 122; **~ dog** sosisli sandöviç 110; **~ spring** kaplıca; **~ water** sıcak su 25

hotel otel 21, 123,

hour saat 97, 117; **in an ~** bir saat içinde 84

house ev; **~wife** ev kadını 121

hovercraft hovercraft 81

how? nasıl 17; **~ long?** ne kadar sürüyor? 23, 68, 74, 75, 77, 88, 94, 98, 106, 135; **~ many?** kaç? 15, 79, 80; **~ many times?** kaç kere? 140; **~ much** ne kadar 15, 21, 65, 68, 79, 89, 100, 109, 136, 140; **~ old …?** … ne kadar eski? 155; **~ are you?** nasılsınız? 118

hundred yüz 217

hungry: I'm ~ karnım aç

hurry: I'm in a ~ acelem var

hurt, to acımak 164; **to be ~** yaralanmak 92; **my … hurts** … acıyor 162

husband koca 120, 162

I I'd like ... ... istiyorum 18

ice buz 38; ~ cream dondurma 40; ~-cream parlor dondurmacı 35

icy buzlu 117; to be ~ buzlu olmak 122

identification kimlik belgesi

I've lost ... ... kaybettim

ill: I'm ~ hastayım

illegal: is it ~? kanuna aykırı mı?

imitation taklit 134

in (place) -de 12, 88; (within period of time) içinde 13; ~ front of önünde 125

include dahil 24; is ... included? ... dahil mi? 86, 98

incredible inanılmaz 101

indicate, to belirtmek

indigestion hazımsızlık

indoor pool kapalı havuz 116

inexpensive ucuz 35

infected: to be ~ iltihaplanmak 165

infection iltihap 167

inflammation iltihap 165

informal (dress) spor

information bilgi 97; ~ desk danışma masası 72; ~ office danışma bürosu 96

injection iğne yapmak 168

injured, to be yaralı olmak 92, 162

innocent masum

insect böcek 25; ~ bite böcek sokması 141, 162; ~ repellent böcek kovucu 141; ~ sting böcek sokması 162

inside içerde 12

insist: I insist ısrar ediyorum

insomnia uykusuzluk

instant coffee neskafe 158

instead of ... ... yerine 38

instructions kullanım talimatları 135

instructor eğitmen

insurance sigorta 86, 89, 93, 160, 168; ~ claim sigortadan para almak 160; ~ card [certificate] sigorta kartı 93

interest (hobby) ilgi alanı 121

interesting ilginç 101

interpreter tercüman 160

intersection kavşak 95

into -e 70

introduce oneself, to tanıtmak 118

invite, to davet etmek 124

iodine tentürdiyot

Ireland İrlanda 119

is it ...? ... mi? 17

is there ...? ... var mı? 17

it is ... -dir

Italian İtalyan 35

itch: it itches kaşınıyor

item eşya 69

itemized bill dökümlü hesap 32

J jacket ceket 144

jam reçel 157

jammed: to be ~ tutukluk yapmak 25

January Ocak 218

jaw çene 166

jazz caz 111

jeans kot pantolon 144

jellyfish deniz anası

jet lag: I'm jet lagged saat değişikliği beni çarptı

jeweler kuyumcu 130, 149

job: what's your ~? işiniz ne?

join, to girmek 116, 117; can we join you? size katılabilir miyiz? 124

joint eklem 166; ~ passport ortak pasaport 66

level *(even)* düz 31
library kitaplık
lie down, to uzanmak 164
lifebelt can simidi
lifeboat cankurtaran sandalı
lifeguard cankurtaran 116
lifejacket can yeleği
lift *(elevator)* asansör 26, 132; **~ pass** teleferik pasosu 117
light *(not dark)* aydınlık 14; *(not heavy)* hafif 14, 134; *(color)* açık 134, 143
light *(electric)* ışık 25; *(on vehicle)* far 83; **~ bulb** ampul 148
lighter *(cigarette)* çakmak 150
like, to beğenmek 101, 119, 121, 135; **I like it** hoşuma gidiyor; **I don't like it** hoşuma gitmiyor; **I'd like ...** ... istiyorum 37, 40, 141, 157
limousine limuzin
line *(subway)* metro hattı 80
linen keten 145
lip dudak 166; **~stick** ruj
liqueur likör
liquor store tekel bayii 131
liter litre 87
little *(small)* küçük; **a little** biraz 15
live, to yaşamak 119; **~ together** beraber yaşamak 120
liver ciğer 166
living room oturma odası 29
lobby *(theater, hotel)* lobi
local yerel 35, 37
lock kilit 25; **~ oneself out** kapıda kalmak 27
log on, to girmek 153
long uzun 144, 146; **~-distance bus** şehirlerarası otobüs 77; **~-sighted** yakını görme bozukluğu 167

look: ~ for aramak 18, 133; **I'm looking for ...** ... arıyorum 143; **I'm just looking** bakıyorum; **~ like** benzemek 71
loose bol 146
lorry kamyon
lose, to kaybetmek 28, 138, 160; **I've lost ...** ... kaybettim. 71, 100, 160; **I'm lost** kayboldum 106
lost-and-found [lost property office] kayıp eşya bürosu 72
lot: a lot çok 15; **lots of fun** çok eğlendirici 101
louder daha yüksek 128
love, to beğenmek 119; **I love you** seni seviyorum
lovely güzel 122, 125
low düşük 122, 163; **~-fat** az yağlı
lower *(berth)* alt 73
luck: good luck iyi şanslar 219
luggage bavullar 71; **~ carts [trolleys]** el arabası 71
lump şiş 162
lunch öğle yemeği 98, 152
lung ak ciğer

M **machine washable** makinede yıkanabilir 145
madam madam
magazine dergi 150
magnificent muhteşem 101
maid hizmetçi 28
mail mektup 27, 152; **by ~** mektup ile 22; **~box** posta kutusu 152
main ana 130; **~ street** ana sokak 95
make up, to hazırlamak 140
make-up makyaj
male erkek 159
mallet tokmak 31

morning: in the ~ sabah 221

mosque cami 105

mosquito bite sivrisinek sokması

mother anne 120

motion sickness yol tutması 141

motorbike motorsiklet 83

motorboat motorlu tekne 116

motorway otoyol 92, 94

mountain dağ 107; ~ bike dağ bisikleti; ~ pass dağ geçidi 107; ~ range sıra dağ 107

moustache bıyık

mouth ağız 164, 166; ~ ulcer ağız yarası

move, to taşınmak 25, 92; don't move him! hareket ettirmeyin 92

movie film 108, 110; ~ theater sinema 110

Mr. Bay

Mrs. Bayan

much çok 15

mugged: to be ~ soyulmak 160

mugging hırsızlık 159

mugs kupa 148

mumps kabakulak

muscle kas 166

museum müze 99

music müzik 112, 121

musician müzisyen

must: I must mecburum

mustard hardal 38

my benim 16

myself: I'll do it myself kendim yaparım

N name ad 22, 36, 93, 118, 120; my ~ is adım 118; what's your ~? adınız nedir? 118

napkin peçete 39

nappies bebek bezi 142

narrow dar 14

national ulusal

nationality uyruk 23

native yerel 155

nature reserve milli park 107

nausea mide bulanması

near yakın 12, 35; ~ sighted uzağı görme bozukluğu 167

nearby yakında 21, 87, 115

nearest en yakın 80, 92, 127, 130, 140

necessary gerekli 112

neck boyun 166

necklace kolye 149

need: I need to ... ... gerek 18

nephew yeğen

nerve sinir

nervous system sinir sistemi

never hiçbir zaman 13; never mind önemli değil 10

new yeni 14; New Year Yeni Yıl 219

New Zealand Yeni Zelanda

newspaper gazete 150

newsstand [newsagent] gazete bayii 131, 150

next bir sonraki 68, 75, 77, 80, 81, 94, 100; ~ to yanında 12, 95; next stop! bir sonraki durak! 79

nice iyi 14

niece yeğen

night: at ~ gece 221; for two nights (hotel) iki gece için 22; ~club gece klübü 112

no hayır 10; no one hiç kimse 16; no way! asla! 19

noisy gürültülü 14, 24

non-alcoholic alkolsüz

non-smoking sigara içilmeyen 36, 69

none hiç 15

nonsense! saçma! 19

noon öğlen 220

north kuzey 95
nose burun 166
not: ~ **bad** fena
degil 19; ~ **yet** henüz
degil 13
nothing hiçbir şey 16; ~ **else**
bu kadar 15
notify, to bildirmek 167
November Kasım 218
now şimdi 13, 32, 84
number numara 138; ~ **plate** plaka;
sorry, wrong number affedersiniz,
yanlış numara
nurse hemşire
nylon naylon

O **o'clock: it's ... o'clock**
saat ... 220
occasionally bazen
occupied meşgul 14
October Ekim 218
of course tabii 19
off-licence tekel bayii 131
off-peak kalabalık saatler dışında
office ofis
often sık sık 13
oil sıvı yağ 38
okay tamam 10
old eski 14; (person) yaşlı 14; ~ **town**
eski kent 99
olive oil zeytin yağı
omelet omlet 40
on (day, date) -de 13; ~ **foot**
yürüyerek 17, 95; ~ **the left**
solda 12; ~ **the right** sağda 12;
on/off switch açma/kapama
düğmesi
once bir kere 217; ~ **a day** günde
bir tane 75
one-way (ticket) sırf gidiş
65, 68, 73, 79

open (adj.) açık 14; ~~-**air pool** açık
havuz 116
open, to (store, etc.)
açılmak 132, 140, 152; (unfasten
window, etc.) açmak 76
opening hours açılış saatleri 100
opera opera 108, 111; ~ **house**
opera binası 99
operation ameliyat
opposite karşıda 12, 95
optician göz doktoru 167
or ya da 19
orange (color) portakal rengi 143
oranges portakal 158
orchestra orkestra 111
order, to sipariş vermek 37, 41, 135
our(s) bizim 16
outdoor açık havada
outrageous pahalı 89
outside dışında 12; dışarda 36
oven fırın
over: ~ **here** burada 157; ~ **there**
orada 36, 157
overcharge: I've been overcharged
benden fazla para alındı
overdone çok pişmiş 41
overheat fazla ısınmak
overnight bir gece 23
owe, to borç 168; **how much do I**
owe? borcum ne kadar?
own: on my ~ tek başıma 65, 120;
I'm on my ~ tek başımayım 66
owner sahip

P **p.m.** öğleden sonra
pacifier (for baby) emzik
pack, to hazırlamak 69
package paket 153
packed lunch kutuya konulmuş
yemek

paddling pool çocuk havuzu 113

padlock asma kilit

pail kova 155

pain: to be in ~ acı içinde olmak 167; **~killer** ağrı kesici 141, 165

paint, to resim yapmak

painter ressam

painting resim

pair: ~ of bir çift 217

palace saray 99

palpitations çarpıntı

panorama manzara 107

pants (trousers) pantolon 144

panty hose tayt 144

paper napkins kağıt peçete 148

paracetamol parasitimol

paraffin parafin 31

paralysis felç

parcel paket 153

pardon? efendim? 11

parents ana baba 120

park park 96, 99, 107

parking: ~ lot otopark 26, 87, 96; **~ meter** parkometre 87

parliament building parlamento binası 99

partner (boyfriend/girlfriend) arkadaş

party (social) parti 124

pass, to (a place) geçmek 77

passport pasaport 23, 66, 69, 160; **~ number** pasaport numarası 23

pasta makarna 38

pastry store pastane 131

patch, to yamamak 137

pavement: on the ~ kaldırımda

pay, to ödemek 42, 136; **can I pay in ...** ... cinsinden ödeyebilir miyim 67; **pay phone** paralı telefon

payment ödeme

peak tepe 107

pearl inci 149

pebbly (beach) çakıllı 116

pedestrian: ~ crossing yaya geçidi 96; **~ zone [precinct]** yaya bölgesi 96

pen kalem 150

people insanlar 92, 119

pepper biber 38

per: ~ day günlük 30, 87, 115; **~ hour** saatliği 87, 115, 153; **~ night** geceliği 21, 24; **~ week** haftalığı 24, 83, 86; **~ round** (golf) bir tur 115

perhaps belki 19

period (menstrual) aybaşı 167; **~ pains** aybaşı ağrısı 167

perm, to perma yapmak 147

person kişi 93

petrol benzin 88; **~ station** benzin istasyonu 87

pewter kurşun kalay alaşımı 149

pharmacy eczane 131, 140, 156

phone telefon; **~ call** telefon görüşmesi 159; **~ card** telefon kartı 127, 153

phone, to telefon etmek

photocopier fotokopi makinesi 153

photograph fotoğraf 98

photographer fotoğrafçı

phrase deyim 11; **~ book** konuşma kılavuzu

pick up, to almak 28

A-Z

picnic piknik; **~ area** piknik alanı 107

piece (item) parça 69; **a ~ of …** bir parça … 40

pill hap; **the Pill** (contraceptive) doğum kontrol hapı 167

pillow yastık 27; **~ case** yastık kılıfı

pilot light şofbende devamlı olarak yanan alev

pink pembe 143

pipe (smoking) pipo

pitch (for camping) kazık

pizzeria pizzacı 35

place yer 123; **~ a bet,** bahis oynamak 114

plane uçak 68

plans planlar 124

plant (noun) bitki

plaster yara bandı 141

plastic: ~ bags naylon torba; **~ wrap** plastik ambalaj kağıdı 148

plate tabak 39, 148

platform peron 72, 76

platinum platin 149

play (theater) tiyatro oyunu 108; **~wright** oyun yazarı 110

play: to ~ oynamak 114, 121; (music) çalmak 111; **~ group** oyun grubu 113; **~ground** çocuk parkı 113

playing field spor alanı 96

pleasant hoş 14

please lütfen 10

plug elektrik fişi 148

pneumonia akciğer iltihabı 165

point to, to göstermek 11

poison zehir

police polis 92, 159; **~ report** polis raporu 160; **~ station** polis karakolu 96, 131, 159

pollen count çiçek tozu ölçümü 122

polyester poliester

pond gölcük 107

popcorn patlamış mısır 110

popular beğenilen 111

port (harbor) liman

porter taşıyıcı 71

portion porsiyon 39, 40

possible: as soon as ~ mümkün olduğu kadar çabuk

post (mail) posta; **~ office** postane 96, 131, 152; **~box** posta kutusu 152

post, to postaya vermek

postage pul parası 152

postcard kartpostal 152, 154

potatoes patates 38; **potato chips** patates cipsi 157

pottery çanak çömlek

pound (sterling) İngiliz sterlini 67, 138

powdery yumuşak 117

power: ~ cut elektrik kesilmesi; **~ points** elektrik prizi 30

pregnant, to be hamile olmak 163

premium (gas [petrol]) süper 87

prescribe, to reçete yazmak 165

prescription reçete 140, 141

present (gift) armağan

press, to ütülemek 137

pretty güzel

price fiyat 24

priest rahip

primus stove gaz ocağı 31

prison hapisane

produce store manav 131

profession meslek 23

program program 108, 109

pronounce, to telaffuz etmek

Protestant Protestan 105

pub bar

pump *(gas [petrol] station)* benzin pompası 87

puncture patlak 83, 88

puppet show kukla gösterisi

pure saf 145

purple mor 143

purse cüzdan 160

push-chair puşet

put, to koymak 22; **where can I put ...?** ... -i nereye koyabilirim?; **can you put me up for the night?** bu gece sizde kalabilir miyim?

Q quality kalite 134

quarter çeyrek 217; **~ past** çeyrek geçiyor 220; **~ to** çeyrek var 220

queue, to sırada beklemek 112

quick çabuk 14

quickest: what's the ~ way? en çabuk hangi yoldan gidilir?

quickly çabucak 17

quiet sessiz 14

quieter daha sessiz 24, 126

R rabbi haham

racetrack [racecourse] hipodrom 114

racket *(tennis, squash)* raket 115

railroad [railway] demiryolu

rain, to yağmur yağmak 122

raincoat yağmurluk 144

rape tecavüz 159

rapids ivinti yeri 107

rare *(steak)* az pişmiş; *(unusual)* ender

rash kaşıntı 162

razor jilet; **~ blades** jilet 142

reading okumak 121

ready, to be hazır olmak 89, 126, 137, 151

real *(genuine)* gerçek 149

rear arka 83

receipt fiş 32, 42, 136, 151, 168

reception resepsiyon

receptionist resepsiyon memuru

reclaim tag teslim etiketi 71

recommend, to önermek 21, 37; **can you recommend ... ?** ... önerebilir misiniz? 35, 97, 108, 112

record *(L.P.)* plak 155; **~ store** müzik dükkânı 131

red kırmızı 143; **~ wine** kırmızı şarap 40

reduction *(in price)* indirim

refreshments hafif yiyecek ve içecekler 77

refrigerator buzdolabı 29

refund para geri almak 137

refuse bags çöp torbası 148

region bölge 106; **in the ~ of ...** *(price)* ... civarında 134

registered mail taahhütlü mektup 153

registration form kayıt formu 23

regular *(portion)* orta boy 40; *(gas [petrol])* normal 87

reliable güvenilir 113

religion din

remember: I don't remember hatırlamıyorum

rent, to kiralamak 29, 83, 86, 115, 116, 117

rental car kiralık araba 160

repair, to onarmak 89, 137, 168

repairs *(car, etc.)* onarım 89

Saturday Cumartesi 218
sauce sos 38
sauna sauna 22
sausage sosis 158
say: how do you say ...? ... nasıl denir?
scarf eşarp 144, 154
scheduled flight tarifeli uçuş
sciatica siyatik 165
scissors makas 148
scooter skuter
Scotland İskoçya 119
screwdriver tornavida 148
sea deniz 107; **~front** deniz kıyısı
seasick: I feel ~ beni deniz tuttu
season ticket abonman bilet
seat (train, etc.) koltuk 73, 76; (theater, movies) yer 108, 109
second ikinci 217; **~ class** ikinci sınıf 73; **~-hand** ikinci el
secretary sekreter
sedative sakinleştirici
see, to görmek 18, 24, 37, 93, 124; (witness) tanık olmak; **see you soon!** görüşmek üzere 126
self-employed: to be ~ kendi işi olmak 121
self-service (gas [petrol] station) kendi kendine doldurma 87
sell, to satmak
send, to göndermek 153
senior citizen yaşlı 74, 100
separated: to be ~ ayrı olmak 120
separately ayrı ayrı 42
September Eylül 218
serious ciddi
service (to customer) servis 42
service (church) ayin
serviette peçete 39
set menu fiks mönü 37
sex (act) cinsel ilişki

shade (color) ton 143
shady gölgede 31
shallow sığ
shampoo şampuan 142; **~ and set** şampuanla yıkama 147
share, to (room) aynı odada kalmak
sharp keskin 69
shaving: ~ brush tıraş fırçası; **~ cream** tıraş kremi
she o
sheath (contraceptive) prezervatif
sheet (bed) çarşaf 28
ship gemi 81
shirt (men's) gömlek 144
shock (electric) elektrik çarpması
shoes ayakkabı 145; **shoe repair** ayakkabı tamiri; **shoe store** ayakkabıcı 131
shopping: ~ area alışveriş merkezi 99; **~ basket** alış veriş sepeti; **~ mall [centre]** alışveriş merkezi 130; **~ cart [trolley]** alış veriş arabası; **to go ~** alış verişe çıkmak
short kısa 14, 144, 146, 147; **~-sighted** uzağı görme bozukluğu 167
shorts şort 144
shoulder omuz 166
shovel kürek 155
show, to göstermek 18, 94, 134; **can you show me?** bana gösterebilir misiniz? 106
shower duş 21, 26, 30
shut (closed) kapalı 14
shut, to kapanmak 132; **when do you shut?** ne zaman kapatıyorsunuz?
shutter panjur 25
sick: I'm going to be sick kusacağım?

side: ~ **order**
yanında 38; ~ **street**
ara sokak 95

sights görülecek yerler

sightseeing: ~ **tour** tur 97;
to go ~ gezmeye çıkmak

sign *(road)* işaret 93, 95; ~**post** yol
işareti

silk ipek

silver gümüş 149; ~ **plate** gümüş
kaplama 149

singer şarkıcı 155

single *(ticket)* sırf gidiş
65, 68, 73, 79, 81; ~ **room**
tek kişilik oda 21; **to be** ~
bekar olmak 120

sink lavabo 25

sister kız kardeş 120

sit, to oturmak 36, 76, 126; **sit down**
oturun

size beden 146

skates paten 117

ski: ~ **boots** kayak çizmesi 117;
~ **poles** kayak sopaları 117;
skis kayak 117

skin deri 166

skirt etek 144

sleep, to uyumak 167

sleeping: ~ **bag** uyku
tulumu 31; ~ **car** yataklı
vagon 73, 77; ~ **pill** uyku hapı

sleeve kol 144

slice: a slice of ... bir dilim ... 40

slippers terlik 145

slow *(speed)* yavaş 14; *(clock)*
geri 221; **to be** ~ yavaş olmak;
slow down! yavaşlayın!

slowly daha yavaş 128; *(speak)*
yavaş 11

SLR camera SLR fotoğraf
makinesi 151

small küçük 14, 24, 40, 110,
117, 134; ~ **change** bozuk
para 138

smaller daha küçük 134

smell: there's a bad smell kötü bir
koku var

smoke, to sigara içmek 126

smoking sigara içilen 36, 69

snack bar büfe 72

snacks hafif yiyecek

sneakers lastik ayakkabı

snorkel şnorkel

snow kar 117

snow, to kar yağmak 122

soap sabun 27, 142; ~ **powder**
sabun tozu

soccer futbol 114

socket priz

socks çorap 144

soft drink alkolsüz içecek 110, 157

sole *(shoes)* alt

soluble aspirin eriyen aspirin

some bazı

something bir şey 16; **something to
eat** yiyecek bir şeyler 70

sometimes bazen 13

son oğul 120, 162

soon yakında 13

sore: it's ~ acıyor; ~ **throat** boğaz
ağrısı 141, 163

sorry! özür dilerim! 10

soul music soul müziği 111

sour ekşi 41

south güney 95

South Africa Güney Afrika

South African Güney Afrikalı

souvenir hediyelik eşya 98, 154;
~ **guide** hediyelik eşya rehberi 154;
~ **store** hediyelik eşya
dükkanı 131

tower kule 99
town kent 70, 94; **~ hall** belediye binası 99
toy oyuncak 155
traditional geleneksel 35
traffic trafik; **~ jam** trafik tıkanıklığı; **~ light** trafik ışığı 95; **~ violation [offence]** trafik suçu
trailer karavan 30, 81
train tren 13, 72, 75, 76, 123; **~ station** tren garı 72, 84, 96
trained eğitimli 113
tram tramvay 79
transfer transfer
transit, in transitte
translate, to tercüme etmek
translation tercüme
translator tercüman
trash çöp 28; **~cans** çöp bidonları 30
travel: ~ agency seyahat acentası 131; **~ sickness** yol tutması 141
traveler's check [cheque] seyahat çeki 136, 138
tray tepsi
tree ağaç 106
trim uçlarından alma 147
trip yolculuk 75, 77
trolley el arabası 156
trousers pantalon 144; **trouser press** pantalon ütüsü
truck kamyon
true: that's not true bu doğru değil
try on, to (clothes) denemek 146
Tuesday Salı 218
tumor tümör 165
tunnel tünel
Turkey Türkiye

Turkish Türkçe 11, 110, 126
Turkish liras Türk lirası 67
turn: to ~ down (volume, heat) kısmak; **~ off** kapatmak 25; **~ on** açmak 25; **~ up** (volume, heat) açmak
TV televizyon 22
tweezers cımbız
twice iki kere 217; **~ a day** günde iki tane 75
twin beds iki yataklı 21
twist: I've twisted my ankle ayak bileğimi burktum
two-door car iki kapılı araba 86
type tür 109; **what type of ...?** ne tür...? 112
typical tipik 37
tyre lastik 83

U **U.K.** Birleşik Krallık 119
U.S. ABD (Birleşik Devletler) 119
ugly çirkin 14, 101
ulcer ülser
umbrella şemsiye 117
uncle amca 120
uncomfortable rahatsız 117
unconscious: to be ~ kendinde olmamak 92; **he's ~** baygın 162
under altında
underdone az pişmiş 41
underpants külot 144
understand, to anlamak 11; **do you understand?** anladınız mı? 11; **I don't understand** anlamadım 11, 67
undress, to soyunmak 164
uneven (ground) bozuk 31
unfortunately ne yazık ki 19
uniform üniforma

unit *(phone card)* kredi 153

United States Birleşik Devletler

unleaded petrol kurşunsuz benzin

unlimited mileage sınırsız kilometre hakkı

unlock, to açmak

unpleasant hoş değil 14

unscrew, to sökmek

until kadar 221

up to -e kadar 12

upper (berth) üst 73

upset stomach mide bozukluğu 141

urine idrar 164

USA ABD

use, to kullanmak 139

use: for my personal ~ kişisel kullanımım için 67

V V-neck V yaka 144

vacant serbest 14

vacation tatil 123; on ~ tatil için 66

vaccinated against karşı aşılanmak 164

vaginal infection vajina iltihabı 167

valid geçerli 74

validate, to onaylamak

valley vadi 107

valuable değerli

valve vana 28

vanilla *(flavor)* vanilyalı 40

VAT KDV 24; VAT receipt KDV fişi

vegan: to be ~ hiçbir hayvansal ürün yememek

vegetables sebze 38

vegetarian *(person)* vejetaryen 35; *(meal)* etsiz 39

vein damar 166

venereal disease bulaşıcı cinsel hastalık 165

ventilator havalandırma camı

very çok 17; ~ good çok iyi 19

video: ~ game video oyunu; ~ recorder (VCR) video; ~cassette video kaseti 155

view: with a ~ of the sea deniz manzaralı; ~point manzara seyretme yeri 107

village köy 107

vinaigrette sirkeli salata sosu 38

vinegar sirke 38

vineyard bağ 107

visa vize

visit ziyaret 119

visit, to ziyaret etmek 123, 167

visiting hours ziyaret saatleri

vitamin tablet vitamin 141

volleyball voleybol 115

voltage voltaj

vomit, to kusmak 163

W wait, to beklemek 41, 140; ~ for beklemek 76, 89; wait! bekleyin! 98

waiter garson 37

waiting room bekleme salonu 72

waitress garson 37

wake *(someone)* uyandırmak 27, 70

Wales Galler Ülkesi 119

walking: ~ boots yürüyüş çizmeleri 145; ~ route yürüyüş yolu 106

wallet cüzdan 42, 160

ward *(hospital)* koğuş 167

warm ılık 14, 122

warmer daha sıcak 24

washbasin lavabo

X Y Z

Dictionary
Turkish – English

This Turkish-English Dictionary covers all the areas where you may need to decode written Turkish: hotels, public buildings, restaurants, shores, ticket offices, and on transportation. It will also help with understanding forms, maps, product labels, road signs, and operating instuctions (for telephones, parking meters, etc.). If you can't locate the exact sign, you may find key words or terms listed separately.

A

AB üyesi ülkelerden olmayanlar non-EU citizens
AB vatandaşı EU citizens
acil durum emergency
acil durum çıkışı emergency exit
acil durum freni emergency brake
acil durum hizmetleri emergency services
acil durum numarası emergency number
acil durumda camı kırınız break glass in case of emergency
acil servis emergency medical service
açık open
açık arazide kayak cross-country skiing
açık hava open air
açık yüzme havuzu open-air swimming pool
açılır köprü drawbridge
açmak için itin press to open
ağ network
ağır iş kamyonu truck
ağızdan alınmaz not to be taken orally
Ağustos August
ahize receiver *(telephone)*
akan su running water

akaryakıt fuel
alarmı çalıştırmak için kolu çekiniz pull for alarm
alışveriş merkezi shopping mall [centre]
alışveriş sepeti shopping basket
altgeçidi kullanınız use the underpass
altın gold
altyazılı subtitled
ana yol main road
anahtarları resepsiyonda bırakınız leave keys at reception
Anayol main highway [A-road]
anne mother
antikacı antique store
apartman apartment building
ara yoktur no intermissions
araba güvertesi car deck *(on ferry)*
araba güvertesinde sigara içilmez no smoking on car decks
araba kiralama car rental
araba plaka numarası license plate number
arabanızı birinci viteste bırakınız leave your car in first gear
arayol lane

arıza halinde ... numaralı telefonu arayınız in case of breakdown, phone / contact ...

arıza hizmetleri breakdown services

arka merdivenler backstairs / service stairs

arka/ön kapıdan çıkınız exit by the rear / front door

armağan free gift

asansör elevator [lift]

aşağı kat downstairs

A.Ş. Inc. [Ltd.] *(company)*

ata binme horseback riding

ateş/mangal yakılmaz no fires / barbecues

atlama tahtası diving board

avcılık hunting

avlu yard

avukat lawyer

ayakkabı shoes

ayakkabı tamircisi shoe repair

ayakta durulmaz no standing

ayakta tedavi outpatients *(hospital department)*

aylık monthly

ayrı ayrı yıkayınız wash separately

ayrılmadan önce çantalarınızı gösteriniz show your bags before leaving

ayrılmış reserved

ayrılmış yol reserved lane

B **bagaj dolapları** luggage lockers

bagaj kontrolu baggage check

bagaj sınırı baggage allowance

bağış donations

bağlantı yolu bypass *(road)*

bahçe merkezi garden center

bahçe seviyesinde apartman dairesi garden apartment

bahşiş tip

balık avlamak yasaktır no fishing

balık avlanabilir fishing permitted

balık oltası fishing rod

balıkçı fish stall

banka bank

banka komisyon ücreti bank charges

banliyöler suburbs

banyo bathroom

banyo kabini cabana [bathing hut]

banyolu with bathroom

bar bar

barınma accommodation

basamağa dikkat edin watch your step

başlık crash helmet

başlık takmak zorunludur crash helmets required

bataklık swamp / marsh

batı west(ern)

bavul talep bandı baggage claim

bavullarınızın başından ayrılmayınız do not leave baggage unattended

bay gentlemen *(toilets)*

Bay Mr.

bayan giyimi ladieswear

bayan ladies *(toilets)*

Bayan Miss / Mrs.

bekleme salonu waiting room

belediye binası town hall

belli bir mesafeyi koruyunuz keep your distance

benzin gas [petrol]

benzin istasyonu gas [petrol] station

berber barber

beyan edecek bir şey yok nothing to declare

biçimini kaybetmez will not lose its shape

A-Z

bilet ticket
bilet acentası ticket agency
bilet bitti sold out
bilet gişesi box office/ticket office
bilet metroda geçer ticket valid for subway [metro]
bileti öncama yerleştiriniz place ticket on windshield [windscreen]
bileti sokunuz insert ticket
biletinizi alın take ticket
biletinizi bekleyiniz wait for your ticket
biletinizi deldiriniz punch your ticket
biletinizi onaylatınız/deldiriniz validate/punch your ticket
biletinizi onaylatmayı unutmayınız don't forget to validate your ticket
bilgisayar computers
bina bakıcısı caretaker
biniş boarding (airport)
biniş kartı boarding pass (airport)
bir sonraki toplama ... next collection at ...
bira beer
birinci balkon dress circle
birinci kat second floor [U.K. first floor]
birinci sınıf first class
Birleşik Devletler United States
Birleşik Krallık United Kingdom
bisiklet ve motorsikletliler giremez no access to cyclists and motorcyclists
bisiklet yolu cycle lane/path
bit pazarı flea market
bodrum basement
borsa stock exchange
boş vacancies/vacant
boşluğa dikkat edin watch your step (subway)

bozuk out of order
bozuk parayı koyunuz insert coin
bölüm department
bu gece tonight
bu gece için biletler tickets for tonight
bu koltuk hasta ve yaşlılara ayrılmıştır please give up this seat to the elderly or disabled
bu makine bozuk para verir this machine gives change
bu odanın temizlenmesi gerek this room needs to be made up
bu otobüs ... -e gidiyor this bus is going to ...
bu öğlesonrası this afternoon
bu sabah this morning
bu tren ... -de duruyor this train stops at ...
bugün today
buhar banyosu sauna
buharlı gemi steamship
buluşma yeri meeting place [point]
bulvar boulevard
bungalov bungalow
burada here
buradan kesiniz tear here
buz pateni ice-skating
buzlu zemin icy road

C cami mosque
can yelekleri life jackets
cankurtaran sandalları lifeboats
cankurtaran lifeguard
Cumartesi Saturday

Ç çabuk pişer fast-cooking
çalışma saatleri business [opening] hours
çamaşır laundry

çantanızı burada bırakınız leave your bags here

çarşaf ve örtüler household linen

Çarşamba Wednesday

çelik steel

çıkış exit/way out

çıkış yoktur no exit

çıkmaz dead end

çıplaklar plajı nudist beach

çiçekçi florist

çift yönlü yol two-lane highway

çift/tek günlerde park yapılır parking allowed on even/odd days

çiftlik farm

çiğnenebilir chewable (tablets, etc.)

çimlere basmayınız keep off the grass

çocuk giyimi babies wear

çocuk havuzu children's pool

çocuklar children

çocuklar tek başlarına alınmaz no unaccompanied children

çocuklardan uzak tutunuz keep out of reach of children

çocukların açamayacağı kapak childproof cap (on bottle, etc.)

çok yavaş very slow

çoklu paket multipack

çöp trash [rubbish]

çöp atmayınız no littering

çöp dökmeyiniz no dumping

çöp yeri garbage disposal

D dağ mountain

dağcılık mountaineering

dahil included (in the price)

dahil değildir not included (in the price)

dalış yapılmaz no diving

damla drops (medication)

danışma masası information desk

dar yol narrow road

darbelere dayanıklı shockproof

değerli eşyalarınızı arabada bırakmayınız do not leave valuables in your car

değiştirme exchange

değiştirmek ya da paranızı geri almak isterseniz fişinizi saklayınız keep your receipt for exchange or refund

değirmen windmill

demir atılmaz no docking [anchorage]

demiryolu geçidi railroad [level] crossing

denetimli yüzme supervised swimming

deneyimli kayakçılar için for advanced skiers

deniz sea

deniz feneri lighthouse

deniz manzaralı with sea view

deniz seviyesi sea level

denizden yükseklik height above sea level

depoyu doldurmadan önce benzin bedelini ödeyiniz pay for gas before filling car

depozitolu returnable

depozitolu şişe returnable bottle

dere stream

dergiler magazines/periodicals

deri leather

derin yeri deep end (swimming pool)

dış çevre yolu outer roadway

dış hat için ... tuşlayın dial ... for an outside line

A-Z

diğer bir yol alternate route

diğer ilaçlarla etkileşim may interfere with other drugs

dikkat caution

dikkat köpek var beware of dog

dikkatli sürünüz drive carefully

dinlenme alanı rest area

dispanser infirmary

diş doktoru dentist

diyet diet

dizel diesel

doğrudan hizmet direct service

doğu east(ern)

doğum tarihi date of birth

doğum yeri place of birth

dolu full up

donmuş frozen

donmuş gıda frozen foods

donmuş halinde pişiriniz cook from frozen

döviz foreign currency

döviz bürosu currency exchange office

döviz kuru exchange rate

dua prayers

duran tren local service (train)

durulmaz no stopping

duşlar showers

duşlu with shower

duvar wall

dükkanlara/denize yakın within easy reach of stores/the sea

E eczane pharmacy

eğim incline (road sign)

ehliyet driver's license

ekmek bread

ekpres paket postası express parcel mail

ekpres posta express mail

el arabası carts

el yapımı handmade

elçilik embassy

elde dokunmuş hand-woven

elektrik sayacı electric meter

elektrikli eşyalar electrical goods

emlakçı estate agent

emniyet kemeri life preserver [belt]

emniyet şeridi hard shoulder

emniyet şeridi sonu end of hard shoulder

en az minimum (requirement)

en az ücret minimum charge

erkek giyimi menswear

eşin adı name of spouse

ev adresi home address

ev mobilyaları home furnishings

evde yapılmış homemade

F fabrika mağazası factory outlet

farlarınızı açın/yakın turn on/use headlights

fazla bagaj excess baggage

fırın bakery

fırtına uyarısı storm warning

fidanlık wood

fişinizi/biletinizi saklayınız keep your receipt/ticket

fiyatlar indirildi prices slashed

fotoğraf çekilmez no photography

fuar fair

G galeri gallery

gazete bayii newsstand [newsagent]

gece night

gece ayini evening service

gece bekçisi night porter

gece yarısı midnight

gece zili night bell
gecikme olabilir delays likely
gecikmeli delayed
geçiş ücreti toll
geçiş yoktur dead end
geçilmez no passing
geçit pass *(mountain)*
geliş arrivals
geliştirilmiş improved
gemi ship
gemi gezileri cruises/boat trips
genç young adult/youth
gençlik yurdu youth hostel
genel amaçlı mağaza general store
geri ödeme refund
gevşek zemin loose clippings
gidiş dönüş round-trip
giriş entrance/admission
giriş ücreti admission fee
giriş ya da çıkış izni clearance
girişi kapatmayınız do not block entrance
girişte ödeyiniz pay on entry
girilmez no access/no entry
glütensiz gluten-free
göl lake
gölcük pond
gönderen sender
görüş açısı viewpoint
gösteri performance/show
gösteri başladıktan ... dakika sonra kapılar kapanır doors close ... minutes after performance begins
gözlükçü optician
gruplara açıktır parties welcome
gümrük customs
gümrük kontrolu customs control
güncelleştirilmiş updated
günde ... kere ... times a day
güneş banyosu sonrası kremi after-sun lotion

güneş geçirmez krem sun-block cream
güneşte bırakmayınız do not expose to sunlight
güney south(ern)
günlük per day
günün yemeği dish of the day
günün yemek listesi menu of the day
güverte deck
güzellik salonu beauty parlor

H haberler news
hafif yemek verilir refreshments available
hafta içi weekdays
haftalık per week/weekly
hamam baths/Turkish bath
hastane hospital
hava pompası/hava air pump/air *(gas station)*
hava raporu weather forecast
havaalanı airport
havai fişek fireworks
havalandırmalı air conditioned
Haziran June
hemşire nurse
heyelan landslide
hırdavatçı hardware store
hız rampası speed bumps
hız sınırı speed limit
hızlı kasa express checkout
hostes flight attendant
hoşgeldiniz! welcome

I ırmak river
ırmak kıyısı river bank
ırmak yatağı river bed
ıslak boya wet paint

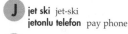

İ iade kabul edilmez non-returnable

iç çamaşırı lingerie/underwear

iç çevre yolu inner roadway

içilmez not to be taken internally

içkiler drinks

içme suyu drinking water

idari bölge administrative district

ihtiyari durak request stop

iki kişilik for two

ikinci el eşya dükkanı secondhand store

ikinci etap second leg

ilk yardım first aid

ilkbahar spring

indirim discount

indirim yoktur no discounts

indirimli eşyalar değiştirilmez sale goods cannot be exchanged

indirimli fiyatlar reduced prices

indirimli mallar dükkanı discount store

İngiliz sterlini pound sterling

İngilizce English

İngilizce konuşulur English spoken

inşa halinde under construction

inşa halinde yol road under construction

ipek silk

iple atlama bungee-jumping

iple iniş abseiling

iptal canceled

iş bölgesi business district

itfaiye firefighters

itfaiye istasyonu fire station

itiniz push

izleme galerisi viewing gallery

izni olmayan araçlar çekilir unauthorized vehicles will be towed

J jet ski jet-ski

jetonlu telefon pay phone

K kadar until

kadın dergisi women's magazine

kahvaltı breakfast

kahvaltı salonu breakfast room

kalacak yer vardır accommodations available

kaldırım sidewalk [pavement]

kale castle

kalite standardı quality standard

kamara güvertesi cabin decks

kambiyo currency exchange

kamyon truck

kamyon çıkışı truck exit

kamyon yolu truck route

kan grubu blood type

kapalı closed/covered

kapalı pazar covered market

kapalı yüzme havuzu indoor swimming pool

kapatma turn off

kapıyı çalın ve girin knock and enter

kapıyı kapalı tutunuz keep gate shut

kapıyı kapatınız close the door

kapsül capsules *(medication)*

karayolu road

karne booklet *(of tickets)*

karşıya geçmeyiniz do not cross

kartı/bozuk parayı sokunuz insert card/coins

kasa cashier/checkout

kasada ödeyiniz pay at cashier

kasadan fiş alınız buy a token at cashier

kasap butcher

kat floor *(level in building)*

kat otoparkı multistory parking lot [car park]

katkınız için teşekkür ederiz thank you for your contribution

katlanabilir koltuk deck chair

kavşak intersection [junction]/ traffic circle [roundabout]

kaya tırmanma rock climbing

kayak skis

kayak güzergahı ski trail

kayıp eşya lost and found [lost property]

kayıt belgelerinizi gösteriniz show your car registration documents

kemerlerinizi bağlayınız fasten your seat belt

kendin pişir kendin ye kır evi/ apartman dairesi self-catering cottage/apartment

kent merkezi downtown area

kent surları city wall

kesik bağlantı disconnected

kırtasiyeci stationer

kış winter

kızlık soyadı maiden name

kilise church

kimlik ID card

kiralık for rent

kiralık ev house for rent

kiralık odalar rooms for rent

kirli eşya soiled goods

kitapçı bookstore

klinik clinic

koltuk numarası seat number

konferans salonu conference room

koridor kenarı aisle seat

korna çalmak yasaktır use of horn prohibited

koruma altında bina protected [listed] building

koruma altında tarihi bina protected [listed] historical building

koruma bölgesi conservation area

koşulmaz no running

köprü bridge *(deck on ship)*

körfez bay

kötü zemin/bozuk zemin poor/uneven road surface

kredi kartını sokunuz insert credit card

kredi kartları geçer we accept credit cards

kredi kartları geçmez no credit cards

kuaför hairdresser

kullanılmış bilet used tickets

kullanım talimatları instructions for use

kullanmadan önce doktorunuza başvurunuz consult your doctor before use

kurşunlu leaded *(gasoline)*

kurşunsuz unleaded *(gasoline)*

kuru temizleyici dry cleaner

kuyumcu jeweler

kuzey north(ern)

küçük small

kütüphane library

L liman port/harbor

lise high school [secondary school]

litre fiyatı price per liter

lunapark amusement park

lütfen ... please ...

lütfen ayakkabılarınızı siliniz please wipe your feet

lütfen bekleyiniz please wait

lütfen engelin arkasında bekleyiniz please wait behind barrier

lütfen yardım isteyiniz please ask for assistance

lütfen zili çalınız please ring the bell

M **madeni para kabul edilir** coins accepted

mağara cave/department store

mağaza rehberi store guide

mahalle parish

mahkeme courthouse

makarna pasta

makinede yıkanabilir machine washable

makineye para koyup bileti alınız insert money in machine and take ticket

manav greengrocer

mandıra dairy

Mart March

Mayıs May

metro subway [metro]

mevsime göre according to season

mevsimlik bilet season ticket

meydan square

meyve suları fruit juices

mezarlık cemetery

mikrodalga fırında pişirilebilir microwaveable

miktar dosage

misafirhane guest house

mizah dergileri comic books

mobilya furniture

motoru durdurunuz turn off your engine

muayenehane doctor's office [surgery]

mutfak kitchen

müdür manager

müşteri danışma customer information

müşteri hizmetleri customer service

müşteri park yeri customer parking lot

müze museum

N **nakit** cash

nakit ödeyiniz pay cash

nalbur hardware store

nehir gemileri riverboats

nemlendirici moisturizer

net ağırlık net weight

Nisan April

Noel Christmas

normal benzin regular (gasoline)

nöbetçi eczane all-night pharmacy

O **Ocak** January

oda servisi room service

oda ücreti room rate

oda ve kahvaltı bed and breakfast

odanızı ... -e kadar boşaltınız vacate your room by ...

okul school

olay event

olta ile balık tutma angling

onarım repairs (car, etc.)

orijinal dilinde film film in original version

orman forest

orta derecede bilenler için pist ski trail for intermediate skiing

orta düzey intermediate level

otobüs bus

otobüs durağı bus stop

otobüs garajı bus station/depot

otobüs yolu bus lane/route

otomatik bulaşık makinelerine dayanıklı dishwasher-proof

otomatik genel tuvalet automated public toilet

otomatik kapı automatic doors

otoyol highway [motorway]

otoyol çıkışı highway [motorway] exit

otoyol kavşağı highway interchange [motorway junction]

otoyol polisi highway [motorway] police

otoyoldan önceki son benzin istasyonu last gas station before highway [motorway]

oturma salonu lounge

oyun salonu game room

oyuncak mağazası toy store

oyuncaklar toys

Ö ödeme gişesi toll booth

ödemeli collect call [reverse-charge call]

ödendi (teşekkür ederiz) paid (with thanks)

öğleden önce a.m.

öğleden sonra p.m.

öğlen noon

öğrenci student

öğretmen teacher/instructor

ölçek: 1:100 scale: 1:100

ölüm tehlikesi danger of death

ön sıralar orchestra [stalls] *(area of theater)*

önce inen yolculara yer veriniz let passengers off first

önceden yer ayırtma advance reservations

öncelik hakkı right of way

önemli tarihi özellik important historical feature

önerilir recommended

örneğin e.g.

özel private

özel mülkiyet private property

P paket package

paket yemek take-away food

para çekme withdrawals

para havalesi money orders

para yatırma ve çekme deposits and withdrawals

paralı yol toll road

Paramatik ATM/cash machine

park public gardens/park

park bileti parking ticket

park yapılır parking permitted

park yapılmaz no parking

park yasağı sonu end of no parking zone

park yeri için ödeme pay for parking space

park yeri numaranızı unutmayınız note your parking space number

parkometre parking meter

parkometreye ödeyiniz pay at the meter

pastane pastry shop

patika path/footpath

pavyon pavilion

pazar market

Pazar Sunday

Pazar günleri kapalıdır no Sunday service

Pazartesi Monday

pencere kenarı window seat

pencerelerden sarkmayınız do not lean out of windows

perde açıldı curtain up

A-Z

peron platform
Perşembe Thursday
peynir cheese
piknik alanı picnic area
PIN numaranızı tuşlayın enter your PIN
piskopos bishop
pist dışında kayak yapılmaz no off-trail [off-piste] skiing
pişirme önerileri cooking instructions
piyango lottery
plaka numarası license [number] plate
plakçı music store
planörcülük gliding/hanggliding
polis karakolu police station
posta kutusu post office box
posta reklamı direct mail
postane post office
pratisyen doktor general practitioner (*doctor*)
prezervatif condom
pul stamps

R **rahatsız etmeyiniz** do not disturb
rampa ramps
reçete prescription
rehber tour guide
rehberinize bahşiş vermeyi unutmayınız remember to tip your guide
resepsiyon reception
resepsiyon için ... tuşlayın dial ... for reception
resepsiyon merkezi reception center
resepsiyona sorun ask at reception
resmi bina public building
resmi giyim formal wear
resmi tatil national holiday

rezervuar reservoir
roman fiction (*section in bookstore*)
roman dışında kitaplar non-fiction (*section in bookstore*)
römork trailer
rüzgar sörfü windsurfing
rüzgar uyarısı gale warning

S **saat** hour
saatçi watchmaker
sabah ayini morning mass
saç kurutma makinesi hairdryer
sağdan gidiniz keep to the right
sağlıklı yiyecekler satan dükkan health food store
sağlıklı yiyecekler health food
sahil coast
Salı Tuesday
salon hall
sanayi bölgesi industrial complex
santral operator (*telephone*)
sapma yol detour [diversion]
satılan mal geri alınmaz/değiştirilmez goods cannot be refunded/exchanged
savaş alanı battle site
savaş anıtı war memorial
sebzeler vegetables
self servis lokanta self-service restaurant
serbest free
serin bir yerde saklayınız keep in a cool place
servis service
servis dahil service included
servis hariç service not included
servis ücreti service charge
servis ücreti dahildir service charge included
servis yolu service road
seslendirmeli dubbed

seyahat acentası travel agent
sıcak hot *(water)*
sığ yeri shallow end
sıra row/tier
sırf gidiş one-way trip [journey]
sigara içilir smoking
sigara içilmez no smoking
sigorta kartı insurance card
sinyal sesini bekleyiniz wait for the tone
siparişe göre made to order
sis fog
sis tehlikesi risk of fog
site housing area
siz beklerken anahtar yapılır keys cut while you wait
soğuk cold/chilled
soğuk servis yapınız best served chilled
sokak street
soldan gidiniz keep to the left
son çağrı last call
son giriş akşam ... latest entry at ... p.m.
son kullanma tarihi expiration [expiry] date/use-by date
son satış tarihi sell-by date
sonbahar fall [autumn]
sorularınız için ... -i görünüz for inquiries see ...
soyadı last name
soyunma odası fitting room
sörf tahtası surfboard
stadyum stadium
standart menü ... lira set menu ... lira
stüdyo studio
su içilmez do not drink the water
su kayağı waterskiing
su musluğu faucet [tap]
suda erir dissolve in water

sunma önerileri serving suggestions
süper benzin premium [super] *(gasoline)*
sürekli gösteri continuous showings
sürekli servis shuttle service
sürücü ile konuşmayınız do not talk to the driver
süt ürünleri dairy products

Ş **şarap tatma** wine tasting
şarküteri delicatessen
şehirlerarası tren intercity trains
şeker sugar
şekerci candy store [confectioner]
şekersiz sugar-free
şemsiye umbrellas
Şubat February

T **taahhütlü mektup** registered letter
tablet pills/tablets
tadilat nedeniyle kapalı closed for renovations
tahliye nedeniyle ucuzluk going out of business [closing-down] sale
tahta top oyunu bowls [boules]
taksi durağı taxi stand
tali yol secondary road [B-road]
tam pansiyon American Plan (A.P.) [full board]
tam para exact change
tam ücret exact fare
tamirhane body shop *(mechanic)*
tarla field
tasarımcı hairstylist
tasarruf bankası savings bank
tatil nedeniyle kapalı closed for vacation [holiday]
tatil programı holiday timetable

A-Z

tatlandırma flavoring
taze fresh
tek yön one-way street
teleferik vagonu cable car
telefon kartı phone card
Temmuz July
tepe hill
tepe aşağı kayak downhill skiing
ters yönden trafik traffic from the opposite direction
terzi işi made to measure
top oyunu oynanmaz no ball games
toplama saatleri times of collection
toplantı salonu convention hall
trafik polisi traffic police
trafik sıkışıklığı; gecikme olabilir traffic jams; delays likely
trafiğe kapalı closed to traffic
tren garı train station
tren yolcuları için park yeri parking for train users
TTOK (Türkiye Turing ve Otomobil Kurumu) Turkish Automobile Association
turistler için for tourists
turizm bürosu tourist office
Türk Lirası Turkish lira
tuş dial
tuz salt

U ucuzluk clearance [sale]
uçak plane
uçurum cliff
uçuş danışma flight information
uçuş kapısı gate (boarding)
uçuş kaydı masası check-in desk (airport)
uçuş kaydı yaptırmak check-in (airport)
uçuş numarası flight number

uyarı warning
uzak durunuz keep out
uzun araç long vehicle
uzun/kısa süreli park yeri long-/short-term parking

Ü ücretsiz arama toll-free number
ütülemeyiniz do not iron

V varış yerini/bölgesini seçin select destination/zone
varsa subject to availability
vejetaryenler için uygundur suitable for vegetarians
vergisiz mallar satan dükkan duty-free shop
vergisiz mallar duty-free goods

Y yabancı foreign
yabancı diller foreign languages
yağ içeriği fat content
yağlı oily/greasy
yağsız fat-free
yalnızca only
yalnızca biletliler ticket holders only
yalnızca elde yıkayın handwash only
yalnızca gazeteler newspapers only
yalnızca giriş access only
yalnızca hafta içi weekdays only
yalnızca izni olanlara permit-holders only
yalnızca mallar deliveries only
yalnızca mevsimlik bileti olanlara season ticket holders only
yalnızca sakinler için residents only
yalnızca tıraş makineleri için razors [shavers] only

yalnızca yük freight only
yan etkiler side effects
yangın çıkışı fire exit
yangın halinde ... in the event of fire ...
yangın kapısı fire door
yangın söndürücü fire extinguisher
yardım hattı help line
yarı fiyat half price
yarım pansiyon Modified American Plan (M.A.P.) [half-board]
yarımada peninsula
yarın tomorrow
yarından sonra the day after tomorrow
yarış alanı racetrack [racecourse]
yarışma contest
yavaş trafik akışı slow traffic
yavaşla slow down
yaya pedestrians
yaya bölgesi pedestrian zone
yaya geçidi pedestrian crossing
yaz summer
yaz saati summertime
yaz tarifesi summer timetable
yelken öğretmeni sailing instructor
yelkencilik klubü sailing club
yemek dahil with food/meals
yemek salonu dining room
yemeklerden önce before meals
yemeksiz without food
yemekten sonra take after meals (medication)
yeni new
Yeni Yıl New Year
yeni başlayanlar için pist skiing trail for beginners
yeni çıkanlar new titles/releases

yeni trafik sistemi başladı new traffic system in operation
yeraltı garajı underground garage
yeraltı geçidi underpass
Yılbaşı gecesi New Year's Eve
Yılın ilk günü New Year's Day
yoğun bakım intensive care
yol çalışması sonu end of roadwork
yol çukuru potholes
yol haritası road map
yol kapalı road closed
yol vermek yield [give way]
yolculuk sırasında araba güvertesine girilmez no access to car decks during crossing
yolu açık tutunuz keep clear
yön gösterme directions (map)
yukarı upstairs
yukarıda salonumuz vardır seats upstairs
yumuşak refüj soft shoulder [verges]
yutan kum quicksand
yük sınırı load limit
yüksek voltaj high voltage
yükseklik ... headroom ... (height restriction)
yün wool
yürüyen merdiven escalator
yüzme swimming
yüzme başlıkları giyilmelidir bathing caps must be worn

Z **zemin kat** first floor [U.K. ground floor]
zincir ya da kar lastiği kullanınız use chains or snow tires
ziyaret saatleri visiting hours

Numbers

GRAMMAR

Large numbers are formed using the components below. The only difference between English and Turkish in this respect is that "and" is not used in Turkish numbers after "hundred" (**yüz**). For example:

7,312,817 = **yedi milyon, üç yüz on iki, bin sekiz yüz on yedi**

0	**sıfır** *ser-fer*		16	**on altı** *on alter*
1	**bir** *beer*		17	**on yedi** *on yedee*
2	**iki** *ikee*		18	**on sekiz** *on sekeez*
3	**üç** *ewch*		19	**on dokuz** *on dokooz*
4	**dört** *durrt*		20	**yirmi** *yirmee*
5	**beş** *besh*		21	**yirmi bir** *yirmee beer*
6	**altı** *alter*		22	**yirmi iki** *yirmee ikee*
7	**yedi** *yedee*		23	**yirmi üç** *yirmee ewch*
8	**sekiz** *sekeez*		24	**yirmi dört** *yirmee durrt*
9	**dokuz** *dokooz*		25	**yirmi beş** *yirmee besh*
10	**on** *on*		26	**yirmi altı** *yirmee alter*
11	**on bir** *on beer*		27	**yirmi yedi** *yirmee yedee*
12	**on iki** *on ikee*		28	**yirmi sekiz** *yirmee sekeez*
13	**on üç** *on ewch*		29	**yirmi dokuz** *yirmee dokooz*
14	**on dört** *on durrt*		30	**otuz** *otooz*
15	**on beş** *on besh*		31	**otuz bir** *otooz beer*

32	**otuz iki** *otooz ikee*	three times	**üç kere** *ewch kereh*
40	**kırk** *kerk*	a half	**yarım** *yarerm*
50	**elli** *ell-ee*	half an hour	**yarım saat** *yarerm sa-art*
60	**altmış** *altmersh*	half a tank	**yarım depo** *yarerm depo*
70	**yetmiş** *yetmish*	half eaten	**yarısı yenmiş** *yarer-ser yenmish*
80	**seksen** *sek-sen*	a quarter	**bir çeyrek** *beer chay-rek*
90	**doksan** *dok-san*	a third	**üçte bir** *ewch-teh beer*
100	**yüz** *yewz*	a pair of ...	**bir çift ...** *beer chift*
101	**yüz bir** *yewz beer*	a dozen ...	**bir düzine ...** *beer dewzeeneh*
102	**yüz iki** *yewz ikee*	1999	**bin dokuz yüz doksan dokuz** *been dokooz yewz dok-san dokooz*
200	**ikiyüz** *ikee yewz*		
500	**beşyüz** *besh yewz*		
1,000	**bin** *been*		
10,000	**on bin** *on been*	the 1990s	**bin dokuz yüz doksanlar** *been dokooz yewz dok-san-lar*
35,750	**otuz beş bin yedi yüz elli** *otooz besh been yedee yewz ell-ee*		
1,000,000	**bir milyon** *beer meel-yon*	the year 2000	**iki bin yılı** *ikee been yer-ler*
first	**birinci** *beerinjee*	2001	**iki bin bir** *ikee been beer*
second	**ikinci** *ikeenjee*	the Millennium	**Binyıl Başı** *beenyerl basher*
third	**üçüncü** *ewchewn-jew*		
fourth	**dördüncü** *dur-dewn-jew*		
fifth	**beşinci** *besheenjee*		
once	**bir kere** *beer kereh*		
twice	**iki kere** *ikee kereh*		

Days Günler

Monday	**Pazartesi** *pazarteh-see*
Tuesday	**Salı** *sa-ler*
Wednesday	**Çarşamba** *charshamba*
Thursday	**Perşembe** *pair-shembeh*
Friday	**Cuma** *jooma*
Saturday	**Cumartesi** *joomarteh-see*
Sunday	**Pazar** *pazar*

Months Aylar

January	**Ocak** *ojak*
February	**Şubat** *shoo-bat*
March	**Mart** *mart*
April	**Nisan** *nee-san*
May	**Mayıs** *my-yers*
June	**Haziran** *hazeer-an*
July	**Temmuz** *temmooz*
August	**Ağustos** *aa-ostos*
September	**Eylül** *eh-lewl*
October	**Ekim** *ekeem*
November	**Kasım** *kaserm*
December	**Aralık** *aralerk*

Dates Tarih

It's ...	**Bugün ...** *boo-gewn*
July 10	**10 temmuz** *on temmooz*
Tuesday, March 1	**1 Mart, Salı** *beer mart sa-ler*
yesterday	**dün** *dewn*
today	**bugün** *boo-gewn*
tomorrow	**yarın** *yarern*
this .../last ...	**bu .../geçen ...** *boo/getchen*
next week	**gelecek hafta** *geleh-jek hafta*
every month/year	**her ay/yıl** *hair eye/yerl*
on [at] the weekend	**hafta sonunda** *hafta sonoonda*

Seasons Mevsimler

spring	**ilkbahar** *eelk-bahar*
summer	**yaz** *yaz*
fall [autumn]	**sonbahar** *son-bahar*
winter	**kış** *kersh*
in spring	**ilkbaharda** *eelk-baharda*
during the summer	**yazın** *yazern*

Greetings Kutlama

Happy birthday!	**Doğum gununüz kutlu olsun!** *do-oom gewn-ewnewz kootloo olsun*
Merry Christmas!	**İyi Noeller!** *eeyee noel-lair*
Happy New Year!	**Yeni Yılınız kutlu olsun!** *yenee yerl-er-nerz kootloo olsun*
Best wishes!	**En iyi dilekler!** *en eeyee deelek-lair*
Congratulations!	**Tebrikler!** *tebreek-lair*
Good luck!/All the best!	**İyi şanslar!** *eeyee shans-lar*
Have a good trip!	**İyi yolculuklar!** *eeyee yol-jewlook-lar*
Give my regards to …	**… -e selam söyleyin.** *… eh selam sow-lay-yeen*

Public holidays Resmi tatiller

The following are Turkey's secular holidays, when banks, schools, offices, and most stores are closed.

1 January	New Year's Day
23 April	National Independence and Children's Day
19 May	Atatürk's Commemoration and Youth and Sports Day
30 August	Victory Day
29 October	Republic Day

There are also two national Muslim holidays, each of around three to four days' duration. These dates are dictated by the lunar calendar, and they occur about 11 days earlier each year, moving throughout the calendar. During these periods, normal business is interrupted, and transportation and seaside accommodations can be booked solid. The most notable of these holidays are the Festival of Sweetmeats (**Şeker Bayramı**) and the Festival of Sacrifice (**Kurban Bayramı**).

The holy month of Ramadan (**Ramazan**), during which devout Muslims fast from sunrise to sunset, occupies the four weeks preceding the Festival of Sweetmeats.

Time Zaman

saat ...
beş geçiyor
beş var
on var
on geçiyor
... çeyrek var
... çeyrek geçiyor
yirmi var
yirmi geçiyor
yirmi beş var
yirmi beş geçiyor
... buçuk

Excuse me. Can you tell me the time?	**Afedersiniz, saat kaç?** _<u>a</u>ffedair-seeniz sa-art katch_
It's ...	**Saat ...** _sa-art_
five past one	**biri beş geçiyor** _beeree besh getch<u>ee</u>-yor_
ten past two	**ikiyi on geçiyor** _ikee-yee on getch<u>ee</u>-yor_
a quarter past three	**üçü çeyrek geçiyor** _ewch-ew <u>chay</u>rek getch<u>ee</u>-yor_
twenty past four	**dördü yirmi geçiyor** _durd-ew yirmee getch<u>ee</u>-yor_
twenty-five past five	**beşi yirmi beş geçiyor** _besh-ee yirmee besh getch<u>ee</u>-yor_
half past six	**altı buçuk** _alter boo<u>chook</u>_
twenty-five to seven	**yediye yirmi beş var** _yedee-yeh yirmee besh var_
twenty to eight	**sekize yirmi var** _se<u>keez</u>-eh yirmee var_
a quarter to nine	**dokuza çeyrek var** _do<u>kooz</u>-ah <u>chay</u>rek var_
ten to ten	**ona on var** _onah on var_
five to eleven	**on bire beş var** _on beer-eh besh var_
twelve o'clock (noon/midnight)	**on iki (öğlen/gece yarısı)** _on ikee (owe-len/geh-jeh <u>yar</u>er-ser)_

at dawn	**şafak sökerken** *shafak surkair-ken*
in the morning	**sabah** *sabah*
during the day	**gün içinde** *gewn itchin-deh*
before lunch	**öğle yemeğinden önce** *owe-leh ye-may-yeenden urn-jeh*
after lunch	**öğle yemeğinden sonra** *owe-leh ye-may-yeenden sonra*
in the afternoon	**öğleden sonra** *owe-leden sonrah*
in the evening	**akşam** *aksham*
at night	**gece** *geh-jeh*
I'll be ready in five minutes.	**Beş dakika içinde hazır olacağım.** *besh dakeeka itchin-deh hazzer olah-jy-yerm*
He'll be back in a quarter of an hour.	**Bir çeyrek içinde dönecek.** *beer chayrek itchin-deh durn-ejek*
She arrived half an hour ago.	**Yarım saat önce geldi.** *yarerm sa-art urn-jeh geldee*
The train leaves at …	**Tren saat … -de kalkacak.** *tren sa-art … deh kalkah-jak*
13:04	**On üç sıfır dört** *on ewch ser-fer durrt*
00:40	**sıfır sıfır kırk** *ser-fer ser-fer kerk*
The train is 10 minutes late/early.	**Tren 10 dakika geç/erken.** *tren on dakeeka getch/air-ken*
It's 5 minutes fast/slow.	**Saat 5 dakika ileri/geri.** *sa-art besh dakeeka eelair-ee/geree*
from 9:00 to 5:00	**9.00'dan 5.00'e kadar** *dokooz-dan besh-eh kaddar*
between 8:00 and 2:00	**8.00 ile 2.00 arası** *sekeez eeleh ikee ara-ser*
I'll be leaving by …	**Saat … -den önce gideceğim.** *sa-art … den urn-jeh gid-eh-jay-yim*
Will you be back before …?	**Saat … -den önce geri gelecek misiniz?** *sa-art … den urn-jeh geree gel-ejek miseeniz*
We'll be here until …	**Saat … -e kadar burada olacağız.** *sa-art … eh kaddar boorada olah-jy-yerz*

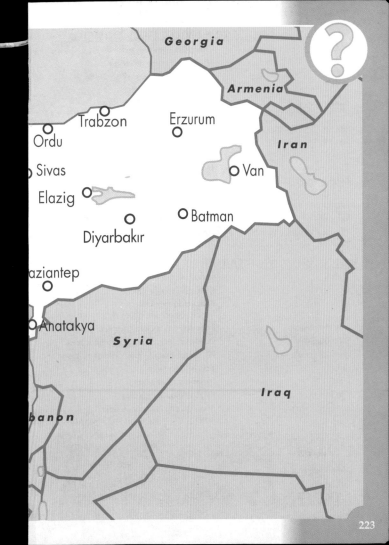

Quick reference Hızlı başvuru

Good morning.	**Günaydın.** gewn-_eye_-dern
Good afternoon.	**İyi günler.** eeyee gewn_lair_
Good evening.	**İyi akşamlar.** eeyee ak-_sham_-lar
Hello.	**Merhaba.** mer-ha_bah_
Good-bye.	**Hoşçakal. /Güle güle.** _hosh_-cha kal/gew-leh gew-leh
Excuse me.	**Afedersiniz.** _aff_-edair-seeniz
Excuse me? [Pardon?]	**Efendim?** eh-_fen_dim
Please.	**Lütfen.** _lewt_-fen
Thank you.	**Teşekkür ederim.** teshek_kewr_ ederim
Do you speak English?	**İngilizce biliyor musunuz?** eengee_leez_-jeh beelee-yor musoonuz
I don't understand.	**Anlamadım.** an_la_maderm
Where is …?	**… nerede?** … neredeh
Where are the bathrooms [toilets]?	**Tuvalet nerede?** too-_va_-let neredeh

Emergency Acil durum

Help!	**İmdat!** eemdat
Go away!	**Çekil git!** che_keel_ geet
Leave me alone!	**Beni yalnız bırakın!** benee _yal_nerz ber-_a_kern
Call the police!	**Polis çağırın!** polees _char_-erern
Stop thief!	**Durdurun, hırsız!** dur_door_un her-serz
Get a doctor!	**Bir doktor bulun!** beer dok-tor bul_loon_
Fire!	**Yangın!** _yan_gern
I'm ill.	**Hastayım.** has-_ty_-yerm
I'm lost.	**Kayboldum.** ky-_bol_dum
Can you help me?	**Bana yardım edebilir misiniz?** bana _yar_derm edeh-bee_leer_ miseeniz

Emergency ☎		
Police **155**	Ambulance **112**	Fire **110**
Embassies ☎		
Canada **(0312) 459 9200**	U.K. **(0312) 455 3344**	U.S. **(0312) 445 5555**